PRAISE FOR
POLITICS—ACCORDING TO THE BIBLE

"Wayne Grudem is one of the outstanding biblical scholars in America. He's going to handle very well any subject he tackles. I particularly appreciate his work in this area..... There are sections of this book that are uncannily timely.... This can be a wonderful resource as we face growing tensions from an ever more powerful state."

—Chuck Colson, Founder, Prison Fellowship

"If you read this year only one Christian book on politics, read *Politics— According to the Bible*.... Grudem's biblically-based good sense overwhelms the nostrums of Jim Wallis and the evangelical left ... and shows why those seeking a vacation from politics need to rise up and go to work."

—Marvin Olasky, editor-in-chief, *World*, and provost, The King's College, New York City

"Conservative and hard-hitting both biblically and culturally, Grudem's treatise is essentially a giant tract for the times, covering the whole waterfront of America's political debate with shrewd insight and strong argument. This book will be a valued resource for years to come, and right now no Christian can afford to ignore it. An outstanding achievement!"

—James I. Packer, Board of Governors Professor of Theology, Regent College, Vancouver.

"Wayne Grudem's call for men and women of faith to be engaged in the public life of our great country is precisely and exactly the call the rising generation needs to hear."

—Timothy Goeglein, Vice President, External Relations, Focus on the Family

Zondervan Books and Products by Wayne Grudem

Systematic Theology

Bible Doctrine

Christian Beliefs

Systematic Theology Laminated Sheet

The Making Sense Series

Are Miraculous Gifts for Today? 4 Views (General Editor)

Politics — According to the Bible

Voting as a Christian: The Economic and Foreign Policy Issues

VOTING AS A CHRISTIAN

THE SOCIAL ISSUES

PREVIOUSLY PUBLISHED IN
POLITICS–ACCORDING TO THE BIBLE

WAYNE GRUDEM

ZONDERVAN.com/
AUTHORTRACKER
follow your favorite authors

ZONDERVAN

Voting as a Christian: The Social Issues
Copyright © 2010, 2012 by Wayne Grudem

Previously published in *Politics — According to the Bible*

This title is also available as a Zondervan ebook. Visit www.zondervan.com/ebooks.

Requests for information should be addressed to:

Zondervan, *Grand Rapids, Michigan 49530*

This edition: ISBN 978-0-310-49598-7 (softcover)

The Library of Congress has cataloged the original edition as:

Grudem, Wayne A.
    Politics — according to the Bible : a comprehensive resource for understanding
    modern political issues in light of scripture / Wayne Grudem.
        p. cm.
    Includes bibliographical references.
        ISBN 978-0-310-33029-5 (hardcover, printed) 1. Politics in the Bible. 2. Bible
    and politics. 3. Christianity and politics. 4. Church and social problems. I. Title.
    BS680.P45G78 2010
    261.7 — dc22   201002252

Cover design: Rob Monacelli
Cover photography: SuperStock / Masterfile
Interior design: Matthew Van Zomeren

Printed in the United States of America

12 13 14 15 16 17 18 /DCI/ 21 20 19 18 17 16 15 14 13 12 11 10 9 8 7 6 5 4 3 2 1

To Jack and Pammy Markle, special friends,
who have encouraged Margaret and me in multiple ways,
and whose lives been examples
of Christians seeking to influence government for good

CONTENTS

PUBLISHER'S PREFACE

Wayne Grudem's *Politics—According to the Bible: A Comprehensive Resource for Understanding Modern Political Issues in Light of Scripture* was first published in the fall of 2010. Systematic and wide-ranging, it filled a niche for a thorough resource of conservative biblical thought on politics. Every significant political issue facing the nation was covered—more than 50 areas of public policy—often in great depth. Many thousands of readers purchased the book, and it will rest on their shelves for years to come, ready to be pulled down when considering a variety of topics.

Yet the very strengths of that book also made it unapproachable for some. At 640 pages, it is admittedly a daunting volume to pick up, let alone to crack open and read. Furthermore, we know that many readers who resonate with Prof. Grudem's political vision are more interested in certain issues than others. Many also have limited reading time.

So we've created two abridged volumes of his larger work. The first is this book you're holding, which unpacks from a biblical perspective the social issues of enduring concern to so many Christian voters. Abortion, homosexual marriage, freedom of speech and religion—all of these and more are tackled in the following pages.

A second book, entitled *Voting as a Christian: The Economic and Foreign Policy Issues*, centers on issues related to national defense, the U.S. economy, and the size of the federal government, topics that dominate political debates during election seasons.

We trust that these accessible, affordable books will aid you in biblically assessing the important decisions confronting our nation, and we hope they will be useful as you consider your own decisions the next time you head to your local polling place.

Paul E. Engle
Senior Vice President and Publisher
Church, Curriculum, Academic, and Reference Resources
Zondervan

FOREWORD

This new book by Wayne Grudem is a rare and valuable contribution. It is not the typical, facile, and simplistic linking of the Bible with a set of preferred set of positions; rather, it is a deep, thoughtful, and comprehensive exploration of what the Bible really has to say about current hot-button issues. No one is more qualified to write this book, and no one could have executed it better.

While at Dartmouth College as an undergrad, I had an experience that I think many others share. I came to the campus with an underdeveloped understanding of Christianity. And when I faced the liberal thinking and attacks on religion on campus, I, in a sense, rejected my faith because I did not think that it had any defense in the face of sophisticated liberalism. However, conservatism made sense to me, and I poured my efforts into *The Dartmouth Review* and, along with a handful of friends, exposed the liberal, political correctness that had so gripped the campus during those years. I was passionate about conservative principles, and I went on to serve in the Reagan White House.

However, it was years later after being at the Hoover Institute at Stanford and the American Enterprise Institute that I came to realize that many of the conservative principles I so valued and upheld were themselves found and rooted in the Bible. I never abandoned my faith, but I had a long, dry season when I thought that the Bible had little to say about the issues and problems we face today. For many Americans the Bible is simply too old and "irrelevant" to be meaningful today. That has led to American Christians taking a back seat in politics or at least allowing their religious views to take a back seat to the political issues of these times.

What Grudem points out so effectively is that the hot-button "social issues" are not something to be avoided by Christians. Rather, they are something to take seriously in light of the Bible and its relevance to all matters of life. Grudem shows how the teachings of the Bible give rise to the Christian political values of today. Grudem has aimed this book specifically at the Christians who are concerned for the future of this country.

While the left and media paint Christians' support of conservative political positions and social issues as being merely a political strategy, Grudem shows the reasons Christians support these positions. In fact, he shows that the biblical position on these issues is not "blind faith," but rather a very thoughtful, consistent stance that ascribes value to the people and things that God cares about most.

Grudem provides a challenge to each and every Christian in America—and those outside of our country as well. However, this book will also challenge pastors and Christian leaders. Too often Christian leadership means *not* taking a position on politics. Instead, leaders tend to have a hands-off approach and leave politics to itself. If what Dr. Grudem proposes is right—and I think it is—Christian leaders should be the first to teach and advocate the biblical positions on how we approach government, protect life, support marriage and family, and also how we understand valued American freedoms. (I think most Americans, both in and outside of the church, would be shocked to hear that the Bible teaches that Christianity should not be compelled by the government.)

Ultimately, this is a thoughtful analysis of the very issues that dominate the headlines in this country from a perspective very often marginalized or misunderstood. Christians would do well to study it to reaffirm their conservative positions and understand more fully the meaning behind their vote.

Dinesh D'Souza
President, The King's College NYC

INTRODUCTION

This book is a shortened version of my longer book, *Politics — According to the Bible: A Comprehensive Resource for Understanding Modern Political Issues in Light of Scripture* (Zondervan, 2010, 624 pages). In this volume I focus solely on what are commonly called the "social issues" — especially the protection of life, marriage, and the family.

I have not written this book from the perspective of a lawyer or journalist or professional politician, but from the perspective of a professor with a Ph.D. in New Testament studies and thirty years of experience in teaching the Bible at the M.Div. and (for several years) the Ph.D. level. I wrote this book because I was convinced that God intended the Bible to give guidance to every area of life — including how governments should function!

I support political positions in this book that would be called more "conservative" than "liberal." That is because of my conclusions about the Bible's teaching on the role of government and a biblical worldview. It is important to understand that I see these positions as *flowing out of the Bible's teachings* rather than positions that I hold prior to, or independently of, those biblical teachings. My primary purpose in the book is not to be liberal or conservative, or Democratic or Republican, but to explain a biblical worldview and a biblical perspective on key social issues being debated today.

I hope that Christians who take the Bible as a guide for life will find these political discussions encouraging. I believe the Bible's teachings about politics will bring hope and beneficial change to people in every nation where they are put into practice. When these teachings are put into practice in a nation, it will be good news for those who are oppressed, good news to those who long for justice, good news to those who long for peace, good news for young and old, weak and powerful, rich and poor — good news for everyone who will follow the wonderful paths of freedom and sound government that are taught in the pages of the Bible. The prophet Isaiah extolled the beautiful sound of the feet of a messenger who came running with good news from God himself:

> How beautiful upon the mountains are the feet of him who brings good news, who publishes peace, who brings good news of happiness, who publishes salvation, who says to Zion, "Your God reigns" (Isa. 52:7).

Therefore I hope that as people and nations follow these principles for government, they will begin to see a reversal of the continual decline in peace, civility, liberty, and civic goodness that we have seen in recent decades in our societies, and instead we will begin to see regular progress toward increasingly good, pleasant, productive, low-crime, free, and happy civil societies in which we can live.

I am well aware that the Bible is not an American book, for it was finished nearly 1,700 years before the United States existed! The principles and teachings in the Bible contain wisdom that is helpful for *all* nations and all governments. Therefore I have tried to keep in mind that people in other nations might read this book and find it useful for formulating their own positions on the political issues that they face in their own nations. Yet in my examples and my choice of political issues, I focus primarily on the United States, because that is the country I know best, the country I am proud to be a citizen of, and the country I deeply love.

What about readers who don't believe the Bible to be from God or who may not be sure what they think about the Bible? I hope they will still consider the arguments in this book on their own merits and find them useful—perhaps even persuasive—in formulating their own opinions. If not, their right to disagree with me is still very important to any government that follows the principles in this book. I believe there should be strong protections for freedom of religion in every nation, and I earnestly desire to protect each person's freedom to make decisions about religious belief for himself or herself, totally without any compulsion from government. I want to protect other people's right to disagree with me and to express that disagreement publicly in any nation.

I also want to say at the beginning that I do not hold with equal confidence every position I support in this book. On some issues I think the overall teaching of the Bible is *clear, direct, and decisive*, such as the idea that civil governments are set up by God to punish evil and reward good (see Rom. 13:1–7; 1 Pet. 2:13–14) and the idea that laws in a nation should protect people's lives, particularly the lives of preborn children (chap. 2).

There is a second set of issues where I depend on *arguments from broader principles*. In these cases I reason not from direct, specific biblical teaching on the topic but from broader biblical principles (such as the equality of all people in the image of God). That kind of argument from broader principles requires wise judgment in applying those principles correctly to a modern situation, and thus there is a greater possibility of making a mistake or failing to balance the principle with other principles that might modify one's conclusions.

Then I have used a third type of argument: *an appeal to facts in the world*. In some sections, much of my argument depends on one's evaluation of the *actual results* of certain policies. Such arguments are different from arguments from *direct biblical statements*, and they are different from arguments from *broader biblical principles*, for they depend not on the Bible but on *an evaluation of the relevant facts* in the world today.

I have not distinguished these three types of argument in the pages that follow. I have not made explicit where I am depending on *direct teachings of the Bible*, where I am depending on *broader biblical principles*, where I am depending on an *evaluation of facts* in the world today, and where I am depending on some combination of these three. But I hope readers will be able to make those distinctions for themselves as they weigh the arguments that I present. And in the end, I hope that most readers will find themselves persuaded by the book.

Many people helped in the writing of the larger book on which this one is based, and I thanked them all in that book. Here I want especially to mention again the irreplaceable research help of Craig Osten, the encouragement of Alan Sears, Ben Bull, and Cathi Herrod, the legal advice of Joe Infranco, Jordan Lorence, Steve Oman, and Jeff Ventrella, the material support of the partners of Marketplace One, and the prayer support of many friends who regularly pray for me and my writing projects. Even more, I am continually thankful for the help and daily encouragement of my wonderful wife, Margaret. Above all of these, I am thankful to the Lord who gives me strength to keep writing and, I hope, some measure of good judgment along the way.

Chapter 1

HOW CHRISTIANS SHOULD BE INVOLVED IN GOVERNMENT

Should Christians try to influence laws and politics? Before explaining my own understanding of this question, I need to mention what I think are five wrong views. After that I will propose what I think is a better, more balanced solution.

A. WRONG VIEW #1: GOVERNMENT SHOULD COMPEL RELIGION

The first wrong view (according to my judgment) is the idea that civil government should compel people to support or follow one particular religion.

Tragically, this "compel religion" view was held by many Christians in previous centuries. It played a large role in the Thirty Years' War (1618–48) that began as a conflict between Protestants and Roman Catholics over control of various territories, especially in Germany. There were many other "wars of religion" in Europe, particularly between Catholics and Protestants, in the sixteenth and seventeenth centuries.

Eventually more and more Christians realized that this position is inconsistent with the teachings of Jesus and inconsistent with the nature of faith itself. Today I am not aware of any major Christian group that holds to the view that government should try to compel people to follow the Christian faith.

But other religions still promote government enforcement of their religion. This is seen in countries such as Saudi Arabia, which enforces laws compelling people to follow Islam and where those who fail to comply can face severe penalties from the religious police. The law prohibits public practice of any religion other than Islam and prohibits Saudis from converting to other religions. But it must be noted that other Muslims also favor democracy and allowing for varying degrees of freedom of religion.

In the early years of the United States, support for freedom of religion in the American colonies increased because many of the colonists had fled from religious persecution in their home countries. For example, the New England Pilgrims had fled from England where they had faced fines and imprisonment for failing to attend services in the Church of England and for conducting their own church services.

Several teachings of the Bible show that "government should compel religion" is an incorrect view, one that is contrary to the teachings of the Bible itself.

1. Genuine faith cannot be forced

Government should never try to compel any religion because, according to the Bible, genuine religious belief cannot be compelled by force. Jesus and the New Testament apostles always *taught* people and *reasoned* with them and then *appealed* to them to make a personal decision to follow Jesus as the true Messiah. Jesus invited people, "Come to me, all who labor and are heavy laden, and I will give you rest" (Matt. 11:28; compare Acts 28:23; Rom. 10:9–10; Rev. 22:17).

Anyone who has brought up children knows that not even parents can force children to believe in God. You can bring them to church and you can teach them the Bible, but each child must make a personal decision to trust in Jesus as his or her own Lord and Savior. Genuine faith cannot be forced.

Someone might object, "But what about laws in the Old Testament that ordered severe punishments for anyone who tried to teach another religion (see Deut. 13:6–11)? Wasn't that part of the Bible?"

The answer is that those laws *were only for the nation of Israel for that particular time.* They were never imposed on any of the surrounding nations. Such Old Testament laws enforcing religion were never intended for people after Jesus came and established his "new covenant" (Heb. 8:8–9:28).

2. Jesus distinguished the realms of God and of Caesar

Another biblical argument against the "compel religion" view comes from Jesus' teachings about God and Caesar. Jesus' Jewish opponents were trying to trap him with the question, "Is it lawful to pay taxes to Caesar, or not?" (Matt. 22:17). Taking his opponents by surprise, Jesus said, "Show me the coin for the tax," and "they brought him a denarius" (v. 19). Jesus said to them, "Whose likeness and inscription is this?" They said, "Caesar's." Then he said to them, "Therefore render to Caesar the things that are Caesar's, and to God the things that are God's" (Matt. 22:20–21).

This is a remarkable statement because Jesus shows that there are to be *two different spheres of influence*, one for the government and one for the religious life of the people of God. Some things, such as taxes, belong to the civil government ("the things that are Caesar's"), and this implies that the church should not try to control these things. On the other hand, some things belong to people's religious life ("the things that are God's"), and this implies that the civil government should not try to control those things.

Jesus did not specify any list of things that belong to each category, but the mere distinction of these two categories had monumental significance for the history of the world. It signaled a *different system* from the nation of Israel in the Old Testament, where everybody in the nation was considered a part of the people of God and they all had to obey the religious laws.

3. Freedom of religion is a biblical value

Jesus' new teaching that the realms of "God" and "Caesar" are distinct implies freedom of religion. It implies that all civil governments — even today — should give people freedom regarding the religious faith they follow (or don't follow), and regarding the religious doctrines they hold, and how they worship God. "Caesar" should not control such things, for they are "the things that are God's."

Therefore Christians in every nation should support freedom of religion and oppose any attempt by government to compel any single religion. In fact, *complete freedom of religion* should be the first principle advocated and defended by Christians who seek to influence government.

B. WRONG VIEW #2: GOVERNMENT SHOULD EXCLUDE RELIGION

The opposite error from the "compel religion" view is "exclude religion." This is the view that says we should completely exclude religion from government and politics. According to this view, religious beliefs should never be mentioned in governmental functions or on government property and should never play a role in decision-making processes in politics or government.

This is the view promoted today by the American Civil Liberties Union (ACLU). According to it, religious belief should be kept at home and quiet. There should be no influence from religious groups in the political process.

Examples of this view are seen when people object to prayers being given at the beginning of a city council meeting, or when groups demand that the Ten Commandments be removed from public places. Supporters of this view seek to prohibit religious expression in high schools, student-led Bible studies, prayers before sporting events, or even a valedictorian talking about his or her faith at graduation.

1. It changes freedom of religion into freedom from religion

The "exclude religion" stance is wrong from a constitutional viewpoint, because it twists the positive ideal of "freedom *of* religion" to mean "freedom *from* all religious influence" — which is entirely different and something the signers of the Declaration of Independence and the framers of the US Constitution never intended.

In fact, the "exclude religion from politics" view would invalidate the very reasoning of the Declaration of Independence, on which the United States of America was first founded. The first two sentences mention God twice in order to say that God's laws authorize independence from Great Britain and that God is the one who gives human beings the rights that governments must protect:

> When in the Course of human events, it becomes necessary for one people to dissolve the political bands which have connected them with another, and to assume among the Powers of the earth, the separate and equal station to which the Laws of Nature *and of Nature's God* entitle them, a decent respect to the opinions of mankind requires that they should declare the causes which impel them to the separation.
>
> We hold these truths to be self-evident, that all men are created equal, that they are *endowed by their Creator* with certain unalienable Rights, that among these are Life, Liberty, and the pursuit of Happiness. That to secure these rights, Governments are instituted among Men....

In other words, the fifty-six signers of the Declaration of Independence proclaimed that both the laws of nature and of God gave our country the right to become an independent nation. They claimed *divine authorization* for the very existence of the United States of America! Furthermore, the signers said that the purpose of government is to protect the rights that are given to people by God ("endowed by their Creator"). This is hardly "excluding religion" from government or important government publications.

The First Amendment to the Constitution likewise declared: "Congress shall make no law *respecting an establishment of religion,* or *prohibiting the free exercise thereof;* or abridging the freedom of speech." What they meant by "an establishment of religion" was an established state church, a government-sponsored or government-endorsed denomination or specific religion. But they did not intend this amendment to exclude all religious speech and activity from government building and activities, for our nation's early political leaders continued praying publicly to God at government events, even having church services in the Capitol for many years.

The phrase "separation of church and state" does not occur anywhere in the Constitution. It was first seen in a letter from Thomas Jefferson in 1802, in which he assured some Baptists in Connecticut (the Danbury Baptists) that the government would never interfere with the affairs of their church. The First Amendment was never intended to guarantee that government should be free from religion or religious influence. The only "freedom of religion" that was intended was freedom from government sponsorship of one particular religion or denomination.

2. It wrongly restricts freedom of religion and freedom of speech

The First Amendment also excluded any law "prohibiting the free exercise" of religion. This is directly opposed to the "exclude religion from government" view, which actually seeks to *prohibit* Christians and Jews and others from exercising their religious freedom when speaking or giving a prayer at a public event. Their free exercise of religion is taken away from them.

This view also wrongly restricts individual freedom of speech. Why should a high school valedictorian not be free to express his own viewpoint in his graduation speech? *Speaking* a religious opinion in public is not *compelling* people to accept that viewpoint!

3. It was never adopted by the American people

The "exclude religion" view was never adopted by the American people through any democratic process, but it is being imposed on our nation by the exercise of "raw judicial power" by our courts, and especially by the Supreme Court. This has been an increasing problem for the last several decades in America.

The Supreme Court decision *Lemon v. Kurtzman* (1971) was especially significant. In that case the court said that government actions "must not have the primary effect of advancing or inhibiting religion." It did not say "advancing or inhibiting *one particular religion*" but "religion" in general. (An earlier decision in 1947, *Everson v. Board of Education*, had said something similar.) This kind of "exclude religion" view was never adopted or approved by the American people but simply decreed by our Supreme Court, taking to itself powers it never legitimately had.

4. It removes from government God's teaching about good and evil

The Bible says that a government official is "God's servant for your good" (Rom. 13:4), but how can government officials effectively serve God if no one is allowed to tell them what they believe God expects of them? The Bible says that government officials are sent "to punish those who do evil and to praise those who do good" (1 Peter 2:14), but how can they do that if no spokesmen from any of the world's religions are allowed to give them counsel on what is "good" and what is "evil"?

Such a viewpoint has to assume that there is no God, or if there is, his moral standards can't be known. And by rejecting the idea of absolute moral standards that come from God, this viewpoint leads toward the moral disintegration of a society.

We see the payoff of this view in the rampant moral relativism among today's young adults who were taught as children in "exclude religion" schools, schools where "because God says so" could no longer be used as the strong foundation for moral conduct as it had been for the first 200 years of this nation.

C. WRONG VIEW #3: ALL GOVERNMENT IS EVIL AND DEMONIC

According to this third view, all use of government power is deeply infected by evil, demonic forces. The realm of government power is the realm of Satan and his forces, and therefore all governmental use of "power over" someone is worldly and not the way of life that Jesus taught.

1. Support from Luke 4:6

This viewpoint has been strongly promoted by Minnesota pastor Greg Boyd in his influential book *The Myth of a Christian Nation* (Grand Rapids: Zondervan, 2005). Boyd's views in this book have had a large impact in the United States, especially on younger evangelical voters.[1]

Boyd says that all civil government is "demonic" (p. 21). His primary evidence is Satan's statement to Jesus in Luke 4:

> And the devil took him up and showed him all the kingdoms of the world in a moment of time, and said to him, "To you I will give all this authority and their glory, *for it has been delivered to me*, and I give it to whom I will. If you, then, will worship me, it will all be yours" (Luke 4:5–7).

Boyd emphasizes Satan's claim that all the authority of all the kingdoms of the world "has been delivered to me" and then says that Jesus "doesn't dispute the Devil's claim to own them. Apparently, the authority of all the kingdoms of the world has been given to Satan."

Boyd goes on to say, "Functionally, Satan is the acting CEO of all earthly governments" (p. 22). This is indeed a thoroughgoing claim!

2. The mistake of depending on Luke 4:6

Greg Boyd is clearly wrong at this point. Jesus tells us how to evaluate Satan's claims, for he says,

> When he lies, he speaks out of his own character, for he is a liar and the father of lies (John 8:44).

Jesus didn't need to respond to *every* false word Satan said, for his purpose was to resist the temptation itself, and this he did with the decisive words, "It is written, 'You shall worship the Lord your God, and him only shall you serve'" (Luke 4:8).

And so we have a choice: Do we believe *Satan's words* that he has the authority of all earthly kingdoms, or do we believe *Jesus' words* that Satan is a liar and the father of lies? The answer is easy: Satan wanted Jesus to believe a lie, just as he wanted Eve to believe a lie (Gen. 3:4), and he wants us to believe a lie as well, that he is the ruler of earthly governments.

---

1. For example, echoes of Boyd's writing can be seen at various places in Shane Claiborne and Chris Haw, *Jesus for President* (Grand Rapids: Zondervan, 2008).

By contrast, there are verses in the Bible that tell us how we should think of civil governments. These verses do not agree with Satan's claim in Luke 4:6 or with Boyd's claim about Satan's authority over all earthly governments. Rather, these verses where *God* is speaking (not Satan) portray civil government as a gift from God, something that is subject to God's rule and used by God for his purposes. Here are some of those passages:

> *The Most High rules the kingdom of men* and gives it to whom he will and sets over it the lowliest of men (Dan. 4:17).

> Let every person be subject to the governing authorities. For *there is no authority except from God, and those that exist have been instituted by God....* For rulers are not a terror to good conduct, but to bad. Would you have no fear of the one who is in authority? Then do what is good, and you will receive his approval, for *he is God's servant for your good ...* the *authorities are the ministers of God* (Rom. 13:1–6).

Peter sees civil government as doing the *opposite* of what Satan does: civil governments are established by God "to *punish* those who do evil," but Satan *encourages* those who do evil! Civil governments are established by God "to *praise* those who do good" (1 Pet. 2:14), but Satan *discourages and attacks* those who do good.

The point is that Satan wants us to believe that all civil government is under his control, but that is not taught anywhere in the Bible. The only verse in the whole Bible that says Satan has authority over all governments is spoken by the father of lies, and we should not believe it. Greg Boyd is simply wrong in his defense of the view that "government is demonic."

D. WRONG VIEW #4: DO EVANGELISM, NOT POLITICS

A fourth wrong view about Christians and politics is promoted by evangelicals who essentially say, "We should just preach the Gospel, and that is the only way Christians can hope to change peoples' hearts and change our society." I call this the "do evangelism, not politics" view. It claims that the church is only called to "preach the Gospel," not to preach about politics.

1. God calls Christians to do "good works"

Of course, we must insist that people can never earn their salvation by doing "good works." The Bible insists that "all have sinned and fall short of the glory of God" (Rom. 3:23), and it also says, "by works of the law no human being will be justified in his sight" (Rom. 3:20).

But after people have trusted in Jesus Christ for forgiveness of sins, then what should they do? How should we live now as Christians? The Bible says we should be doing "good works." In fact, right in the place where Paul writes a magnificent proclamation of justification by faith alone, he adds an important sentence about good works. First he says,

> For by grace you have been saved through faith. And this is not your own doing; it is the gift of God, not a result of works, so that no one may boast (Eph. 2:9).

Then he immediately adds,

> For we are his workmanship, created in Christ Jesus *for good works*, which God prepared beforehand, that we should walk in them (Eph. 2:10).

In another place he says, "As we have opportunity, let us do good to everyone, and especially to those who are of the household of faith" (Gal. 6:10). Certainly that means that we should do good to others, as we have opportunity, by being a good influence on laws and government and by having a good influence on the political process.

Jesus left us here on earth in part because he wants to allow our lives to give glory to him in the midst of a fallen and sinful world: "Let your light shine before others, *so that they may see your good works* and give glory to your Father who is in heaven" (Matt. 5:16).

If a pastor teaches his people how to raise their children, that's "good works." If he teaches them how to have good marriages, that's "good works." If he teaches them to love their neighbors as themselves (Matt. 22:39), that's "good works."

Should churches teach their people how to do "good works" in families, in hospitals and in schools, and in businesses and in neighborhoods, but not in government? Why should that area of life be excluded from the influence of the "good works" of believers that will "give glory to your Father who is in heaven"?

2. Influencing government for good is a way to love our neighbors

Jesus' command, "You shall love your neighbor as yourself" (Matt. 22:39) means that I should seek *good laws* that will protect preborn children. It means that I should seek *good laws* that protect marriages and families. It means I should seek *good laws* that protect children from corrupting moral influences that want to use classrooms to teach that all kinds of sexual experimentation outside of marriage are fine and that there is nothing wrong with pornography.

In short, Jesus' command to "love your neighbor" means that I should seek the good of my neighbors in every aspect of society, *including government, by seeking to bring about good government and good laws.*

3. Obeying what God tells us is doing spiritual good because it glorifies God

I cannot agree with people who say that Christian political involvement will do "no spiritual good." If it is commanded in the Bible and it's what God tells us to do, then by definition it *is* doing spiritual good. "This is the love of God, that we keep his commandments" (1 John 5:3) — therefore, following his teachings regarding government is one way of showing love to him.

In addition, when Christian influence brings about good laws that do good for society, we should expect that some people will realize how good God's moral standards are and they will glorify God as a result. People will "see your good works and give glory to your Father who is in heaven" (Matt. 5:16). Even in the Old Testament, Moses told the people of Israel:

> [The other nations] when they hear all these statutes, will say, "Surely this great nation is a wise and understanding people" (Deut. 4:6).

4. Good and bad governments make a huge difference in people's lives, and in the church

When people say that the kind of government we have doesn't make any difference to the church or to the spiritual lives of Christians, I think of the difference between North Korea and South Korea. These countries have the same language, the same ethnic background, the same cultural history, and live in the same location of the world. The only difference between them is that South Korea is a robust, thriving democracy with free people and North Korea is a Communist country with the most repressive, totalitarian government in the world.

And what a difference that makes in people's lives. There is just a handful of Christians in North Korea, and they must exercise their faith in secret. Severe, persistent persecution has hindered the church so greatly that there is no missionary activity, no public worship, no publication of Christian literature. Millions of North Koreans are born, live, and die without ever hearing the Gospel of Jesus Christ. By contrast, the church in South Korea, where the government has allowed freedom of religion, is growing, thriving, and sending missionaries around the world. It has one of the highest percentages of evangelical Christians of any nation (around 25%).

What is the only difference? The kind of government they have. One country is free and one is totalitarian. And in between these extremes fall many other nations of the world, governments more or less free and more or less conformed to God's principles for government as taught in Scripture. Where God's principles are followed more fully and people are allowed more freedom, the church will often thrive and people's lives are better in hundreds of ways.

Governments do make a difference to the church and to the work of God's kingdom. This is why Paul urged that prayers be made "for kings and all who are in high positions, that we may lead a peaceful and quiet life, godly and dignified in every way" (1 Tim. 2:2). Good governments help people to live a "peaceful" and "godly" life, and bad governments hinder that goal.

Governments can allow churches to meet freely and evangelize or they can prevent these things by force of law (as in Saudi Arabia and North Korea). They can hinder or promote literacy (the latter enabling people to read a Bible). They can stop murderers and thieves and drunk drivers and child predators or allow them to terrorize society and destroy lives. They can promote and protect marriages or hinder and even destroy them. Governments do make a significant difference for the work of God in the world, and we are to pray and work for good governments around the world.

5. Christians have influenced governments positively throughout history

Historian Alvin Schmidt points out how the spread of Christianity and Christian influence on government was primarily responsible for outlawing infanticide, child abandonment, and abortion in the Roman Empire (in AD 374);[2] outlawing the brutal battles-to-the-death in which

---

2. Alvin Schmidt, *How Christianity Changed the World* (Grand Rapids: Zondervan, 2004; formerly published as *Under the Influence*, 2001), 51, 53, 59.

thousands of gladiators had died (in 404);[3] granting of property rights and other protections to women;[4] banning polygamy (which is still practiced in some Muslim nations today);[5] prohibiting the burning alive of widows in India (in 1829);[6] outlawing the painful and crippling practice of binding young women's feet in China (in 1912);[7] persuading government officials to begin a system of public schools in Germany (in the sixteenth century);[8] and advancing the idea of compulsory education of all children in a number of European countries.[9]

During the history of the church, Christians had a decisive influence in opposing and often abolishing slavery in the Roman Empire, in Ireland, and in most of Europe (though Schmidt frankly notes that a minority of "erring" Christian teachers have supported slavery in various centuries).[10] In England, William Wilberforce, a devout Christian, led the successful effort to abolish the slave trade and then slavery itself throughout the British Empire by 1840.[11]

In the United States, though there were vocal defenders of slavery among Christians in the South, they lost the argument, and they were vastly outnumbered by the many Christians who were ardent abolitionists, speaking, writing, and agitating constantly for the abolition of slavery in the United States. Schmidt notes that two-thirds of the American abolitionists in the mid-1830s were Christian clergymen who were preaching "politics" from the pulpit, saying that slavery should be abolished.[12]

The American civil rights movement that resulted in the outlawing of racial segregation and discrimination was led by Martin Luther King Jr., a Baptist pastor, and supported by many Christian churches and groups.[13]

There was also strong influence from Christian ideas and influential Christians in the formulation of the Magna Charta in England (1215)[14] and

---

3. Ibid., 63.
4. Ibid., 111.
5. Ibid., 115.
6. Ibid., 116–17.
7. Ibid., 119.
8. Ibid., 179.
9. Ibid., 179–80. Although this is not a matter of merely influencing laws, Schmidt also points out the immense influence of Christians on higher education: By the year 1932 there were 182 colleges and universities in the United States, and of that number, 92 percent had been founded by Christian denominations (p. 190).
10. Ibid., 274–76.
11. Ibid., 276–78.
12. Ibid., 279.
13. Ibid., 287–89.
14. Ibid., 251–52.

of the Declaration of Independence (1776) and the Constitution (1787)[15] in the United States. These are three of the most significant documents in the history of governments on earth, and all three show the marks of significant Christian influence in the foundational ideas of how governments should function. These foundations for British and American government did not come about as a result of the "do evangelism, not politics" view.

Schmidt also argues that several specific components of modern views of government had strong Christian influence in their origin and influence, such as individual human rights, individual freedom, the equality of individuals before the law, freedom of religion, and separation of church and state.[16]

As for the present time, Charles Colson's insightful book *God and Government*[17] (previously published as *Kingdoms in Conflict*) reports dozens of encouraging narratives of courageous, real-life Christians who in recent years, in causes large and small, have had significant impact for good on laws and governments around the world.

When I look over that list of changes in governments and laws that Christians incited, I think God *did* call the church and thousands of Christians within the church to work to bring about these momentous improvements in human society throughout the world. Or should we say that Christians who brought about these changes were *not* doing so out of obedience to God? That these changes made *no difference* to God? This cannot be true.

I believe those changes listed above were important to the God who declares, "Let justice roll down like waters, and righteousness like an ever-flowing stream" (Amos 5:24). God *cares* how people treat one another here on earth, and these listed changes in government *do* have eternal value in God's sight.

If the Christian church had adopted the "do evangelism, not politics" view throughout its history, it would never have brought about these immeasurably valuable changes among the nations of the world. But these changes did happen, because Christians realized that if they could influence laws and governments for good, they would be obeying the command of their Lord, "Let your light shine before others, so that they *may see your good works* and give glory to your Father who is in heaven" (Matt. 5:16). They influenced governments for good because they knew that "we are his

---

15. Ibid., 253–58.

16. Ibid., 258–70.

17. Charles W. Colson, *God and Government: An Insider's View on the Boundaries between Faith and Politics.* Grand Rapids: Zondervan, 2007.

workmanship, created in Christ Jesus *for good works*, which God prepared beforehand, that we should walk in them" (Eph. 2:10).

6. Doesn't the Bible say that persecution is coming?

Sometimes people ask me, "Why should we try to improve governments when the Bible tells us that persecution is coming in the end times before Christ returns? Doesn't that mean that we should expect governments to become more and more anti-Christian?" (They have in mind passages like Matt. 24:9–12, 21–22; 2 Tim. 3:1–5.)

The answer is that we do not know if Christ will return next year or 500 years from now. What we do know is that while we have opportunity, God tells us not to give up but to go on preaching "the whole counsel of God" (Acts 20:27) and doing "good works" (Eph. 2:10) and loving our neighbors as ourselves (Matt. 22:39). That means we should go on *trying to influence governments for good* as long as we are able to do so.

If all the Christians who influenced governments for good in previous centuries had given up and said, "Persecution is coming and governments will become more evil, so there is nothing we can do," then none of those good changes in laws would have come about. Instead of giving in to such a hopeless attitude, courageous Christians in previous generations sought to do good for others and for governments, and God often blessed their efforts.

7. But won't political involvement distract us from the main task of preaching the Gospel?

At this point someone may object that while political involvement may have *some* benefits and may do *some* good, it can so easily distract us, turn us away from the church, and cause us to neglect the main task of pointing people toward personal trust in Christ.

Yet the proper question is not, "Does political influence take resources away from evangelism?" but, "Is political influence something God has called us to do?" If God has called some of us to some political influence, then those resources would not be blessed if we diverted them to evangelism—or to the music ministry, or to teaching Sunday School to children, or to any other use.

In this matter, as in everything else the church does, it would be healthy for Christians to realize that God may call *individual Christians* to different emphases in their lives. This is because God has placed in the church "varieties of gifts" (1 Cor. 12:4) and the church is an entity that has "many members" but is still "one body" (v. 12).

Therefore God might call someone to devote almost all of his or her time to the music ministry, someone else to youth work, someone else to evangelism, someone else to preparing refreshments to welcome visitors, and someone else to work with lighting and sound systems. "But if Jim places all his attention on the sound system, won't that distract the church from the main task of preaching the Gospel?" No, not at all. That is not what God has called Jim to emphasize (though he will certainly share the Gospel with others as he has opportunity). Jim's exclusive focus on the church's sound system means he is just being a faithful steward in the responsibility God has given him.

I think it is entirely possible that God called Billy Graham to emphasize evangelism and say nothing about politics and also called James Dobson to emphasize a radio ministry to families and to influencing the political world for good. Aren't there enough Christians in the world for us to focus on more than one task? And does God not call us to thousands of different emphases, all in obedience to him?

The whole ministry of the church will include many emphases. And the teaching ministry from the pulpit should do nothing less than proclaim "the whole counsel of God" (Acts 20:27). It should teach, over the course of time, on all areas of life and all areas of Bible knowledge. That certainly must include, to some extent, what the Bible says about the purposes of civil government and how that should apply to our situations today.

E. WRONG VIEW #5: DO POLITICS, NOT EVANGELISM

The fifth view says that the church should just try to change the laws and the culture and should not emphasize evangelism. I do not know of any responsible evangelical leaders or prominent Christian groups today who hold this view or say that Christians should just "do politics, not evangelism."

But this was a primary emphasis of the Social Gospel movement in the late nineteenth and early twentieth centuries, with its campaigns to get the church to work aggressively to overcome poverty, slums, crime, racial discrimination, and other social evils. These were good causes in themselves, but this movement placed little if any emphasis on the need for individuals to place personal trust in Christ as Savior or the need to proclaim the entire Bible as the Word of God and worthy of our belief. The Social Gospel movement gained followers primarily among liberal Protestants rather than among more conservative, evangelical Protestant groups.

Christians who encourage greater Christian involvement in politics today need to hear an important word of caution: If we (and I include myself here) ever begin to think that *good laws alone* will solve a nation's problems or bring about a righteous and just society, we will have made a huge mistake. Unless there is simultaneously an inner change in people's hearts and minds, good laws alone will only bring about grudging, external compliance with the minimum level of obedience necessary to avoid punishment. Good government and good laws can prevent much evil behavior, and they can teach people and show what society approves, but they cannot by themselves produce good people.

Genuine, long-term change in a nation will only happen (1) if people's *hearts* change so that they seek to do good, not evil; (2) if people's *minds* change so that their moral convictions align more closely with God's moral standards in the Bible; and (3) if a nation's *laws* change so that they more fully encourage good conduct and punish wrong conduct. Item 1 comes about through personal evangelism and the power of the Gospel of Jesus Christ. Item 2 takes place both through personal conversation and teaching and through public discussion and debate. Item 3 comes about through Christian political involvement. All three are necessary.

This "do politics, not evangelism" view is certainly wrong. The church must above all proclaim that "the wages of sin is death, but the free gift of God is eternal life in Christ Jesus our Lord" (Rom. 6:23). People definitely experience a change in their hearts when they believe in Christ: "Therefore, if anyone is in Christ, he is a new creation. The old has passed away; behold, the new has come" (2 Cor. 5:17).

What then? Is there a correct view that is different from these five wrong views? The view I propose next is "significant Christian influence on government." "Significant Christian influence on government" is not *compulsion* (view 1), it is not *silence* (view 2), and it is not *dropping out of the process* (views 3 and 4), nor is it thinking *the government can save people* (view 5). It is different from each of these wrong views, and I think it is much closer to the actual teaching of the Bible.

F. A BETTER VIEW: SIGNIFICANT CHRISTIAN INFLUENCE ON GOVERNMENT

The "significant influence" view says that Christians *should* seek to influence civil government according to God's moral standards and God's purposes for government as revealed in the Bible (when rightly understood). But while Christians exercise this influence, they must simultaneously insist on protecting freedom of religion for all citizens.

1. Old Testament support for significant Christian influence

The Bible shows several examples of believers in God who influenced secular governments.

For instance, the Jewish prophet Daniel exercised a strong influence on the secular government in Babylon. Daniel said to Nebuchadnezzar,

> "Therefore, O king, let my counsel be acceptable to you: *break off your sins* by *practicing righteousness*, and your iniquities by *showing mercy to the oppressed*, that there may perhaps be a lengthening of your prosperity" (Dan. 4:27).

Daniel's approach is bold and clear. It is the opposite of a modern multicultural approach that might say something like this:

> "O King Nebuchadnezzar, I am a Jewish prophet, but I would not presume to impose my Jewish moral standards on your Babylonian kingdom. Ask your astronomers and your soothsayers! They will guide you in your own traditions. Then follow your own heart! It would not be my place to speak to you about right and wrong."

No, Daniel boldly told the king, "*Break off your sins* by practicing righteousness, and your iniquities by showing mercy to the oppressed."

At that time Daniel was a high official in Nebuchadnezzar's court. He was "ruler over the whole province of Babylon" and "chief prefect over all the wise men of Babylon" (Dan. 2:48). He was regularly "at the king's court" (v. 49). Therefore it seems that Daniel had a significant advisory role to the king. This leads to a reasonable assumption that, though it is not specified in the text, Daniel's summary statement about "sins" and "iniquities" and "showing mercy to the oppressed" (Dan. 4:27) was followed by a longer conversation in which Daniel named specific policies and actions of the king that were either good or evil in the eyes of God.

The counsel that Jeremiah proclaimed to the Jewish exiles in Babylon also supports the idea of believers having influence on laws and government. Jeremiah told these exiles, "*Seek the welfare of the city* where I have sent you into exile, and pray to the LORD on its behalf, for in its welfare you will find your welfare" (Jer. 29:7). But if believers are to seek to bring good to such a pagan society, that must include seeking to bring good to its government (as Daniel did). The true "welfare" of such a city will be advanced through governmental laws and policies that are consistent with God's teaching in the Bible, not by those that are contrary to the Bible's teachings.

Other believers in God also had high positions of governmental influence in non-Jewish nations. Joseph was the highest official after Pharaoh, king of Egypt, and had great influence in the decisions of Pharaoh (see Gen. 41:37–45; 42:6; 45:8–9, 26). Later, Moses boldly stood before the Pharaoh and demanded freedom for the people of Israel, saying, "Thus says the LORD, 'Let my people go'" (Exod. 8:1). Nehemiah was "cupbearer to the king" (Neh. 1:11), a position of high responsibility before King Artaxerxes of Persia.[18] Mordecai "was second in rank to King Ahasuerus" of Persia (Esth. 10:3; see also 9:4). Queen Esther also had significant influence on the decisions of Ahasuerus (see Esth. 5:1–8; 7:1–6; 8:3–13; 9:12–15, 29–32).

In addition, there are several passages in the Old Testament prophets that address the sins of foreign nations around Israel: see Isaiah 13–23; Ezekiel 25–32; Amos 1–2; Obadiah (addressed to Edom); Jonah (sent to Nineveh); Nahum (addressed to Nineveh); Habakkuk 2; Zephaniah 2. These prophets could speak to nations outside of Israel because the God who is revealed in the Bible is the God of *all peoples* and *all nations* of the earth. Therefore the moral standards of God as revealed in the Bible are the moral standards to which God will hold all people accountable. This includes more than the way people conduct themselves in their marriages and families, in their neighborhoods and schools, and in their jobs and businesses. It also concerns the way people conduct themselves *in government offices*. Believers have a responsibility to bear witness to the moral standards of the Bible by which God will hold all people accountable, including those people in public office.

2. New Testament support for significant Christian influence

A New Testament example of influence on government is found in the life of John the Baptist. During his lifetime the ruler of Galilee (from 4 BC to AD 39) was Herod Antipas, a "tetrarch" who had been appointed by the Roman emperor and was subject to the authority of the Roman Empire. Matthew's gospel tells us that John the Baptist rebuked Herod for a specific personal sin in his life:

---

18. "The position of cupbearer to the king was a high office and involved regular access to the king," ESV *Study Bible* (Wheaton, IL: Crossway, 2008), 825.

For Herod had seized John and bound him and put him in prison for the sake of Herodias, his brother Phillip's wife, because John had been saying to him, "It is not lawful for you to have her" (Matt. 14:3–4).

But Luke's gospel adds more detail:

[John the Baptist] preached good news to the people. But Herod the tetrarch, who had been reproved by him for Herodias, his brother's wife, *and for all the evil things that Herod had done*, added this to them all, that he locked up John in prison (Luke 3:18–20).

Certainly "all the evil things that Herod had done" included evil actions that he had carried out as a governing official in the Roman Empire. John the Baptist rebuked him *for all of them*. He boldly spoke to officials of the empire about the moral right and wrong of their governmental policies. In doing this, John was following in the steps of Daniel and many Old Testament prophets. The New Testament portrays John the Baptist's actions as those of "a righteous and holy man" (Mark 6:20). He is an excellent example of a believer who had what I call "significant influence" on the policies of a government (though it cost him his life: see Mark 6:21–29).

Another example is the apostle Paul. While Paul was in prison in Caesarea, he stood trial before the Roman governor Felix. Here is what happened:

After some days Felix came with his wife Drusilla, who was Jewish, and he sent for Paul and heard him speak about faith in Christ Jesus. And *as he reasoned about righteousness and self-control and the coming judgment*, Felix was alarmed and said, "Go away for the present. When I get an opportunity I will summon you" (Acts 24:24–25).

While Luke does not give us any more details, the fact that Felix was "alarmed" and that Paul reasoned with him about "righteousness" and "the coming judgment" indicates that Paul was talking about moral standards of right and wrong and the ways in which Felix, as an official of the Roman Empire, had obligations to live up to the standards that are given by God. Paul no doubt told Felix that he would be accountable for his actions at "the coming judgment" and that this was what led Felix to be "alarmed." When Luke tells us that Paul "reasoned" with Felix about these things, the word (Greek *dialegomai*) indicates a back-and-forth conversation or discussion. It is not difficult to suppose that

Felix asked Paul, "What about this decision that I made? What about this policy? What about this ruling?" It would be an artificial restriction on the meaning of the text to suppose that Paul *only* spoke with Felix about his "private" life and not about his actions as a Roman governor. Paul is thus another example of attempting to exercise "significant Christian influence" on civil government.

Clearly, examples of godly believers' influence on governments are not minor or confined to obscure portions of the Bible, but are found in Old Testament history from Genesis all the way to Esther (the last historical book), in the canonical writing prophets from Isaiah to Zephaniah, and in the New Testament in both the Gospels and Acts. And those are just the examples of God's servants bringing "significant influence" to pagan kings who gave no allegiance to the God of Israel or to Jesus in the New Testament times. If we add to this list the many stories of Old Testament prophets bringing counsel and encouragement and rebuke to the good and evil kings of Israel as well, then we would include the histories of all the kings and the writings of all the prophets — nearly every book of the Old Testament. And we could add in several passages from Psalms and Proverbs that speak of good and evil rulers. Influencing government for good on the basis of the wisdom found in God's own words is a theme that runs through the entire Bible.

3. Romans 13 and 1 Peter 2

In addition to these examples, *specific Bible passages that teach about government* present an argument for "significant Christian influence." Why do we think God put Romans 13:1–7 and 1 Peter 2:13–14 and other related passages (as in Psalms and Proverbs) in the Bible? Are they in the Bible simply as a matter of intellectual curiosity for Christians who will read them privately but never use them to speak to government officials about how God understands their roles and responsibilities? Does God intend this material to be *concealed* from people in government and *kept secret* by Christians who read it and silently moan about "how far government has strayed from what God wants it to be"?

Certainly God put such passages there not only to inform Christians about how *they* should relate to civil government, but also in order that *people with governmental responsibilities* could know what God himself expects from them. This also pertains to other passages in the Bible that instruct us about God's moral standards, about the nature and purpose of human beings made in God's image, about God's purposes for the earth, and about principles concerning good and bad governments.

All of these teachings are relevant for those who serve in governmental office, and we should speak and teach about them when we have opportunity to do so.

4. The responsibility of citizens in a democracy to understand the Bible's teaching

There is still another argument for "significant Christian influence" on government that applies to anyone who lives in a democracy, because in a democracy a significant portion of the ruling power of government is entrusted to the citizens generally, through the ballot box. Therefore all citizens who are old enough to vote have a *responsibility* before God to know what God expects of civil government and what kind of moral and legal standards he wants government to follow. But *how can citizens learn what kind of government God is seeking?* They can learn this only if churches teach about government and politics from the Bible.

I realize that pastors will differ in the degree of detail they wish to teach with regard to specific political issues facing a nation (for example, whether to teach about issues such as abortion, euthanasia, care for the poor, the military and national defense, use and care of the environment, or the nature of marriage). But surely it is a responsibility of pastors to teach on *some* of these specific policies in ways that go beyond the mere statement, "You have a responsibility to vote intelligently."

After all, who else is going to teach these Christians about *exactly how* the Bible applies to specific political issues? Would pastors think it right to leave their congregations with such vague guidance in other areas of life? Would we say, "You have a responsibility to bring up your children according to Christian principles," and then never explain to them what those Christian principles are? Would we think it right to say to people in the business world, "You have a responsibility to work in the business world according to Christian principles," and then never give them any details about what these Christian principles are? No, the responsibility of pastors is to give wise biblical teaching, *explaining exactly how the teachings of the Bible apply to various specific situations in life*, and that should certainly include instruction about some policy matters in government and politics.

G. FINAL THOUGHTS

There is a view among a few Christians in the United States today called "Theonomy." Theonomists argue that the Old Testament laws that God gave to Israel in the Mosaic covenant should be the pattern for civil laws in nations today. This would include carrying out the death penalty for such things as blasphemy or adultery or homosexual conduct!

The error of Theonomists is that they misunderstand the unique place that these laws for Israel had in the history of the whole Bible, and they misunderstand the New Testament teaching of the distinction between the realm of the church and the realm of the state that Jesus established when he said, "Render to Caesar the things that are Caesar's, and to God the things that are God's" (Matt. 22:21).

Furthermore, when I speak about "significant Christian influence" on government, I want to be very clear that *I do not mean that Christians should only vote for other Christian candidates for office*, or even that Christians should generally prefer an evangelical candidate over others who are running. The relevant principle is this: Christians should support candidates who best represent moral and political values consistent with biblical teaching, no matter their religious background or convictions.

Two concluding observations: First, without Christian influence, governments will have no clear moral compass, and second, Christian citizens have an obligation to exercise such influence.

1. Without Christian influence, governments will have no clear moral compass

Try to imagine what a nation and its government would be like *if all Christian influence on government were suddenly removed*. Within a few years no one would have any moral absolutes beyond their individual moral sentiments and moral intuitions, which can be so unreliable. In addition, most people would have no moral authority beyond that of individual human opinion. Therefore, how could a nation find any moral guidance?

Consider the many political issues facing the United States (and other nations) that have significant moral components to them. For example: war, same-sex marriage, abortion, pornography, poverty, care for the environment, capital punishment, and public education. There are many other issues as well. The United States has a tremendous need for moral guidance, and I am convinced that Christians should study and discuss and then speak publicly about them.

If pastors and church members say, "I'll let somebody else speak about that," where will the nation's moral standards come from? Where will people learn about ethics? Perhaps from Hollywood movies? From friends at work or at the local bar? From professional counselors? From elementary school teachers? But where do *these* people learn about right and wrong?

The simple fact is that if Christians do not speak publicly about what the Bible teaches regarding issues of right and wrong, there aren't many other good sources for finding any transcendent source of ethics, any source outside of ourselves and our own subjective feelings and consciences.

As Christians, we need to remember that the entire world is locked in a tremendous spiritual battle. There are demonic forces, forces of Satan, that seek to oppose God's purposes and bring evil and destruction to every human being that God created in his own image, and also bring destruction to every human society and every nation. If pastors and church members say, "I'm going to be silent about the moral and ethical issues that we face as a nation," that will leave a moral vacuum, and it will not be long until the ultimate adversaries of the Gospel — Satan and his demons — will rush in and influence every decision in a way contrary to biblical standards.

2. The political obligations of all Christian citizens

I believe that every Christian citizen who lives in a democracy has at the very least a minimal obligation to be well-informed and to vote for candidates and policies that are most consistent with biblical principles. The opportunity to help select the kind of government we will have is a *stewardship* that God entrusts to citizens in a democracy, a stewardship that we should not neglect or fail to appreciate.

Furthermore, I want to ask every Christian in the United States to consider whether he or she has a higher obligation than merely voting. The question is whether someone thinks it is morally right *to receive great benefits from a nation but to give almost nothing in return*. The great freedoms that citizens have in the United States came only as a result of great sacrifice on the part of millions of others. The original signers of the Declaration of Independence knew that they were publicly declaring themselves to be guilty of treason against Britain, and they knew they would be subject to the death penalty and to confiscation of their property if the British caught them or defeated them.[19] Nor could they have any great confidence that they would win a war against the most powerful nation on earth at that time. Therefore the last line in the Declaration of Independence says this:

---

19. Pauline Maier, *American Scripture: Making the Declaration of Independence* (New York: Alfred A. Knopf, 1998), 59, 118, 125, 147, 152.

And for the support of this declaration, with a firm reliance on the protection of divine Providence, we mutually pledge to each other our lives, our fortunes, and our sacred honor.[20]

Independence from Britain did not come cheaply. In the War of Independence, approximately 4,500 Americans died. Later wars were even more costly. All told, hundreds of thousands of men (and many women as well) *sacrificed their lives* to protect the nation and preserve the freedoms we enjoy today. *Is it right that we simply enjoy these freedoms while giving back to our nation nothing in return?* Should we not participate at least at some level in giving money or giving time to support specific candidates and issues? Or writing letters or helping to distribute literature? Or even running for office or volunteering to serve in the military? Is it not right that all of us at least do *something* more than merely voting to preserve and protect this nation?

---

20. Declaration of Independence, adopted July 4, 1776. www.archives.gov/national_archives_experience/charters/declaration_transcript.html.

THE PROTECTION OF LIFE: ABORTION

A. ABORTION

1. The issue

With regard to the question of abortion, the political question is this:

> Should governments make laws to protect the lives of preborn children?

If the answer to that question is yes, then there are more specific questions, such as:

> Should the preborn child be protected from the moment of conception to the moment of birth, or only from some later point in pregnancy?

> What should the preborn child be called—a "fetus," a "preborn child," an "unborn child," or a "baby"?

> What kind of penalties should attach to taking the life of a preborn child?

Even for those who do not think governments should make laws protecting the lives of preborn children, other policy questions remain:

> Should governments pay for women to have abortions?

> Should physicians and other health-care providers who think abortion is morally wrong be compelled to perform abortions?

Should government policies promote or discourage abortions? (This would include educational policies, policies regarding aid to other nations, and so forth.)

2. Relevant biblical teaching

a. The preborn should be treated as a person from the moment of conception

Several passages in the Bible suggest that a preborn child should be thought of as a person from the moment of conception. For example, before the birth of John the Baptist, when his mother, Elizabeth, was in about her sixth month of pregnancy, she was visited by her relative, Mary, who was to become the mother of Jesus. Luke reports:

> And when Elizabeth heard the greeting of Mary, the baby leaped in her womb. And Elizabeth was filled with the Holy Spirit, and she exclaimed with a loud cry,... "Behold, when the sound of your greeting came to my ears, *the baby in my womb leaped for joy*" (Luke 1:41–44).

Under the influence of the Holy Spirit, Elizabeth calls the preborn child in the sixth month of pregnancy a "baby" (Greek *brephos*, "baby, infant"). This is the same Greek word that is used for a child after it is born, as in Luke 2:16, where Jesus is called a "baby [*brephos*] lying in a manger" (see also Luke 18:15; 2 Tim. 3:15). Elizabeth also says that the baby "leaped for joy," which attributes personal human activity to him. He was able to hear Mary's voice and somehow, even prior to birth, feel joyful about it. (Note that modern medical research shows that preborn children can distinguish and become familiar with the voices of their father, mother, or other family members.)

In the Old Testament, King David sinned with Bathsheba and then was rebuked by Nathan the prophet. Afterward, David wrote Psalm 51, in which he pleads with God, "Have mercy on me, O God, according to your steadfast love" (v. 1). Amidst confessing his sin, he writes,

> Behold, I was brought forth in iniquity, and *in sin did my mother conceive me* (Ps. 51:5).

David thinks back to the time of his birth and says that he was "brought forth" from his mother's womb as a sinner. In fact, his sinfulness as a person extended back even prior to his birth, for David, under the direction of the Holy Spirit says, "In sin did my mother conceive me."

He is not talking about his mother's sin in any of the preceding verses, but is talking about the depth of his own sinfulness as a human being. Therefore, in this verse he is talking about himself as well. He is saying that from the moment of conception he had a sinful nature. This means that *he thought of himself as a distinct human being, a distinct person, from the moment of conception.* He was not merely part of his mother's body, but was distinct in his personhood. And this goes all the way back to the point of conception.

David also thinks of himself as a person while he was growing in his mother's womb, for he says,

> You formed my inward parts; you knitted *me* together in my mother's womb (Ps. 139:13).

Here also he speaks of himself as a distinct person ("me") when he was in his mother's womb. The word translated "inward parts" is Hebrew *kilyah*, literally "kidneys," but in contexts such as this one, it refers to the innermost parts of a person, including his deepest inward thoughts and emotions (see its uses in Pss. 16:7; 26:2; 73:21; Prov. 2:16; Jer. 17:10).

In an earlier example, Rebekah, the wife of Isaac, was pregnant with the twins who were to be named Jacob and Esau. We read:

> The children [Hebrew *banim*, plural of *ben*] struggled together within her, and she said, "If it is thus, why is this happening to me?" So she went to inquire of the LORD. And the LORD said to her, "Two nations are in your womb, and two peoples from within you shall be divided; the one shall be stronger than the other, the older shall serve the younger" (Gen. 25:22–23).

Once again, the preborn children are viewed as "children" within her womb. (Hebrew *ben* is the ordinary word used more than 4,900 times in the Old Testament for "son" or—plural—"children.") These twins are viewed as already struggling together. Before the point of birth they are thought of as distinct persons, and their future is being predicted.

For the question of abortion, perhaps the most significant passage of all is found in the specific laws God gave Moses for the people of Israel during the time of the Mosaic covenant. One particular law spoke of the penalties to be imposed in case the life or health of a pregnant woman or her preborn child was endangered or harmed:

> When men strive together and hit a pregnant woman, so that her children come out, *but there is no harm*, the one who hit her shall surely be fined, as the woman's husband shall impose

on him, and he shall pay as the judges determine. But *if there is harm*, then you shall pay life for life, eye for eye, tooth for tooth, hand for hand, foot for foot, burn for burn, wound for wound, stripe for stripe (Exod. 21:22–25).[1]

This law concerns a situation when men are fighting and one of them accidentally hits a pregnant woman. Neither one of them intended to do this, but as they fought they were not careful enough to avoid hitting her. If that happens, there are two possibilities:

1. If this causes a premature birth but *there is no harm to the pregnant woman or her preborn child,* there is still a penalty: "The one who hit her shall surely be fined" (v. 22). The penalty was for carelessly endangering the life or health of the pregnant woman and her child. We have similar laws in modern society, such as when a person is fined for drunken driving, even though he has hit no one with his car. He recklessly endangered human life and health, and he deserved a fine or other penalty.

2. But *"if there is harm"* to either the pregnant woman or her child, then the penalties are quite severe: "Life for life, eye for eye, tooth for tooth ..." (vv. 23–24). This means that both the mother and the preborn child are given equal legal protection. The penalty for harming the preborn child is just as great as for harming the mother. Both are treated as persons, and both deserve the full protection of the law.[2]

This law is even more significant when we put it in the context of other laws in the Mosaic covenant. In other cases in the Mosaic law where someone *accidentally* caused the death of another person, there was no requirement to give "life for life," no capital punishment. Rather, the person who accidentally caused someone else's death was required to

---

1. The phrase "so that her children come out" is a literal translation of the Hebrew text, which uses the plural of the common Hebrew word *yeled,* "child," and another very common word *yâtsâ',* which means "go out, come out." The plural "children" is probably the plural of indefiniteness, allowing for the possibility of more than one child. Other translations render this as "so that she gives birth prematurely," which is very similar in meaning (so NASB, from 1999 editions onward; similarly: NIV, TNIV, NET, HCSV, NLT, NKJV).

2. Some translations have adopted an alternative sense of this passage. The NRSV translates it, "When people who are fighting injure a pregnant woman so that there is a miscarriage, and yet no further harm follows ..." (RSV is similar, as was NASB before 1999). In this case, causing a miscarriage and the death of a preborn child results only in a fine. Therefore, some have argued, this passage treats the preborn child as *less worthy* of protection than others in society, for the penalty is less. But the arguments for this translation are not persuasive.

flee to one of the "cities of refuge" until the death of the high priest (see Num. 35:9–15, 22–29). This was a kind of "house arrest," although the person had to stay within a city rather than within a house for a limited period of time. It was a far lesser punishment than "life for life."

This means that God established for Israel a law code *that placed a higher value on protecting the life of a pregnant woman and her preborn child than the life of anyone else in Israelite society.* Far from treating the death of a preborn child as *less significant* than the death of others in society, this law treats the death of a preborn child or its mother as *more significant* and worthy of more severe punishment. And the law does not place any restriction on the number of months the woman was pregnant. Presumably it would apply from a very early stage in pregnancy, whenever it could be known that a miscarriage had occurred and her child or children had died as a result.

Moreover, this law applies to a case of *accidental* killing of a preborn child. But if *accidental* killing of a preborn child is so serious in God's eyes, then surely *intentional* killing of a preborn child must be an even worse crime.

The conclusion from all of these verses is that the Bible teaches that we should think of the preborn child as a person from the moment of conception, and we should give to the preborn child legal protection at least equal to that of others in the society.

Additional note: It is likely that many people reading this evidence from the Bible, perhaps for the first time, will already have had an abortion. Others reading this will have encouraged someone else to have an abortion. I cannot minimize or deny the moral wrong involved in this action, but I can point to the repeated offer of the Bible that God will give forgiveness of sins to those who repent of their sin and trust in Jesus Christ for forgiveness: "If we confess our sins, he is faithful and just to forgive us our

---

The primary argument is that this would make the law similar to a provision in the law code of Hammurabi (about 1760 BC in ancient Babylon). But such a supposed parallel should not override the meanings of the actual words in the Hebrew text of Exodus. The moral and civil laws in the Bible often differed from those of the ancient cultures around Israel. In addition, there is a Hebrew word for a miscarriage (*shakal*, Gen. 31:38; see also Exod. 23:26; Job 21:20; Hosea 9:14), but that word is not used here, nor is *nçphel*, another term for "miscarriage" (see Job 3:16; Ps. 58:8; Eccl. 6:3). However, the word that is used, *yâtsâ'*, is ordinarily used to refer to the live birth of a child (see Gen. 25:26; 38:29; Jer. 1:5). Finally, even on this (incorrect) translation, a *fine* is imposed on the person who accidentally caused the death of the preborn child. This implies that *accidentally* causing such a death is still considered morally wrong. Therefore, *intentionally* causing the death of a preborn child would be much more wrong, even on this translation.

sins and to cleanse us from all unrighteousness" (1 John 1:9). Although such sin, like all other sin, deserves God's wrath, Jesus Christ took that wrath on himself as a substitute for all who would believe in him: "He himself bore our sins in his body on the tree, that we might die to sin and live to righteousness. By his wounds you have been healed" (1 Peter 2:24).

b. Scientific information on the distinct personhood of the preborn child

Dr. Dianne Irving, a biochemist and biologist and professor at Georgetown University, writes:

> To begin with, scientifically something very radical occurs between the processes of gametogenesis and fertilization—the change from a simple *part* of one human being (i.e., a sperm) and a simple *part* of another human being (i.e., an oocyte— usually referred to as an "ovum" or "egg"), which simply possess "human life," to a new, genetically unique, newly existing, individual, whole living human being (a single-cell embryonic human zygote). That is, upon fertilization, parts of human beings have actually been transformed into something very different from what they were before; they have been changed into a single, whole human being. During the process of fertilization, the sperm and the oocyte cease to exist as such, and a new human being is produced.
>
> To understand this, it should be remembered that each kind of living organism has a specific number and quality of chromosomes that are characteristic for each member of a species. (The number can vary only slightly if the organism is to survive.) For example, the characteristic number of chromosomes for a member of the human species is 46 (plus or minus, e.g., in human beings with Down's or Turner's syndromes). Every somatic (or, body) cell in a human being has this characteristic number of chromosomes. Even the early germ cells contain 46 chromosomes; it is only their mature forms—the sex gametes, or sperms and oocytes—which will later contain only 23 chromosomes each. Sperms and oocytes are derived from primitive germ cells in the developing fetus by means of the process known as "gametogenesis." Because each germ cell normally has 46 chromosomes, the process of "fertilization" can not take place until the total number of chromosomes in each germ cell is cut in half. This is necessary so that after their fusion at fertilization

the characteristic number of chromosomes in a single individual member of the human species (46) can be maintained— otherwise we would end up with a monster of some sort.

To accurately see why a sperm or an oocyte are considered as only possessing human life, and not as living human beings themselves, one needs to look at the basic scientific facts involved in the processes of **gametogenesis** and of **fertilization**. It may help to keep in mind that the products of gametogenesis and fertilization are very different. The products of gametogenesis are mature sex gametes with only 23 instead of 46 chromosomes. The product of fertilization is a living human being with 46 chromosomes. Gametogenesis refers to the maturation of germ cells, resulting in gametes. Fertilization refers to the initiation of a new human being.[3]

c. Objections regarding the personhood of the preborn child

Some objections may be raised against the idea that the preborn child should be treated as a person from the moment of conception.

(1) Unable to interact and survive on its own: One objection is that the preborn child is unable to talk or interact with other people or perform moral actions. In addition, it is unable to survive without its mother.

But these factors do not mean that the preborn child is not a person. For instance, a newborn is still unable to talk or perform moral actions. This is also true for a person in a coma due to a serious accident. Moreover, a newborn infant is surely unable to survive without its mother. (In fact, some people would say that most junior high students are unable to survive without their mother!) Such an objection is not persuasive.

(2) Birth defects: Another objection concerns preborn children who are known to have birth defects. Should parents not have the right to abort such children, thus saving themselves much hardship and saving the child from a life of suffering?

But the relevant question here is this: Would we think it right to put such a child to death *after* it is born?

If we have already established that the preborn child should be treated as a person from the moment of conception, then being born or not

---

3. Dianne Irving, Ph.D., "When Do Human Beings Begin? 'Scientific' Myths and Scientific Facts," http://catholiceducation.org/articles/abortion/ab0027.html. Dr. Irving is a former career-appointed bench research biochemist/biologist (NIH, NCI, Bethesda, MD), an M.A. and Ph.D. philosopher (Georgetown University, Washington, DC), and Professor of the History of Philosophy and of Medical Ethics.

yet being born should make no difference in assessment of the child's personhood. If we would not think it right to kill such a child after it is born, then we should not think it right to kill the child before it is born.

Moreover, prior to birth the "possible" or "probable" diagnosis of birth defects can be in error. Sometimes children can be perfectly normal even though there was a diagnosis of a "possible" or "probable" birth defect. Many birth defects can be very small and not have significant impact on the child's life. And even when the birth defect is quite significant (for example, Down syndrome) the child can still lead a happy life and bring much joy and blessing to his or her own family and to many others. In such cases Christians should be encouraged to trust in God's wise providence and his sovereign direction of their lives. The Lord said to Moses, "Who has made man's mouth? Who makes him mute, or deaf, or seeing, or blind? Is it not I, the LORD?" (Exod. 4:11). When Jesus saw a man who had been blind from birth,

> his disciples asked him, "Rabbi, who sinned, this man or his parents, that he was born blind?" Jesus answered, "It was not that this man sinned, or his parents, but that the works of God might be displayed in him" (John 9:2–3).

Randy Alcorn quotes an example of a medical school professor who told about the following case study and asked students what they would do:

> The father had syphilis and the mother had tuberculosis. Of four previous children, the first was blind, the second died, the third was both deaf and dumb, and the fourth had tuberculosis. What would you advise the woman to do when she finds she is pregnant again?

One student answered, "I would advise an abortion." Then the professor said, "Congratulations.... You have just killed Beethoven."[4]

(3) Pregnancies resulting from rape or incest: If a child has been conceived through rape or incest, we must recognize the genuine pain and hardship experienced by the mother, who is involuntarily pregnant and perhaps pregnant at a very young age. Christians who know of such situations should be ready to give encouragement and support in many ways.

But once again the question must be asked, would we think it right to kill a baby conceived through rape or incest *after* it is born? Most people would say, certainly not. Such a child does not lose its right to

---

4. Randy Alcorn, *ProLife Answers to ProChoice Arguments* (Portland, OR: Multnomah, 1992), 175.

live because of the circumstances of its conception. But then we should not think it right to kill the child *before* it is born either. The rape that occurred is not the fault of the child, and the child should not be put to death because of someone else's crime. "Fathers shall not be put to death because of their children, nor shall children be put to death because of their fathers. Each one shall be put to death for his own sin" (Deut. 24:16; compare Ezek. 18:20). In addition, such instances are quite rare, constituting at most 1% of all abortions,[5] but probably much less than that.

Alcorn points out that well-known gospel singer Ethel Waters was born as a result of pregnancy that occurred when her mother was raped at age twelve.[6] There are no doubt other people today who lead useful, productive, fulfilling lives, even though their birth was the result of the horrible crime of rape. We should not justify taking the life of the preborn child in such cases.

(4) Abortion to save the life of the mother: According to the Centers for Disease Control, abortion carried out to save the life of the mother is extremely rare (less than 0.118% of all abortions).[7] Such a situation is different from the others we considered above, because here the choice is between the loss of one life (the baby's) and the loss of two lives (both the baby's and the mother's). I cannot see a reason to say this would be morally wrong, and in fact, I believe it would be morally right for doctors to save the life that can be saved and take the life of the preborn child. This is significantly different from the other cases, because removing the preborn child from the mother's body (for example from the Fallopian tube in the case of an ectopic pregnancy) results from *directly intending to save the life of the mother,* not from *directly intending to take the child's life.* If the medical technology exists to save the child's life in such cases, then of course the child's life should also be saved. But if abortion is necessary to save the mother's life, this would seem to be the only situation in which abortion is morally justified.

Therefore it seems right to me that all mainstream pro-life proposals for legal restrictions on abortion have included an exception to save the life of the mother.

---

5. A. Torres and J. Forest, "Why Do Women Have Abortions?" *Family Planning Perspectives* 20:4 (July/Aug. 1988), 169–76; still the best source of US data according to A. Bankole et al., "Reasons Why Women Have Induced Abortions: Evidence from 27 Countries," *Family Planning Perspectives* 24:3 (Aug. 1998), 117–25, 152.

6. Alcorn, *ProLife Answers,* 179.

7. Jeani Chang et al., "Pregnancy-Related Mortality Surveillance—United States, 1991–1999," Centers for Disease Control, *Morbidity and Mortality Weekly Report* (Feb. 21, 2003). www.cdc.gov/mmwr/preview/mmwrhtml/ss5202a1.htm.

But in politics, proponents of "abortion rights" too often lump together "life" and "health" and declare that they are willing to restrict abortion "except to save the life or health of the mother." Then in actual practice, "health" becomes defined so broadly in legal precedents that it also includes "mental health," including freedom from excessive distress; thus, "except to save the life *or health* of the mother" in practice means abortion is allowed whenever the mother wants to obtain one.

In fact, *Doe v. Bolton*, the companion case to *Roe v. Wade*, defined maternal "health" as "all factors—physical, emotional, psychological, familial, and the woman's age—relevant to the well-being of the patient." These factors are so vague and open-ended that almost any reason can be cited to allow an abortion in the second and third trimesters. Therefore, abortion is legal—and cannot be prohibited—in the fourth, fifth, sixth, seventh, eighth, or ninth month of pregnancy if any of the reasons is invoked.[8]

3. Arguments from reason and evidence apart from the Bible

When talking about abortion with people who do not think of the Bible as God's Word, a case for the personhood of the preborn child can still be argued in several ways. Medical evidence about the distinct genetic identity and distinct DNA of the child can be used to show that the preborn child is far different (in every single cell of its body!) from any other part of the mother's own body. Modern ultrasound technology can give highly realistic images of the preborn child—images that look so much like a real human person that they have great persuasive force. For that reason, many abortion advocates try to discourage pregnant women from seeing such vivid images. Nancy Keenan, president of NARAL Pro-Choice America in Washington, DC, said, "Politicians should not require a doctor to perform a medically unnecessary ultrasound, nor should they force a woman to view an ultrasound against her will."[9] Abortion advocate William Saletan, writing in *Slate* magazine, said, "Ultrasound has exposed the life in the womb to those of us who didn't want to see what abortion kills. The fetus is squirming, and so are we."[10]

---

8. *Doe v. Bolton*, 41 U.S. 179, 192 (1973).

9. Jennifer Parker, "Bill Would Mandate Ultrasound before Abortion," *ABCNews.com* (March 16, 2007). http://abcnews.go.com/US/story?id=2958249&page=1&CMP=OTC-RSSFeeds0312.

10. William Saletan, "Sex, Lies, and Videotape," *Slate.com* (April 28, 2007). www.slate.com/id/2165137/.

As of February 2009, eleven states were considering ultrasound laws, requiring that a woman be given an opportunity to view an ultrasound of her preborn child prior to having an abortion (Connecticut, Indiana, Kansas, Maryland, Missouri, Nebraska, New York, South Carolina, Texas, Virginia, and Wyoming).[11] At present, three states (North Dakota, South Dakota, and Utah) mandate that a woman be given an opportunity to view an ultrasound when seeking abortion.[12]

In addition, the arguments from how we would treat a child after it is born can have significant persuasive force. (For example, would we think it right for our laws to allow a parent to kill a child simply because the parent does not want the child or finds the child a difficult burden?)

Another argument against abortion is the incalculable loss to the nation from the deaths of more than one million babies per year. Since the 1973 Supreme Court decision *Roe v. Wade,* nearly 50 million children have been put to death through abortion.[13] Some of those would now be thirty-seven years old. Others would be thirty-six, and thirty-five, and so on, down to 1,200,000 of them who would be in their first year of life.[14] Many of them by now would be scientists and doctors, engineers and business leaders, entrepreneurs, artists, electricians, poets, carpenters, musicians, sports figures, political leaders, and so forth. Many of them would be mothers taking care of their own children and fathers helping to raise their children. They would be contributing to society in all areas of life—but they never had the chance to be born. They never had the chance to contribute in a positive way to this world.

A further argument can be made simply from the instinctive sense a pregnant woman has that what is growing in her womb is not a piece of tissue or merely a part of her body, but is in fact *a baby.* (Such an instinct is given even to unbelievers by God himself, for the Bible tells us, with respect to Gentiles "who do not have the Law," that "the work of the Law is *written on their hearts,* while their *conscience* also bears witness, and their conflicting thoughts accuse or even excuse them" [Rom. 2:14–15].) This gives us some hope that arguments showing the

---

11. "More States Considering Mandating Ultrasounds before Abortions," *USA Today* (Feb. 8, 2009). www.usatoday.com/news/nation/2009–02–08-abortion-laws_N.htm.

12. Alan Guttmacher Institute, "State Policies in Brief: Requirements for Ultrasound" (Sept. 1, 2009). www.guttmacher.org/statecenter/spibs/spib_RFU.pdf.

13. As of September 2009, National Right to Life calculates the total number of abortions since *Roe v. Wade* to be 49,551,703. www.nrlc.org/abortion/facts/abortionstats.html.

14. Recent statistics show a current rate of 1.2 million abortions per year, down from a peak of 1.6 million per year in 1990. From 1980 to 1992 the average was over 1.5 million per year, but it has been declining slightly ever since then. See ibid.

personhood of the preborn child will eventually be persuasive to the majority of people in a society.

4. Objections

Here are some objections that people have raised against the idea of prohibiting abortions.

a. A wrongful restriction of freedom

Some people will argue that a law prohibiting abortions is a wrongful restriction on individual human freedom. Shouldn't the decision about whether to carry a baby to full term and give birth be a decision made by the mother herself? How can it be right to say that the law should force a woman to endure a pregnancy and bear a child that she does not want? Isn't individual freedom a foundational principle of this country? Sometimes people will say, "I am personally opposed to abortion, but I think that's a decision that should be up to the mother and her doctor."

For example, US Vice President Joe Biden has repeatedly said, "My position is that I am personally opposed to abortion, but I don't think I have a right to impose my view on the rest of society."[15] In 2004, then-presidential candidate John Kerry was asked about his position on abortion on *Meet the Press*. He said, "I don't want abortion. Abortion should be the rarest thing in the world. I am actually personally opposed to abortion. But I don't believe that I have a right to take what is an article of faith to me and legislate it to other people."[16] In the meantime, the 2004 Democratic platform he ran under read, "Because we believe in the privacy and equality of women, we stand proudly for a woman's right to choose, consistent with Roe v. Wade, and regardless of her ability to pay. We stand firmly against Republican efforts to undermine that right...."[17]

In response, individual freedom is of course important and should be protected. But the real question is not freedom in the abstract but what appropriate restrictions the law should place on individual freedom. The law already restricts freedom in many ways that people agree on. The

---

15. Scott Richert, "Where Do Barack Obama and Joe Biden Stand on Abortion?" *About. com*, http://catholicism.about.com/od/thechurchintheworld/p/Dem_Abortion.htm.

16. Carla Marinucci, "Dems Give Abortion Foes Space," *San Francisco Chronicle* (Feb. 7, 2005). www.sfgate.com/cgi-bin/article.cgi?f=/c/a/2005/02/07/ABORTION. TMP&type=printable.

17. "Strong at Home, Respected in the World," 2004 Democratic Party Platform, www. democrats.org/pdfs/2004platform.pdf.

law does not allow me the freedom to drive while intoxicated or steal my neighbor's car or beat up on someone I don't like or fire a gun inside the city limits — and surely it does not allow parents to put their living children to death. So the question is not human freedom, but whether the law should allow people *freedom to take their child's life*. If the preborn child is considered a human person, the question is whether the government should allow people to commit murder against their own children. Certainly it should not.

b. All children should be wanted children

This is another popular phrase used by politicians who advocate abortion. For example, New Jersey Democratic Senator Robert Menendez says on his website, "I support women's reproductive rights, including the right to preventative options and family planning options. Regardless of a person's position on contraception and choice, I think that we can all agree that the ultimate goal is to ensure that all children are wanted children."[18]The benefit of allowing abortions, some people say, is that it gives mothers the freedom not to bear children they really don't want, children that might grow up to be neglected and abused and poorly cared for in any case. Why not allow abortions, so that only mothers who really *want* their children will have them?

But if we consider the preborn child to be a person, then this argument is merely another way of saying that people should be allowed to kill other people that they do not want to care for. In particular, parents should be able to kill the children that they do not want to care for.

Once a child is born, would we say that a parent who does not "want" to care for that child any longer should have the right to put him or her to death because "all children should be wanted children"? Surely not. This is a horrible thought, but it is simply the logical conclusion of the "all children should be wanted children" argument. This is really a bankrupt moral argument, one that so devalues human life that it values a mother's desire for convenience more highly than the right to life of a child made in the very image of God.

c. "I'm personally against abortion, but I just don't support laws against abortion"

This argument is made by a number of politicians who do not want to appear to be *supporting* the idea of killing preborn children, but still are committed to protecting the *legal* right of women to have an abortion

---

18. See http://menendez.senate.gov/issues/reproductiverights.cfm.

if they choose. Presumably, if they were asked for advice by a pregnant woman, they would tell her that they would *personally recommend* that she not get an abortion. But the decision, of course, is still up to her.

This argument fails to understand the difference between personal moral persuasion and governmental laws. If we really believe that an action is taking innocent human lives, then we will not be content to depend on moral influence to stop it. This position would be similar to saying, *"I'm personally opposed to drunk driving, and I wouldn't personally recommend* drunk driving, but I don't support having laws against it, because I think *individual drivers should have the right to decide for themselves* whether to drive when drunk." The fact of the matter is that, apart from legal enforcement by the government, many people will foolishly decide to drive while intoxicated and will actually kill other people through their wrongful choices. Government is instituted by God to protect us from such wrongdoing by others.

This argument is, in fact, a subtle attempt at changing the subject. The whole subject under dispute is not *personal preferences* of individuals, but what *the laws of a government* should prohibit. Just as we would not say, "I'm personally opposed to murder, but I don't think there should be any laws against murder," so it seems naïve and, I think, misleading to say, "I'm personally opposed to abortion, but I don't think that there should be laws against abortion."

d. "We should reduce the causes of abortion but not have laws against abortion"

A similar position to "I'm personally against abortion, but I don't support laws against abortion" is that of Jim Wallis, in his book *God's Politics*. Wallace says that "the abortion rate in America is much too high for a good and healthy society that respects both women and children," and he recommends "really targeting the problems of teen pregnancy and adoption reform, which are so critical to reducing abortion, while offering real support for women, especially low-income women, at greater risk for unwanted pregnancies."[19]

But this is just changing the subject. The subject under discussion is *laws* about abortion. The specific question is *what should the laws about abortion be?* Should laws prohibit abortion (with certain exceptions) or not? Saying we should try to reduce teen pregnancy in order to stop abortion is like saying we should support Alcoholics Anonymous

---

19. Jim Wallis, *God's Politics: Why the Right Gets It Wrong and the Left Doesn't Get It* (New York: Harper SanFransisco, 2005), 299–300.

in order to stop drunk driving, or we should support job creation to stop stealing, or we should support anger management clinics to stop murders. Those are helpful social programs, but they alone will not stop those crimes.

This actually raises the question of our basic assumptions about our worldview. Is the ultimate cause of wrongdoing something in society (and therefore we should just give more support to low-income women who become pregnant), or is it that people make evil choices (to kill their preborn children), so laws should hold people accountable for those choices?

What Jim Wallis refuses to say in *God's Politics* is that we should have *laws* that prevent women from taking the lives of their preborn children. Our laws should protect human life. The main difference between conservatives and liberals on abortion is how they answer this question: *Should it be against the law to kill your preborn child?* I believe it should be against the law (except to save the mother's life). Certainly we *also* should give support to low-income women who are pregnant, but both sides agree on this. The solution is "both-and" — both maternal support and laws. But Wallis and most of his fellow Democrats will not say "both-and." When the question is asked about *what the laws should be*, they simply change the subject to maternal support. They will not support laws to prohibit abortion, and most Democrats actively oppose such laws. (On Wallis's claim to a "consistent ethic of life," see discussion on pp. 61–62.)

e. "Christians should not try to impose their moral standards on other people"

People who make this objection would usually say that it's fine for Christians to think that abortion is wrong for themselves, but they have no right to try to force that conviction on others who do not have a Christian viewpoint.

In response, it must be said that many of our laws are based on moral convictions that are held by the vast majority of the population. The laws against murder are based on a moral conviction that murder is wrong. The laws against stealing are based on the moral conviction that stealing is wrong. Laws against polygamy and incest are based on moral convictions that those things are wrong. Laws against sexual harassment, or adults having sex with minors, are based on convictions that those things are wrong. We could multiply examples by the thousands from all areas of the law.

So the question is not whether laws should be based on *some* moral convictions, but whether laws about abortion should be based on *these* moral convictions.

Which moral standards support laws against abortions? There are two: (1) People should not be allowed to murder other people; (2) the preborn child should be considered a human person and should be protected as a human person. No doubt almost everyone would agree on the first point. So the question really involves the second point, whether the preborn child should be considered a human person worthy of legal protection.

In our system of government, Christians cannot *impose* their moral convictions on anyone. But everyone in the nation is free to attempt to *persuade* others about the moral convictions that should be the basis for various laws. So a more accurate way of phrasing this objection is not that "Christians should not try to impose their moral standards on others," but rather, "Christians should not try to persuade others that the preborn child is a human person and deserves the legal protections due to human persons." Of course, when the objection is stated that way, hardly anyone would agree with it. Surely our nation was founded on the ability of citizens *to speak freely about their convictions and try to persuade others* and thereby try to influence laws. In fact, the First Amendment *guarantees* freedom of speech and freedom of the press, assuring us that people of all persuasions are free to argue and attempt to persuade others about what kinds of laws should be made.

Finally, Christians should not view these convictions about the personhood of the preborn child as "*our* moral convictions." We did not make them up out of our own minds, but found them written in the Bible. And the Bible presents these as not mere human opinion, but the moral standards of God himself, by which he holds all people in every nation accountable.

It does seem right for Christians to attempt to persuade others that the moral standards found in the Bible are correct and should be used in human government. It was on the basis of this conviction that Paul could reason with the Roman governor, Felix, "about righteousness and self-control and the coming judgment" (Acts 24:25). It was on this basis that John the Baptist "reproved" Herod the Tetrarch "for all the evil things that Herod had done" (Luke 3:19). And in the Old Testament, Daniel warned King Nebuchadnezzar of Babylon about his "sins" and "iniquities" (Dan. 4:27), and Jonah warned the entire city of Nineveh to repent (see Jonah 3:4).

5. Recommendations for Political Policies

a. Governments should enact laws prohibiting abortions except to save the life of the mother

One of the fundamental responsibilities of a government is to protect the lives of the people it governs, for if government is to punish those who do evil and to prevent them from harming the innocent, then a government certainly must protect its people from the ultimate harm of being killed (see discussion of Gen. 9:5–6 on pp. 75–78). If preborn children are considered persons, then surely government should protect their lives. In fact, it is *especially* the weak and helpless, those without other means of protection, who should be the objects of governmental protections:

> Give justice to the weak and fatherless; maintain the right of the afflicted and the destitute. Rescue the weak and needy; deliver them from the hand of the wicked (Ps. 82:3–4).

If laws are eventually made to prevent abortions, what penalties should be given to those who perform an abortion? That question should be left to individual state legislatures to decide through a normal political process, just as penalties are determined for all other violations of the law. In a democracy, laws can only be passed with support from a majority of the elected representatives of the people, and ultimately this means that—in ordinary circumstances anyway—laws can only be passed and sustained with the support of the majority of the citizens covered by a law. Therefore, in determining an appropriate penalty for performing an abortion, it would be foolish for pro-life representatives to insist on penalties so severe that they would not gain assent from a reasonable majority of the population or their elected representatives, for then no law would be passed at all. (Prior to *Roe v. Wade*, most state penalties were against the doctor who performed the abortion rather than the woman who got the abortion.)

What if a "compromise" law were proposed that would prohibit abortions except to save the life of the mother or in cases of rape or incest? I think that Christians should support such legislation, since it would still prohibit probably 99 percent of the abortions that are occurring today. After such a law is passed, perhaps further modifications could be made to the law in the future, if public sentiment would support it. But even such a law would do a tremendous amount of good in protecting the lives of the vast majority of preborn children who today are being put to death.

b. No government policies should promote or fund abortions

No government money should be given to pay the medical costs of abortions (while they are still legal). Nor should any government money be given to promote abortions (supporting pro-abortion groups such as Planned Parenthood, for example). Nor should foreign aid be given for the purpose of "population control," which involves paying for abortions in other countries. If abortion is the wrongful taking of a human life, and if civil government is given by God "to punish those who do evil and to praise those who do good" (1 Peter 2:14), then government should surely do nothing to encourage such wrongdoing.

Democratic and Republican presidents have clearly differed on this question. Republican President Ronald Reagan instituted what has become known as the "Mexico City Policy," which forbade government funds going to international "family planning groups" that provide abortions. This ban was lifted by Democratic President Bill Clinton in 1993 and reinstituted by Republican President George W. Bush in 2001. Democratic President Barack Obama lifted the ban again in 2009.[20]

c. No government policy should compel people to participate in abortions or to dispense drugs that cause abortions

In the current situation in the United States, abortions are still legal. This gives women freedom to choose whether or not they will have an abortion. In such a situation it is essential that doctors (as well as nurses and other medical workers) have the freedom to choose whether or not to participate in abortions, both in medical school as part of their training and then in their practice of medicine. It is also essential that pharmacists be allowed to choose not to dispense drugs that cause abortions (such as Mifepristone or RU–486, also otherwise known as the "morning-after" pill). Sadly, some laws and governmental regulations have attempted to deny people freedom of conscience on whether they participate in abortions or dispense such drugs.[21] This is a blatant viola-

---

20. See Jake Tapper, "Obama Overturns 'Mexico City Policy' Instituted by Reagan," *ABCNews.com* (Jan. 23, 2009). http://abcnews.go.com/Politics/International/story?id=6716958&page=1.

21. In January 2009, Alliance Defense Fund attorneys, along with attorneys from the Christian Legal Society, filed motions to intervene in three lawsuits that seek to invalidate a federal regulation protecting medical professionals from discrimination because they refuse to participate in abortions. Abortion advocates are challenging a regulation enacted by the Department of Health and Human Services in December 2008 that prohibits recipients of federal grants from forcing medical professionals to participate in abortions. The regulation requires that grantees certify compliance with existing laws protecting rights of conscience in order to receive government funds.

tion of freedom of conscience, and it is ironic that it is promoted by those who call themselves "pro-choice." They are for anything *but* choice on the part of these doctors and pharmacists.

In Washington state, the pro-life owner of a local pharmacy declined to stock or dispense the morning-after pill and soon found himself in violation of the state law mandating that all pharmacists make the drug available, regardless of their religious beliefs. Attorneys with the Alliance Defense Fund filed a lawsuit on his behalf against the law. On May 2, 2008, the US Court of Appeals for the Ninth Circuit ruled that Washington pharmacists' rights of conscience will be protected while an appeal by state officials who oppose those rights moves forward.[22]

A pro-life nurse at Mount Sinai Hospital in New York was forced in 2009 to participate in a late-term abortion or face loss of her job and nursing license, even though the hospital had known since 2004 that she requested to not be involved in abortions. Hospital administrators threatened senior nurse Cathy Cenzon-DeCarlo with disciplinary measures if she did not honor a last-minute summons to assist in a scheduled late-term abortion. The patient was not in crisis at the time of the surgery, yet the hospital insisted on the nurse's participation in the procedure on the grounds that it was an "emergency" even though the procedure was not classified as such. Again, attorneys with the Alliance Defense Fund have filed suit on her behalf to protect not only her right of conscience, but that of other pro-life medical professionals.[23]

In response to this kind of increasing pressure in society, on November 20, 2009, several Christian leaders released the Manhattan Declaration, which was eventually signed by more than 400,000 people from Roman Catholic, Orthodox, and evangelical Protestant backgrounds. (I thought the statement was excellent, and I was one of the original signers.) Part of this declaration said:

> Because the sanctity of human life, the dignity of marriage as a union of husband and wife, and the freedom of conscience and religion are foundational principles of justice and the common good, we are compelled by our Christian faith to speak and act in their defense....

---

22. "9th Circuit thwarts Wash. state's attempt to stall conscience rights," *ADF News Release* (May 24, 2008). Copy of the order is available at www.telladf.org/UserDocs/StormansWin.pdf.

23. "NY nurse threatened, forced to assist in late-term abortion," *ADF News Release* (July 22, 2009). Copy of complaint is available at www.telladf.org/UserDocs/Cenzon-DeCarlo-Complaint.pdf.

We are Christians who have joined together across historic lines of ecclesial differences to affirm our right—and, more importantly, to embrace our obligation—to speak and act in defense of these truths. We pledge to each other, and to our fellow believers, that no power on earth, be it cultural or political, will intimidate us into silence or acquiescence....

Because we honor justice and the common good, we will not comply with any edict that purports to compel our institutions to participate in abortions, embryo-destructive research, assisted suicide and euthanasia, or any other anti-life act.... We will fully and ungrudgingly render to Caesar what is Caesar's. But under no circumstances will we render to Caesar what is God's.[24]

d. No funding or support should be given to the process of creating human embryos for the purpose of destroying them in medical research

The term "embryo" is applied to preborn children from the moment of conception until the eighth week of pregnancy.

If the Bible encourages us to treat the preborn child as a person from the moment of conception (see arguments above), then the argument here is whether we should create the beginnings of little babies simply to harvest their stem cells and then put them to death. The biblical arguments given above on the personhood of the preborn child would argue against the validity of this action.

The argument in favor of such research is that such stem cells taken from such embryos might be used to grow all sorts of different kinds of useful organs that could be transplanted into people to overcome various diseases and disabilities.

But it is doubtful that such stem cells need to be taken from human embryos, for there are other excellent sources of stem cells being discovered every year. These stem cells can be taken from human adults and used in research with apparently as much potential for medical benefits as embryonic stem cells. Why should we take stem cells from embryos and destroy tiny human lives instead of taking stem cells from other human tissue so that we destroy no human lives?

For example, UCLA stem cell scientists reprogrammed human skin cells into cells with the same unlimited properties as embryonic stem cells, and they did it without using embryos or eggs. The researchers

---

24. See the Manhattan Declaration at http.//manhattandeclaration.org/home.aspx.

used genetic alteration to turn back the clock on human skin cells and create cells that are nearly identical to human embryonic stem cells, which have the ability to become every cell type found in the human body. According to the researchers:

> The implications for disease treatment could be significant. Reprogramming adult stem cells into embryonic stem cells could generate a potentially limitless source of immune-compatible cells for tissue engineering and transplantation medicine. A patient's skin cells, for example, could be reprogrammed into embryonic stem cells. Those embryonic stem cells could then be prodded into becoming various cell types — beta islet cells to treat diabetes, hematopoetic cells to create a new blood supply for a leukemia patient, motor neuron cells to treat Parkinson's disease.[25]

From this perspective, President George W. Bush's decision in 2001 that he would not allow government funding for the creation of *new* embryos to begin *new* stem cell lines was certainly the correct decision.[26] He allowed government funding to continue on stem cell research where the stem cells had already been taken from embryos and the embryos have already been destroyed. But he did not allow government funding to be used for the intentional creation of and destruction of new embryos. His decision *only involved government funding.* It did not affect ongoing research in the *private* sector, nor did it do anything to prohibit *private* research companies from using embryonic stem cells.

However, President Bush's actions (and subsequent vetoes of embryonic stem cell research bills) were widely misrepresented and misreported in the media. Liberal pundit Michael Kinsley called Bush's actions "cynical," writing:

> The week-old embryos used for stem-cell research are microscopic clumps of cells, unthinking and unknowing, with fewer physical human qualities than a mosquito. Fetal-tissue research has used brain cells from aborted fetuses, but this is not that. Week-old, lab-created embryos have no brain cells.... None of this matters if you believe that a microscopic embryo is a human being with the same human rights as you and me.

---

25. "Human Skin Cells Reprogrammed Into Embryonic Stem Cells." *ScienceDaily.com* (Feb. 12, 2008). www.sciencedaily.com/releases/2008/02/080211172631.htm.

26. "President's Remarks on Stem Cell Research," The White House (Aug. 9, 2001). http://usgovinfo.about.com/blwhrelease16.htm.

George W. Bush claims to believe that, and you have to believe
something like that to justify your opposition to stem-cell
research.... If he's got both his facts and his logic wrong—and
he has—Bush's alleged moral anguish on this subject is unim-
pressive. In fact, it is insulting to the people (including me)
whose lives could be saved or redeemed by the medical break-
throughs Bush's stem-cell policy is preventing.[27]

e. The ban on partial-birth abortions

The term "partial-birth abortion" (also known in medical literature by
other terms such as "intact dilation and extraction") is a procedure in
which the preborn child is partially extracted from the mother's womb,
starting with the feet and then delivering the baby as far as the neck.
Then the head is crushed and the brain is sucked out of the baby, and
the dead child is removed completely from its mother's womb. This horrible procedure is most frequently used in late-term abortions, up to and
including the ninth month of pregnancy.

Efforts to produce legislation prohibiting this procedure began in
1995. One bill, written under the leadership of Florida Congressman
Charles Canady (a graduate of Yale Law School), was passed in October 1996 by Congress, but it was vetoed by President Clinton.[28] It was
passed again in October 1997 by both houses of Congress, but was once
again vetoed by President Clinton.[29] Republicans who supported the
bill did not have enough votes to override President Clinton's veto in
either case.[30] Then, in the 2002 congressional elections Republicans
increased their majority in the House and gained a fifty-one-seat
majority in the Senate.[31] This enabled them to pass the Partial-Birth
Abortion Ban Act in the House October 2, 2003,[32] and in the Senate
October 21, 2003.[33] President George W. Bush signed it into law on
November 5, 2003.[34]

---

27. Michael Kinsley, "Taking Bush Personally," *Slate.com* (Oct. 23, 2003).

28. "Clinton Vetoes Partial-Birth Abortion Ban," *AllPolitics.com* (April 10, 1996). www.
cnn.com/ALLPOLITICS/1996/news/9604/10/abortion/index.shtml.

29. "Clinton Again Vetoes Abortion Ban," *AllPolitics.com* (Oct. 10, 1997). www.cnn.com/
ALLPOLITICS/1997/10/10/lateterm.abortion/.

30. "Presidential Vetoes, 1989–2000," www.senate.gov/reference/resources/pdf/presve-
toes.pdf.

31. See www.cnn.com/ELECTION/2002/pages/senate/index.html.

32. "House Passes Ban on Abortion Method," *Washington Times* (Oct. 2, 2003).

33. "Partial-Birth Abortion Ban Heads to President's Desk," *Online News Hour Update*
(Oct. 21, 2003).

34. "Bush Signs Ban on Partial-Birth Abortions," *Fox News* (Nov. 5, 2003).

Pro-abortion forces challenged the ban in several different federal district courts (California, New York, and Nebraska).[35] All three ruled the ban unconstitutional, and the federal courts of appeal (in the Ninth Circuit, Second Circuit, and Eighth Circuit, respectively) affirmed those rulings.[36] At that point the partial-birth abortion ban could still not take effect because, even though it had been passed by Congress and signed by the President, and even though nothing in the Constitution said a word about this procedure or anything related to it, these federal courts had ruled that the law was "unconstitutional."

The three cases were all appealed to the US Supreme Court and were consolidated into one case, *Gonzales v. Carhart*. By a five-to-four majority the Supreme Court upheld the law as constitutional, declaring its decision on April 18, 2007.[37] (Supporting the law were Justices Roberts, Kennedy, Thomas, Scalia, and Alito. Dissenting were Justices Ginsburg, Stevens, Souter, and Breyer.) Therefore, after twelve years of effort, this extremely limited restriction on the right to abortion, applying only to a very tiny percentage of cases, finally became the law of the land.

Although this law applies to all hospitals and medical facilities under *federal* jurisdiction, many *states* still do not have such laws applying to medical facilities under state jurisdiction. Several other states do have such laws.

f. The most important legal goal regarding abortion is appointing Supreme Court justices who will overturn Roe v. Wade because no significant restriction on abortions can be made at either the state or national level until the Supreme Court overturns the Roe v. Wade decision

I do not think that many Christians understand how the key to this entire matter is the appointment of "originalist" Supreme Court justices who will vote to overturn *Roe v. Wade*. Until that Supreme Court decision is changed, the highest law of the land (the US Constitution, as "interpreted" by the Supreme Court) declares that all women in the United States have a *constitutional right* to an abortion at any time in their pregnancy.[38]

---

35. "Supreme Court to Take Up Partial-Birth Abortion Issue," *USA Today* (Feb. 21, 2006). www.usatoday.com/news/washington/2006–02–21-abortion_x.htm.

36. Ibid.

37. *Gonzales v. Carhart* and *Gonzales v. Planned Parenthood,* 550 U.S. (2007). www.supremecourtus.gov/opinions/06pdf/05–380.pdf.

38. Under *Roe* and the companion case *Doe v. Bolton,* the Supreme Court allowed abortion for the mother's health, including emotional and psychological health, which effectively allows abortion at any time in the nine months of pregnancy (see discussion earlier in this chapter, pp. 45–46).

Therefore the US Congress *has no power* to pass a law prohibiting abortions at any stage of pregnancy. The fifty state legislatures *have no power* to pass any law prohibiting abortion. (The prohibition on partial-birth abortion is the only exception, as discussed above.) This is because every law prohibiting abortion has been struck down by the Supreme Court as "unconstitutional" because they say it violates the Constitution's guarantee of a right to abortion! And this is the decision of the court even though the Constitution itself says nothing about abortion.

But will the Supreme Court overturn *Roe v. Wade*? The court now is almost evenly divided between four justices who would always vote to uphold *Roe v. Wade* and four justices who would probably vote to overturn that decision, with one justice in the middle.

Would keep *Roe v. Wade*	Often in middle (perhaps would overturn?)	Would probably overturn *Roe v. Wade*
Stephen Breyer	Anthony Kennedy	John Roberts
Ruth Ginsburg		Samuel Alito
Sonia Sotomayor		Antonin Scalia
Elena Kagan		Clarence Thomas

This is why the election of a President and the elections of US senators are so important to the future of this issue. If a liberal, pro-choice President such as President Obama is allowed to appoint some replacements for the four conservative members of the Supreme Court (when they retire or die), it would solidify a majority in support of upholding *Roe v. Wade* for many years to come. And a Democratic Senate would confirm such appointments. But if a pro-life President (such as Ronald Reagan or George W. Bush) would be allowed to appoint any replacements for the four more liberal justices or for Justice Kennedy (through death or retirement of any one of them), and if there was a Republican majority in the Senate to confirm such justices, then it is likely that a test case would be brought and *Roe v. Wade* would be overturned.

Until such a change comes about in the Supreme Court, no major changes can be made in the law. States can (and should) pass laws requiring parental notification prior to abortion or requiring certain kinds of informed consent, but they cannot pass any laws that prohibit people who want abortions from getting them.

If the *Roe v. Wade* decision were to be overturned by the Supreme Court, what would happen? Then the democratic process could function once again regarding this issue. Members of Congress and the elected representatives of the legislatures of the fifty states would have to consider and decide what laws they would pass regarding abortion. It is difficult to predict in advance what the outcome of those discussions would be, and what laws would result. But at least decisions would be made as they should be in a nation that believes in democracy—by the people themselves and their elected representatives, not by nine unelected and unaccountable justices in the Supreme Court.

Unfortunately, abortion has become a major dividing line—perhaps the principal dividing line—between the Democratic and Republican parties in the United States at this time, at least at a national level. The Democratic leadership is united in supporting abortion rights and, above all, in seeking to appoint activist justices to the Supreme Court who will uphold *Roe v. Wade*, which is by itself keeping the entire abortion industry in place and protecting it from legal interference. But Republicans have consistently nominated pro-life candidates for President and Vice President, and most Republican senators and representatives have supported a pro-life position.

g. What about a "consistent ethic of life"?

How can some evangelicals still vote for Democratic candidates for the US Senate or for President? One approach is to change the subject from discussing laws about abortion to saying we should give more support to women who are pregnant, and so reduce abortion (see discussion on pp. 50–51). Another common approach is the argument of Jim Wallis. He says that Christians should support "a consistent ethic of life," but *neither party* is satisfactory in this area. He defines this ethic as including "the life issues" of "abortion, euthanasia, capital punishment, nuclear weapons, poverty, and racism." He calls these "critical components of a consistent ethic of life."[39] Then he says,

> The tragedy is that in America today, one can't vote for a consistent ethic of life. Republicans stress some of the life issues, Democrats some of the others, while both violate the seamless garment of life on several vital matters....[40]

In other words, no party agrees with "a consistent ethic of life" (according to Wallis) on all of these issues, and therefore people shouldn't think

---

39. Jim Wallis, *God's Politics*, 300–301.
40. Ibid., 301.

that they should vote for Republicans because of the abortion issue, because there are other "life" issues where the Democratic position is better.

But Christians should understand what Wallis is doing here. He is changing the subject from laws prohibiting abortion to laws about a whole range of things and is claiming that a *truly Christian* pro-life position would include things like opposition to capital punishment, opposition to nuclear weapons, and increased government help for the poor (as he explains elsewhere in his book). The effect of this argument by Wallis is to downplay the importance of the abortion issue by saying these are all "life" issues.

I agree that it is important to consider all the issues that Republicans and Democrats stand for before deciding how to vote. But it is hard to see how any issue could have more importance than stopping the wrongful murder of more than 1,000,000 innocent preborn children every year, year after year after year. I think Wallis is wrong to diminish this issue by lumping it with a whole basket of other controversial and complicated questions.

In addition, many Christians sincerely disagree with Wallis about capital punishment, national defense, and solutions to poverty (see discussions in chap. 3). Wallis's phrase "a consistent ethic of life" is a misleading slogan that attempts to make people think that his pacifist views on capital punishment and war, his support for government redistribution of wealth, and his own solutions to racial discrimination are the truly "pro-life" positions. This confuses the argument about the biblical teaching against abortion by changing the subject to many other disputed issues. This slight-of-hand argument should not blind us to the plain fact that every vote for every Democratic candidate for president or Congress undeniably has the effect of continuing to protect 1,000,000 abortions per year in the United States.

6. The importance of this issue

The Old Testament contains sober warnings to a nation that allowed people to put their children to death. In imitation of the practices of other nations, some of the people of Israel had begun "to burn their sons and their daughters in the fire" (Jer. 7:31), which referred to putting their live children into a fire to sacrifice them to Molech and other pagan gods. For allowing this practice to continue, God issued a severe warning of judgment through the prophet Jeremiah:

> For the sons of Judah have done evil in my sight, declares the
> LORD.... And they have built the high places of Topheth, which
> is in the Valley of the Son of Hinnom, *to burn their sons and
> their daughters in the fire*, which I did not command, nor did
> it come into my mind. Therefore, behold, the days are coming,
> declares the LORD, when it will no more be called Topheth, or
> the Valley of the Son of Hinnom, but the Valley of Slaughter;
> for they will bury in Topheth, because there is no room else-
> where. And the dead bodies of this people will be food for the
> birds of the air, and for the beasts of the earth, and none will
> frighten them away. And I will silence in the cities of Judah and
> in the streets of Jerusalem the voice of mirth and the voice of
> gladness, the voice of the bridegroom and the voice of the bride,
> *for the land shall become a waste* (Jer. 7:30–34).

The troubling question with regard to the United States elections
of 2008 concerns the direction the nation has willingly chosen. The
nation freely elected a president who is a strong supporter of abortion
"rights." The White House website states, "President Obama has been
a consistent champion of reproductive choice and believes in preserving women's rights under *Roe v. Wade*."[41] The nation elected a sizable
Democratic majority (sixty) in the Senate, and they strongly support abortion "rights" in the United States. This sets the stage for the
appointment of additional fairly young liberal justices to the Supreme
Court, such as Justice Sotomayor and Elena Kagan.

The nation has willingly chosen to be represented by people with
these convictions. What will God's evaluation of our nation be in light
of this decision? Or do we not think that God is still sovereign over the
affairs of nations?

7. For further reading

Bibliography on abortion:

Randy Alcorn, *Pro Life Answers to Pro Choice Arguments* (Portland,
OR: Multnomah, 1992); Francis Beckwith, *Politically Correct Death:
Answering Arguments for Abortion Rights* (Grand Rapids: Baker, 1992);
John Jefferson Davis, *Evangelical Ethics*, 3rd ed. (Phillipsburg, NJ: P & R,
2004), 137–65; John Feinberg and Paul Feinberg, *Ethics for a Brave New
World* (Wheaton, IL: Crossway, 1993), 47–72; John Frame, *The Doctrine*

---

41. See www.whitehouse.gov/issues/women/.

of the Christian Life (Phillipsburg, NJ: P & R, 2008), 717–32; Richard Ganz, ed., *Thou Shalt Not Kill: The Christian Case against Abortion* (New Rochelle, NY: Arlington House, 1978); Michael J. Gorman, *Abortion and the Early Church* (Eugene, OR: Wipf and Stock, 1982); Randall Hekman, *Justice for the Preborn* (Ann Arbor, MI: Servant Books, 1984); Jeff Hensley, *The Zero People: Essays on Life* (Ann Arbor, MI: Servant Books, 1983); Scott Rae, *Moral Choices*, 3rd ed. (Grand Rapids: Zondervan, 2009), 121–43.

Chapter 3

THE PROTECTION OF LIFE: OTHER ISSUES

A. EUTHANASIA

1. The issue

The word "euthanasia" is derived from the Greek words *eu* ("good") and *thanatos* ("death"), and therefore people sometimes understand it to mean "good death," a rather misleading understanding of the term. Sometimes this procedure is also popularly called "mercy killing," another term that is misleading in portraying such an action in a positive way. It simply means the act of putting to death an elderly person or one who is terminally ill.

The issue in the question of euthanasia is this:

> Should governments make laws against intentionally taking the lives of elderly or dying persons?

This issue often comes to focus in the case of terminally ill patients who are experiencing chronic pain and who no longer want to live and may even wish that they could be put to death. It also is a question in the case of people who have lost much or most of their mental capacities because of a coma or severe dementia, or patients who through severe injury or illness appear to have no reasonable human hope of recovery. What should the law do in such cases?

2. The relevant biblical teaching

a. The command against murder

The primary biblical teaching in this regard is found in the Ten Commandments:

"You shall not murder" (Exod. 20:13).

This commandment, which is affirmed in the New Testament in Matthew 18:19 and Romans 13:9, applies to all human beings created in the image of God. It does not say, "You shall not murder, except when a person is more than eighty or ninety years old," or "You shall not murder except when a very ill person wants to be murdered."

Just as the command against murder prohibits abortion in the very early stages of human life, so the command against murder also prohibits intentionally taking the life of a person in the final stages of human life.

The word translated "murder" in Exodus 20:13 includes both premeditated murder (which is implied by the English word "murder") and also any accidental causing of another person's death. The term is always applied to the murder of human beings, not of animals.

Therefore this biblical command prohibits the action of taking the life of another person, even an elderly or terminally ill person, or a person in great pain.

One other passage of special significance is 2 Samuel 1:1–16. King Saul had recently died in battle, in effect making David king. A few days after the battle where Saul had died, a man came to David and claimed that he had found Saul gravely wounded and that Saul had begged for the man to kill him, and the man had done so. In several ways this was an act of "euthanasia." Yet David's response was to order capital punishment for the man who had done this. Here is the story:

> After the death of Saul, when David had returned from striking down the Amalekites, David remained two days in Ziklag. And on the third day, behold, a man came from Saul's camp, with his clothes torn and dirt on his head. And when he came to David, he fell to the ground and paid homage. David said to him, "Where do you come from?" And he said to him, "I have escaped from the camp of Israel." And David said to him, "How did it go? Tell me." And he answered, "The people fled from the battle, and also many of the people have fallen and are dead, and Saul and his son Jonathan are also dead." Then David said to the young man who told him, "How do you know that Saul and his son Jonathan are dead?" And the young man who told him said, "By chance I happened to be on Mount Gilboa, *and there was Saul leaning on his spear, and behold, the chariots and the horsemen were close upon him.* And when he looked behind him, he saw me, and called to me. And I answered, 'Here I am.' And he said to me, 'Who are you?' I answered him, 'I am an

Amalekite.' And he said to me, *'Stand beside me and kill me, for anguish has seized me,* and yet my life still lingers.' *So I stood beside him and killed him, because I was sure that he could not live after he had fallen.* And I took the crown that was on his head and the armlet that was on his arm, and I have brought them here to my lord."

Then David took hold of his clothes and tore them, and so did all the men who were with him. And they mourned and wept and fasted until evening for Saul and for Jonathan his son and for the people of the LORD and for the house of Israel, because they had fallen by the sword. And David said to the young man who told him, "Where do you come from?" And he answered, "I am the son of a sojourner, an Amalekite." David said to him, "How is it you were not afraid to put out your hand to destroy the LORD's anointed?"

Then David called one of the young men and said, *"Go, execute him." And he struck him down so that he died.* And David said to him, "Your blood be on your head, for your own mouth has testified against you, saying, 'I have killed the LORD's anointed'" (2 Sam. 1:1–16).

This situation had several similarities to modern examples where people might say euthanasia is justified:

(1) The patient (Saul) appeared to be terminally ill, with no reasonable human hope of recovery. (He had fallen on his own sword in an attempt to commit suicide: see 1 Sam. 31:4–5.)

(2) The patient was in extreme pain, and if he did not die, he faced the prospect of even more suffering.

(3) The patient clearly requested, even begged, that someone else would actively put him to death.

(4) This request was also a command from the head of government at that time, because Saul was still the king.

But David, who at that time is clearly portrayed as a man after God's "own heart" (1 Sam. 13:14; cf. Acts 13:22), declares that this man is worthy of capital punishment. In other words, the person who carried out euthanasia is *guilty of murder.*

Three objections may be brought against this interpretation:

(a) This story about the Amalekite messenger killing Saul is not mentioned in 1 Samuel 31:3–6, where Saul's death is first reported. Therefore the Amalekite messenger may be making up this story to show David that he had killed Saul, who was David's enemy.

However, this idea does not nullify the force of this narrative, because even if the story is not true, *David accepts it as true and passes judgment on the man based on the story.* David condemns him based on his own confession of guilt. And thus the narrative of Scripture portrays the decision of this wise king, a man after God's own heart, as *an appropriate and morally right judgment* on the man who has carried out euthanasia. In addition, the Amalekite messenger actually had the crown and the armlet that Saul had been wearing, and he knew that Saul had fallen on his own sword, so it is quite certain that the man was there in the very vicinity of Saul when Saul was dying. Therefore it is certainly possible that it is entirely true and it simply was not included in the summary of Saul's death in 1 Samuel 31. Verse 4 of that chapter does not specify that Saul killed himself, but that he tried to do so: "Saul took his own sword and fell upon it." The next verse says that at some later point Saul's armor-bearer "saw that Saul was dead," but it allows for the Amalekite to end Saul's life before that. In any case, the events probably occurred very quickly in the heat of battle.

(b) Another objection is that this case is unique because Saul was king, and David refers to him as "the LORD's anointed" (2 Sam. 1:14). Therefore this case should not be used to establish a general principle that euthanasia is wrong, but only the specific application that assassination of a king is wrong.

However, this objection is not persuasive, because the wrongfulness of murder does not depend on the status or rank of the victim. Murder is wrong in the Bible because God prohibits it (Exod. 20:13), and more specifically because it is the taking of the life of a person made in the image of God (see Gen. 9:5–6). A king does not possess a greater share of the image of God than others who do not happen to be king! All human beings share equally in the status of being "created in the image of God" (cf. Gen. 1:27). Therefore, if it is wrong to kill a terminally ill king who requests it, then it is also wrong to kill anyone else who requests it.

(c) A final objection is that the sin of the Amalekite messenger was not murder, but rebellion against the king who was "God's anointed." However, this interpretation does not match the actual words of the text, for David does not put the man to death for rebellion, but for killing the king (vv. 14, 16). And in fact, at the time this happened, the Amalekite was not rebelling against the king, but was actually obeying what the king commanded. The sin was murder, and David punished it accordingly.

Therefore this narrative gives significant confirmation of the right-ness of applying "you shall not murder" to the question of euthanasia.

The conclusion is that both Exodus 20:13 and 2 Samuel 1:1–16 indi-cate that it is morally wrong to actively take the life of a terminally ill person.

b. Killing versus letting die

A clear distinction must be made between "killing" and "letting die." *Killing* is actively doing something to a patient that hastens or causes the person's death. On the other hand, *letting die* is passively allowing someone to die from other causes, without interfering with that process. In the first case, the cause of death is the action taken by another person. In the second case, the cause of death is the disease or injury or aging process that has already been occurring in the person who dies. While the Bible prohibits actively killing someone, in the case of letting some-one die the decision is more complex.

We should intervene and try to help a person recover, and *not* pas-sively allow the person to die, when (a) there is a reasonable human hope of recovery, and (b) we are able to help. This would be obeying Jesus' teaching, "You shall love your neighbor as yourself" (Matt. 22:39), and his command, "So whatever you wish that others would do to you, do also to them, for this is the Law and the Prophets" (Matt. 7:12). More-over, in the Parable of the Good Samaritan, Jesus implicitly condemned the priest and the Levite who neglected to do what they could to help a badly injured man (see Luke 10:30–37).

On the other hand, in cases where (a) there is no reasonable human hope of recovery (sometimes called a situation of "futility"), and (b) it is the patient's wish to be allowed to die, and/or (c) we are unable to help (such as a person trapped in a burning car, or where we could not afford the extraordinary expense of some elaborate medical treatments), *then it may be right to allow the person to die.* This is morally distinct from actively murdering a person.

Allowing someone to die may include not starting a medical life-support system (such as an artificial respirator) or stopping an artificial life-support system. Sometimes in Scripture we see examples of people realizing that their death is near, and they trust God and yield their lives into his hands (see Luke 23:46; Acts 7:59; also Gen. 49:33; Heb. 2:15; and 1 Cor. 15:55–57).

In addition, modern medicine should be used to alleviate the pain and suffering of a terminally ill patient (see Matt. 7:12 and 22:39). In the vast majority of cases today (perhaps in all cases), modern medicines, such as morphine or what are known as opioids, are available that will protect people from ongoing, extreme suffering as they near death.[1]

3. Arguments from reason and evidence apart from the Bible

Most people have a conviction that it is wrong to murder another human being. An argument can be made from this general conviction to the specific application that it is wrong to murder elderly or terminally ill persons. Is murder not murder whether the victim is young or old, strong or weak, in good health or suffering? None of these considerations should change the moral status of the person as a human being.

Moreover, concerns about a "slippery slope" in public policy have some persuasive force. If euthanasia is allowed for *some* patients who are suffering, then how can we prevent it from being applied to *more and more* patients who are suffering? And with the increasing cost of healthcare for elderly and extremely ill patients, there will likely be a tendency to put pressure on people to ask that their lives be taken. In fact, "nations that have allowed for physician-assisted suicide find that a society can quickly move from merely *allowing* 'the right to die' to the belief that there is 'an *obligation* to die' on the part of the elderly and the very ill people who are 'draining resources' from the society. In such situations it becomes likely that a number of elderly people will be put to death against their will."[2]

The situation in the Netherlands has become particularly notorious,[3] where a number of elderly people have been put to death against their will. According to the Netherlands' "adult euthanasia vetting commissions," approximately 2,000 people per year are euthanized through a mix of sedatives and a lethal dose of muscle relaxant.[4] Wesley Smith, an attorney for the International Anti-Euthanasia Task Force, has written that the amount is actually much higher:

> The evidence of decades demonstrates that such involuntary euthanasia is rampant. Indeed, in its 1997 ruling refusing to create a constitutional right to assisted suicide (*Washington* v. *Glucksberg*) the United States Supreme Court quoted a 1991

---

1. U.S. Institute of Health, "Last Days of Life." www.cancer.gov/cancertopics/pdq/supportivecare/lasthours/Patient/page2#Keypoint7.

2. *ESV Study Bible*, "The End of Life," p. 2543.

3. A concise summary of the Netherlands' euthanasia law can be read at www.internationaltaskforce.org/hollaw.htm.

4. "Dutch to Set Guidelines for Euthanasia of Babies," Associated Press (Sept. 29, 2005).

Dutch government study finding that in 1990 doctors committed "more than 1000 cases of euthanasia without an explicit request" and "an additional 4,941 cases where physicians administered lethal morphine overdoses without the patients' explicit consent." That means in 1990, nearly 6,000 of approximately 130,000 people who died in the Netherlands that year were involuntarily euthanized—approximately 4 percent of all Dutch deaths. So much for "choice."[5]

Euthanasia advocate Dr. Phillip Nitschke invented the so-called "peaceful pill" to induce suicide, and he also conducted "how to commit suicide" clinics. He said that his personal position is that if we believe that there is a right to life, then we must accept that people have a right to dispose of that life whenever they want."[6] He continued:

> Many people I meet and argue with believe that human life is sacred. I do not. . . . If you believe that your body belongs to God and that to cut short a life is a crime against God, then you will clearly not agree with my thoughts on this issue. I do not mind people holding these beliefs and suffering as much as they wish as they die. For them, redemptive suffering may well pry open heaven's door that little bit wider, and if that is their belief they are welcome to it, but I strongly object to having those views shoved down my neck. I want my belief—that human life is not sacred—accorded the same respect.[7]

The slippery slope has also extended into infant euthanasia. In September 2005 the Dutch government announced its intention to expand its euthanasia policy to allow doctors to end the lives of infants with the parents' consent. Under the "Gronican Protocol," euthanasia would be allowed when it is decided that a child is terminally ill with no prospect of recovery and suffering great pain.

Christine Rosen, author of *Preaching Eugenics*, says:

> The Netherlands' embrace of euthanasia has been a gradual process aided by the growing acceptance (in a much more secular Europe) that some life is "unworthy of life." Indeed,

5. Wesley Smith, "Going Dutch," *National Review Online* (Dec. 18, 2000). www.national-review.com/comment/comment121800d.shtml.

6. Kathryn Jean Lopez, "Euthanasia Sets Sail: An interview with Philip Nitschke, the other 'Dr. Death,'" *National Review Online* (June 5, 2001). www.nationalreview.com/interrogatory/interrogatory060501.shtml.

7. Ibid.

Europe is doing just that. According to the Associated Press, 73 percent of French doctors have admitted to using drugs to end an infant's life, with between 2 and 4 percent of doctors in the United Kingdom, Italy, Spain, Germany, and Sweden confessing the same.[8]

A final argument against euthanasia comes from personal narratives and testimonies from people who were apparently terminally ill or had life-threatening injuries and then have recovered, as well as from elderly people who are still living happy, productive lives.

One recent example of this is Jesse Ramirez of Mesa, Arizona. In May 2007, then-36-year-old Jesse was in a horrific automobile accident while he and his wife were engaged in an argument.[9] Barely ten days after the accident, Jesse's food, water, and antibiotics were withdrawn at the request of his wife. He was then transferred to hospice, where he would have died, but Alliance Defense Fund attorneys, at the behest of Jesse's sister, were successful in restoring food, water, and treatment. While he did go without food and water for six days until it was restored, Jesse recovered and walked out of the hospital in October 2007 and continued his recovery at home.[10] In 2008 the state of Arizona passed "Jesse's Law," which closed a loophole in the decision-making process for patients who are physically unable to communicate their wishes regarding medical care.[11]

4. Objections

The primary objections to the position outlined here emphasize (1) the value of protecting human freedom, even individual freedom to choose to end one's own life, and (2) the need to alleviate pain and frustration felt by the terminally ill patient.

In response, if it is morally wrong to actively murder another person, then the fact that a person would choose to be murdered does not nul-

---

8. Christine Rosen, *Preaching Eugenics: Religious Leaders and the American Eugenics Movement* (Oxford: Oxford University Press, 2004): cited in Kathryn Jean Lopez, "Mercy!" *National Review Online* (March 30, 2005). www.nationalreview.com/lopez/lopez200503300755.asp.

9. Dennis Wagner, "Injured Man's Awakening Called 'Miracle,'" *USA Today* (June 27, 2007). www.usatoday.com/news/nation/2007-06-26-comatose_N.htm?csp=34.

10. Rick Dubek, "Comatose Mesa Man Walks Out of Hospital," *AZCentral.com* (Oct. 19, 2007). www.azcentral.com/12news/news/articles/jesseramirezwalks10192007-CR.html.

11. "ADF Commends Signing of 'Jesse's Law,'" *ADF Press Release* (June 25, 2008). www.telladf.org/news/story.aspx?cid=4583.

lify this moral argument. There are many cases where someone might so despair of life that he or she would say, "I want to die." But should we then say that it is right to murder such a person? If it is morally wrong, then even the person who wants to be murdered cannot make it morally right, for it is still taking a human life. A person's right to life does not depend on the person himself wanting to live.

As for pain and frustration, these are not sufficient reasons for overcoming the moral prohibition against murder. A better solution is to alleviate the pain and do what can be done to overcome the person's frustration.

A final argument is this: (3) since money and medical resources are limited, we should put to death elderly or very ill people so they do not waste money or medical resources. This is not the question of allocating a scarce resource (say, a kidney transplant) to a younger or healthier person. Rather, it is the argument that older or very ill people should not be using so much medical care at all.

But this argument, phrased another way, essentially says that it is right to kill people who are costing us too much to care for. Since more money can always buy more medical resources, in the end this argument is simply a way of saying, "We don't have enough money to care for these elderly and terminally ill people." But is that a justification for taking another person's life? This would change the commandment "You shall not murder" into a different commandment: "You shall not murder unless you do so to spend your money on something else." This objection is hardly acceptable on moral grounds.

It is important to realize that all three of these objections are based on a viewpoint that is contrary to a Christian worldview. These three objections do not value human life as something sacred, something that uniquely carries the image of God in this world. And they do not give full weight to the moral force of God's command, "You shall not murder."

5. Recommendation for political policies

a. Governmental laws against murder should continue to be applied to cases of euthanasia

In most states in the United States, euthanasia is still prohibited and laws against murder apply to it. However, Oregon voters enacted the "Death with Dignity Act," what is called physician-assisted suicide, in 1994,[12] and this was upheld by the US Court of Appeals for the Ninth Circuit in 1997. The

---

12. Death with Dignity Act. www.oregon.gov/DHS/ph/pas/.

US Supreme Court subsequently denied an appeal to the law.[13] In a subsequent challenge involving the federally controlled substance acts overriding the law, the court ruled six-to-three in the law's favor.[14] In November 2008 the citizens of Washington state also legalized physician-assisted suicide.[15] On the other hand, in 1999, Dr. Jack Kevorkian, a physician in Michigan, was convicted for assisting someone to commit suicide in an act that was displayed on television and that violated current Michigan law.[16]

6. The importance of this issue

The direction a society takes on the question of euthanasia is a reflection of how highly it values human life and how highly it values God's command not to murder. In societies where physician-assisted suicide becomes legal, this will set the stage for a further erosion of the protection of human life. Some people will be thought "too old" to deserve medical treatment. Compassion and care for the elderly will diminish, and they will be more and more thought of as burdens to care for, rather than valuable members of the society.

And, unless we experience premature death, all of us reading this chapter will ourselves one day be those "elderly" people who need care and support from others.

7. For further reading

Bibliography on euthanasia:
Davis, *Evangelical Ethics*, 167–201; Feinberg and Feinberg, *Ethics for a Brave New World*, 99–126; Frame, *The Doctrine of the Christian Life*, 732–38; John Kilner, Arlene Miller, and Edmund Pellegrino, eds., *Dignity and Dying: A Christian Appraisal* (Grand Rapids: Eerdmans, 1996); Joni Eareckson Tada, *When Is It Right to Die?* (Grand Rapids: Zondervan, 1992).

B. CAPITAL PUNISHMENT

1. The issue

The question with regard to capital punishment (also called the death penalty) is this:

13. See www.oregon.gov/DHS/ph/pas/about_us.shtml.
14. *Gonzales v. Oregon*, 546 U.S. 243 (2006).
15. "Washington State to Allow Assisted Suicide," *USA Today* (March 2, 2009). www.usatoday.com/news/nation/2009–03–01-washington-assisted_N.htm.
16. "Kevorkian Gets 10 to 25 Years in Prison," *CNN.com* (April 13, 1999). www.cnn.com/US/9904/13/kevorkian.03/.

Should governments take the life of a person who has been convicted of certain crimes?

The crimes for which capital punishment (or execution) is specified as the penalty usually include premeditated murder and treason. Other crimes that are sometimes thought to deserve capital punishment include an attempt to use weapons of mass destruction, espionage that results in loss of life of a country's citizens, and crimes such as aggravated rape, aggravated kidnaping, aircraft hijacking, or perjury that leads to a person's death. (An aggravated crime is one where the intent or actual circumstances add significantly to the guilt of the criminal or the harm to the victim.)

But the primary question is whether governments should have the right to carry out capital punishment *at all*.

2. The relevant biblical teaching

a. Genesis 9:5–6 provides the foundation for human government

In the early history of the human race, Genesis 6–9 relates that God brought a massive flood on the earth, destroying all human beings except the eight who were rescued in the ark: Noah, his wife, his three sons, and their wives.

When the flood ended, Noah and his family came out of the ark and started human society all over again. At that point God gave them instructions regarding the life they were about to begin. Among those instructions is the following passage, which provides the foundation for human government:

> And for your lifeblood I will require a reckoning: from every beast I will require it and from man. From his fellow man I will require a reckoning for the life of man.
>
> "Whoever sheds the blood of man,
> by man shall his blood be shed,
> for God made man in his own image" (Gen. 9:5–6).

The verb "shed" in this statement translates the Hebrew verb *shaphak*, which means "to pour out in large amount, causing death." Therefore, "In this verse, 'shedding blood' refers to the violent, unjustified taking of human life (cf. Gen. 37:22; Num. 35:33; 1 Kings 2:31; Ezek. 22:4)."[17]

---

17. ESV *Study Bible*, p. 2552.

This law says that when someone murders another person, the murderer himself should be put to death: "by man shall his blood be shed."

This execution of the murderer was not going to be carried out directly by God, but by a human agent, "by man." Yet this was not to be seen as human vengeance, but as carrying out God's own requirement of justice, for it explains what God means when he says, "from his fellow man *I will require a reckoning* for the life of man" (v. 5).

The reason God gives for this is the immense value of human life: "*For* God made man in his own image" (v. 6). To be in the image of God is the highest status and highest privilege of anything in all creation, and only human beings share in that status (see Gen. 1:27). To be in God's image means that human beings are more like God than anything else on the earth, and it also means that human beings are God's representatives on the earth (for they are like him and thus can best represent him). Therefore, to murder a human being is to murder someone who is more like God than any other creature on the earth. The murder of another human being is therefore a kind of attack against God himself, for it is an attack against his representative on the earth, an attack against the "image" that he has left of himself on the earth.

In order to give just punishment for such a serious crime, God decrees that the murderer will pay the ultimate price: he will forfeit his own life as a punishment. The punishment will fit the crime: "Whoever sheds the blood of man, by man shall his blood be shed, for God made man in his own image" (Gen. 9:6).

This verse therefore lays the foundational principles for all human governmental authority. At the very beginning of human society after the flood destroyed the earth, God establishes that he will delegate to human beings the authority to carry out punishment on wrongdoers ("by man shall his blood be shed"). Therefore the authority to execute punishment on wrongdoing has not simply been invented by human beings on their own. Rather, it is an authority that has been delegated to human beings by God, and through this authority God carries out his righteous justice on wrongdoers, for he says this is the way in which he "will require a reckoning for the life of man" (v. 5). Therefore the authority to punish wrongdoing (presumably through some form of government that would be established) is given by God to human government. And such authority to punish wrongdoing also implies that human governments will have to decide (a) what wrongdoing is worthy of punishment, (b) what punishment is appropriate for each wrongdoing, and (c) whether or not an individual is guilty of that wrongdoing.

This passage comes long before the establishment of the nation of Israel (at the exodus from Egypt) or the giving of the laws of the Mosaic covenant (in Exodus, Leviticus, Numbers, and Deuteronomy). Therefore the application of this passage is not limited to the nation of Israel for a specific period of time, but is intended to apply to all people, for all time. It is important to recognize that when the New Testament speaks of the "Old Covenant" (see 2 Cor. 3:14), it always refers to the covenant established through Moses with the nation of Israel. (See also Jer. 31:31–32; Luke 22:20; 1 Cor. 13:11; 2 Cor. 3:4–16; and Heb. 8–10). But the covenant God made with Noah after the flood is nowhere called the "Old Covenant," and it is nowhere said to be abolished or no longer in effect. The covenant God made with Noah applies to all human beings on the earth, for all generations:

> "When the bow is in the clouds, I will see it and remember the *everlasting covenant* between God and *every living creature* of all flesh that is on the earth" (Gen. 9:16).

What we conclude from this passage is that God gave to human government the authority to carry out capital punishment and that this is the foundational authority of all governments of the earth.

One objection to this understanding of Genesis 9 is to say that it is a "proverb" and not an actual command from God about how human beings should act. Glen Stassen and David Gushee say this about Genesis 9:6: "As it stands in Genesis, it does not command the death penalty but gives wise advice based on the likely consequence of your action: if you kill someone, you will end up being killed."[18]

But this interpretation is not persuasive, for three reasons.

(1) When verse 5 is connected to verse 6, it shows that execution of the murderer is the way that *God himself will carry out justice in human society*: God says, "from his fellow man *I will require a reckoning* for the life of man" (Gen. 9:5). But Stassen and Gushee say nothing about verse 5.

(2) The last clause of verse 6 (which Stassen and Gushee also fail to mention) gives an *explanation* for the command. The death penalty is to be carried out for murder *because* man is in the image of God. This shows why the crime is so serious. But in Stassen and Gushee's view, this reason would make no sense. They understand this "proverb" to mean, in effect, "If you do something wrong (murder), another wrong will be done to you (another murder)." But how can our creation in

18. Glen Stassen and David Gushee, *Kingdom Ethics* (Downers Grove, IL: InterVarsity Press, 2003), 202.

God's image be a reason for wrongdoing? This is like saying (on their view that capital punishment is wrong), "People will do wrong to each other because they are made in God's image." That ends up saying that God's image is the reason why people do wrong!

(3) Later passages in the Old Testament show that God himself did institute the death penalty for the crime of murder (see Num. 35:16–34).

Because of these three reasons, Stassen and Gushee's interpretation is not persuasive.

b. Romans 13:1–7 is the first of two primary New Testament passages that teach about civil government

I would like to make two comments about Romans 13:1–7. Here is the passage:

> Let every person be subject to the governing authorities. For there is no authority except from God, and those that exist have been instituted by God. Therefore whoever resists the authorities resists what God has appointed, and those who resist will incur judgment. For rulers are not a terror to good conduct, but to bad. Would you have no fear of the one who is in authority? Then do what is good, and you will receive his approval, for he is God's servant for your good. But if you do wrong, be afraid, for he does not bear the sword in vain. For *he is the servant of God, an avenger who carries out God's wrath on the wrongdoer.* Therefore one must be in subjection, not only to avoid God's wrath but also for the sake of conscience. For the dame reason you also pay taxes, for the authorities are ministers of God, attending to this very thing. Pay to all what is owed to them: taxes to whom taxes are owed, revenue to whom revenue is owed, respect to whom respect is owed, honor to whom honor is owed (Rom. 13:1–7).

First, Paul says, the agent of government is "the servant of God, an avenger [Greek *ekdikos,* "one who carries out punishment"] who carries out God's wrath on the wrongdoer" (v. 4). This is consistent with the teaching of Genesis 9 that God requires a reckoning for wrongdoing and that this will be carried out through human agents.

Second, Paul says, the civil government "does not bear the sword in vain" (v. 4). The Greek word for "sword" is *macharia,* which is used in several other verses to speak of the instrument by which people are put to death. Here are some examples:

Acts 12:2: He killed James the brother of John with the *sword*.

Acts 16:27: [The Philippian jailer] drew his *sword* and was about to kill himself, supposing that the prisoners had escaped.

Hebrews 11:37: They were stoned, they were sawn in two, they were killed with the *sword*.

Revelation 13:10: If anyone is to be slain with the *sword*, with the sword must he be slain.

A number of verses in the Septuagint (the Greek translation of the Old Testament) also use the word in this way, such as these:

Deuteronomy 13:15: You shall surely put the inhabitants of that city to the *sword*, devoting it to destruction.

Deuteronomy 20:13: And when the LORD your God gives it into your hand, you shall put all its males to the *sword*.

Therefore the idea, suggested by some, that the sword here is simply a symbol of governmental authority is hardly persuasive. When Paul says that civil government in general is authorized to "bear the sword," he means that it has been given authority from God to use the sword for the purpose for which people used it in the first century, and that is to put people to death.

c. First Peter 2:13 – 14 is the second primary passage on civil government in the New Testament

Be subject for the Lord's sake to every human institution, whether it be to the emperor as supreme, or to governors as sent by him *to punish those who do evil* and to praise those who do good.

The expression translated "to punish" in verse 14 is *eis ekdikçsis*, using the same word that Paul used for "vengeance" that belongs to God (Rom. 12:19) and a word from the same root that Paul uses to say that the civil government is *"an avenger* who carries out God's wrath" (Rom. 13:4). In both Romans 13 and 1 Peter 2 the New Testament teaches that government has a responsibility not only to deter crime, but also actually to bring God's punishment to the wrongdoer. This is consistent with Genesis 9:5 – 6.

d. But is it right to desire that government punish a criminal?

Sometimes Christians may think that if a loved one has been murdered, or if they themselves have been robbed or beaten or severely injured by a drunk driver, they should merely forgive the person and never seek that the wrongdoer be punished by the courts. But that is not the solution Paul gives in Romans 12:19. He does not say, "Beloved, never avenge yourselves, but simply forgive everyone who has done wrong to you." Rather, he tells them to give up any desire to seek revenge themselves and instead give it over to the civil government, for after he says, "Beloved, never avenge yourselves," he says, "*but leave it to the wrath of God.*" Then he goes on to explain that the civil government is "the servant of God, an avenger who carries out *God's wrath* on the wrongdoer" (Rom. 13:4).

In other words, people should not seek to take *personal revenge* when they have been wronged, but they should seek that *justice be done* through the workings of the civil government. Letting the civil government carry out justice frees the believer to do good even to those who have wronged him. As Paul says, "If your enemy is hungry, feed him; if he is thirsty, give him something to drink" (Rom. 12:20). In that way they will "overcome evil with good" (v. 21), and that good comes not only through giving food and water but also through the justice system of the civil government, which is "God's servant for your good" (Rom. 13:4).[19]

But, someone might object, isn't it wrong for a Christian to *desire* vengeance? It depends on what kind of vengeance is desired. If we seek and desire to take *personal vengeance* (to harm the wrongdoer ourselves), then that is disobeying Romans 12 and 13; but if we desire that the government carry out *God's just vengeance* on the wrongdoer, then we are doing exactly what Paul says in 12:19 and are leaving vengeance "to the wrath of God." We are leaving it to the proper purpose of government, who is "the servant of God" when it "carries out God's wrath on the wrongdoer" (13:4). It cannot be wrong for us to desire that God's justice be carried out in this manner, for it is another way how God demonstrates the glory of his attribute of justice on the earth. (Jim Wallis fails to make this distinction between wrongful personal vengeance and a rightful desire for God's vengeance to come through government when he opposes capital punishment, saying it "just satisfies revenge."[20] No, it satisfies God's requirement of justice.)

Therefore it does not seem to me to be wrong when Christians both (1) show personal kindness to and pray for the salvation and eternal

---

19. There were no chapter or verse divisions in the earliest Greek manuscripts, and the connection between what we now know as the end of chapter 12 and the beginning of chapter 13 would have been even clearer to Paul's original readers.

20. Jim Wallis, *God's Politics*, 303.

forgiveness of those who have done them wrong, and (2) simultaneously pursue justice through the civil courts and desire that the wrongdoer be justly paid back for the wrong that he has done. In fact, I have spoken with more than one believer who had a friend or loved one murdered, and who deeply longed for the courts to carry out punishment on the murderer. It seemed to me that this reflected a deep-seated sense of God's justice that he has put in our human hearts and that was crying out for wrong to be punished and for justice to be done.

Another passage that gives confirmation to this is Revelation 6:9–10:

> When he opened the fifth seal, I saw under the altar the souls of those who had been slain for the word of God and for the witness they had borne. They cried out with a loud voice, "O Sovereign Lord, holy and true, *how long before you will judge and avenge* [Greek *ekdikeô*, "punish, take vengeance"] *our blood on those who dwell on the earth?*"

The significant point about this passage is that these "souls" are now completely free from sin, and this means that there is no trace of sinful desire left in their hearts. Yet they are crying out for God to avenge their murderers, to take vengeance on those who had murdered them, "on those who dwell on the earth" (v. 10). Therefore such a desire cannot be seen as morally wrong, nor is it inconsistent with forgiving others and continually committing judgment into the hands of God, even as Jesus did when he was on the cross (see 1 Peter 2:23 and Luke 23:34). In fact, it is exactly this action of committing judgment into the hands of God that allows us to give up the desire to seek it for ourselves and that gives us freedom to continue to show acts of personal mercy to them in this life.

e. What crimes are worthy of capital punishment?

Are any other crimes besides murder also worthy of capital punishment? The Bible does not give us explicit directions on that question, though some principles from it can inform our reasoning process. The main question is whether other crimes are *sufficiently as horrible as murder in the degree of evil they involve*, so that they deserve capital punishment.

The final decision about which crimes deserve capital punishment should be made by each state or nation, ideally as the will of the people finds expression through the laws enacted by their elected representatives. (I certainly do not think this is a question that a democracy should allow to be decided by nine unelected justices on a Supreme Court, as now happens in the United States.)

Christopher Wright points out a significant feature of Old Testament law: "No property offense in normal legal procedure was punishable by death."[21] That is, *people* could not be put to death for stealing *things*, but some kind of monetary retribution had to be made instead. This seems to be a wise principle that should prevent the death penalty from even being considered for crimes involving only property.

However, one word of caution is in order: I do *not* think it right to appeal to the *many kinds of crimes subject to the death penalty* in the laws in the Mosaic covenant (in Exodus, Leviticus, Numbers, and Deuteronomy) to say that those crimes should receive capital punishment today. Those laws were only intended for the people of Israel at that particular time in history. Many of those laws reflected the unique status of Israel as a people for God's own possession who were required to worship him and not allow any hint of allegiance to other gods. There is no suggestion in the rest of the Bible that those particular uses of the death penalty in the Mosaic covenant should ever be applied by civil governments today.

As far as modern governments are concerned, I think that capital punishment should be the penalty for *some other crimes* that were intended to or actually did lead to the death of other people. Some examples might include perjury that resulted in the wrongful death of a falsely accused person, or espionage that resulted in the deaths of some of the citizens of a country. Other examples would be "crimes against the state" such as treason or plotting to use weapons of mass destruction, both of which could result in the deaths of many thousands of people. It also seems to me that a crime such as kidnapping along with brutal rape and beating of another person that did not result in death but resulted in permanent disability to the victim could also fall into the category of a crime worthy of capital punishment. (However, the US Supreme Court took away the right of any state to decide to impose such a death penalty in *Kennedy v. Louisiana*, announced on June 25, 2008, a case involving the brutal rape of a child. In that case the court also ruled out the death penalty for any crime against an individual "where the victim's life was not taken.")[22]

f. Conclusion

God gives to civil government the right and the responsibility to carry out capital punishment for certain crimes, at least for the crime of murder (which is specified in Genesis 9:6).

---

21. Christopher J. H. Wright, *Old Testament Ethics for the People of God* (Downers Grove, IL: InterVarsity Press, 2004), 308.

22. *Kennedy v. Louisiana*, 554 U.S. 36 (2008).

3. Arguments from reason and evidence apart from the Bible

Many private advocacy groups have advanced persuasive arguments for capital punishment based on the fact that it does in fact deter violent crime, that it can be fairly administered, that adequate safeguards can be taken to prevent innocent people from being executed, and that a widespread human sense of justice acknowledges that the crime of premeditated murder can only be adequately punished through taking the life of the murderer. Christians should not be surprised that even unbelievers have an inward sense of the requirements of justice in such a case, because the Bible says that "the work of the law is written on their hearts, while their conscience also bears witness" (Rom. 2:15). This indicates that God has put in the hearts of all people a sense of right and wrong that reflects much of his moral law, and that would include also a sense of a need for justice to be carried out when a wrong has been committed.

4. Objections

a. Objections from the Bible

Some writers have raised objections to the idea that I have presented here, that governments have a right and responsibility to carry out capital punishment at least for premeditated murder. They have based their objections on other passages found in the Bible.[23]

(1) Exodus 20:13

Some have argued that Exodus 20:13, "You shall not murder," prohibits the death penalty. They claim that not even a government should "murder" a criminal.

But that interpretation misunderstands the sense of the Hebrew verb *râtsakh*, which is here translated "murder." This verb is used in the Old Testament to refer to what we would call "murder" (in a criminal sense) today (see Num. 35:20). But the word *râtsach* is *not* the ordinary word that refers to judicial execution; that is Hebrew *muth*, along with other expressions. Thus Numbers 35:16 says, "The murderer [*râtsach*] shall be put to death [*muth*]," a different verb.[24]

---

23. Several of these objections are taken from the extensive argument against the death penalty found in Stassen and Gushee, *Kingdom Ethics*, 197–203.

24. Out of forty-nine instances of *râtsach* in the Old Testament, it is only used once to apply to judicial execution, and that is in a proverbial or axiomatic saying that does not represent the ordinary use of the word, even in the context of that verse: "If anyone kills a person, the murderer [*râtsach*] shall be put to death [*râtsach*] on the evidence of witnesses. But no person shall be put to death [*muth*] on the testimony of one witness" (Num. 35:30).

Therefore this verse should not be used as an argument against capital punishment, for that is not the sense in which the original readers would have understood it. (This also means that the RSV and KJV are misleading when they translate the verse, "You shall not kill," which could be taken by people to mean all sorts of killing, a much broader sense than what is intended by the Hebrew verb.)

In addition, God himself commanded that the death penalty be carried out in the actual laws that he gave for the Mosaic covenant (see, for example, Num. 35:16–21, 30–34). It would not be consistent to think that in Exodus 21:13 God prohibited what he commanded in Numbers 35.

(2) Matthew 5:38–39

This Scripture passage says, "You have heard that it was said, 'An eye for an eye and a tooth for a tooth.' But I say to you, Do not resist the one who is evil. But if anyone slaps you on the right cheek, turn to him the other also."

However, in this verse Jesus is speaking to *individual persons* and talking about how they should be relating to other individuals. It is similar to Romans 12:19, where Paul prohibits personal vengeance. Jesus is not talking about the responsibility of governments or telling governments how they should act with regard to the punishment of crime. We need to pay attention to the context of passages and apply them to the situations they are addressing; Matthew 5 is addressing personal conduct while Romans 13 explicitly addresses the responsibilities of governments.

(3) Matthew 22:39

Here Jesus says, "You shall love your neighbor as yourself." Does this command prohibit putting a murderer to death? Is it possible to love one's neighbor, in obedience to this command, and at the same time put him to death for murder? How can these be consistent with each other? And shouldn't this command of Jesus take precedence over the Old Testament commands about executing the death penalty?

But this objection, if it pits Jesus' command against some Old Testament commands about the death penalty, clearly misunderstands the context from which Jesus took these words. Jesus is actually quoting from the Old Testament, from Leviticus 19:18, where God commanded the people, "You shall not take vengeance or bear a grudge against the sons of your own people, but *you shall love your neighbor as yourself*: I am the LORD." In that same context, God also commanded the death penalty for certain crimes (see Lev. 20:2, 10). Therefore it must have been consistent for God to command love for one's neighbor and also command the death penalty, for example, for people who put their children to death in sacrificing to idols (see 20:2). Love for one's neighbor does not nullify the requirement to carry out God's justice on wrongdoers.

(4) Matthew 26:52

When Jesus was being arrested, Peter drew his sword and struck the servant of the high priest, thinking to defend Jesus against attack. But Jesus said to him, "Put your sword back into its place. For all who take the sword will perish by the sword" (Matt. 26:52). Does this argue against the death penalty?

This verse should not be taken as a command to people serving as agents of a government. That interpretation would fail to take account of who Peter was and what his role was at that point. Jesus was not saying that no soldiers or policemen should ever have weapons; rather, he was telling Peter not to attempt to resist those who were arresting Jesus and would lead him to crucifixion. Jesus did not want to begin a civil uprising among his followers, and he certainly did not want Peter to be killed at that time for attempting to defend and protect him.

But it is also interesting that Peter, who had been traveling with Jesus regularly for three years, was carrying a sword! People carried swords at that time for self-defense against robbers and others who would do them harm, and Jesus apparently had not taught them that it was wrong to carry a sword for self-defense. (He seems to authorize swords for this very purpose in Luke 22:38.) In addition, Jesus did not tell Peter to give his sword away or throw it away, but, "Put your sword back into its place" (Matt. 26:52). It was apparently right for Peter to continue carrying his sword, just not to use it to prevent Jesus' arrest and crucifixion. In that context, "all who take the sword will perish by the sword" must mean that those who take up the sword *in an attempt to do the spiritual work of advancing the kingdom of God* will not succeed in that work, and if Jesus' followers attempted to overthrow the Roman government as a means of advancing the kingdom of God at that time, they would simply fail and perish by the sword.

(5) John 8:2–11

The Old Testament had commanded the death penalty for the crime of adultery (see Deut. 22:23–24), but in the New Testament story of the woman caught in adultery, Jesus first said, "Let him who is without sin among you be the first to throw a stone at her" (John 8:7), and then, when all the accusers had left, he said, "Neither do I condemn you; go, and from now on sin no more" (8:11). Does this imply that Jesus no longer wanted people to enforce the death penalty?

There are several reasons why this passage should not be used as an argument against the death penalty. First, even if this text is used to argue against using the death penalty *for adultery*, which was taught in the Mosaic covenant (see Deut. 22:23–24), it is not a story about a murderer and it cannot be used to apply to the use of the death penalty *for murder*, which was established in God's covenant with Noah long before the time of the covenant with Moses.

Second, the historical context of this passage explains more about Jesus' answer: He did not allow himself to be drawn into a trap in which he would tell the Jewish leaders to carry out the death penalty, whereas the Roman government had prohibited anyone from carrying out the death penalty except the Roman officials themselves.

Third, the entire story is contained in John 7:53–8:11, a passage of doubtful origin, as is plain from the explanatory notes in any modern Bible translation. Although the passage is retained in many Bibles today, it is usually with double brackets or other marks showing that it almost certainly was not a part of the original manuscript of John's gospel. Thus the authority of this text itself is doubtful.

Therefore, on several levels the text does not provide a persuasive objection to the death penalty with respect to crimes such as murder.

(6) "We should follow the teachings of Jesus"

Sometimes opponents of the death penalty say that we should follow the teachings of Jesus on this matter rather than other verses in the Bible, especially some Old Testament passages. Stassen and Gushee, for example, say, "One way to study the biblical teaching on the death penalty is to begin with Jesus Christ as Lord, and with the commitment to be followers of Jesus.... Then we ask first what Jesus taught on the death penalty as a response to murder."[25] They contrast this approach with using as the key passage "not Jesus' teaching but Genesis 9:6."[26]

The primary biblical teaching about the responsibilities of civil government is found in passages such as Genesis 9, Romans 13, and 1 Peter 2, but *Jesus himself* did not give much explicit teaching about civil government. Therefore, when someone says, "We should follow the teaching of Jesus" regarding civil government, he has ruled out most of the relevant

---

25. Stassen and Gushee, *Kingdom Ethics*, 197.
26. Ibid., 199.

teaching in the Bible about civil government! In another sense, however, the whole Bible comes with the authority of Jesus, and we should seek to follow all that it teaches on this topic. Finally, as explained with regard to passages from Matthew above, Stassen and Gushee incorrectly try to apply some of Jesus' teachings to the question of the death penalty as used by governments, a subject that these teachings were not intended to address.

(7) God spared some murderers such as Cain and King David

The final biblical argument against the death penalty is that God's own actions show that murderers should not be put to death, because God himself spared Cain, who murdered his brother Abel (Gen. 4:8–16), and also spared the life of King David when David caused the death of Bathsheba's husband, Uriah (see 2 Sam. 12:13).[27]

But this objection merely changes the subject from the responsibility of civil government to the freedom of God to pardon whomever he wishes. Of course, God can pardon some people until the day of final judgment and execute immediate judgment on others, according to his wise purposes. He is God! In other passages he executed immediate judgment that ended people's lives, as with the fire from heaven on Sodom and Gomorrah (Gen. 19:24–29), or the flood (Gen. 6–9), or Korah, Dathan, and Abiram (Num. 16:31–33), or Nadab and Abihu (Lev. 10:1–2), or Uzzah (2 Sam. 6:7). The simple truth is that God can pardon whom he will until the day of final judgment, and he can carry out immediate judgment on whom he will. But he is *not* telling us in these passages *what he wants civil governments to do!* He has established that clearly in Genesis 9:5–6, in Romans 13:1–7, in 1 Peter 2:13–14, and elsewhere. Where he tells us what he wants governments to do, governments should follow those teachings.

It is characteristic of the opponents of capital punishment that they continue to appeal to passages that *do not* speak explicitly about the subject of civil government, in order to use them to deny the teaching of those passages that *do* speak about civil government. This is hardly sound biblical interpretation.

(8) A "whole life ethic"

Some opponents of the death penalty have said that Christians should apply a "whole life ethic," in which they oppose all intentional taking

---

27. Stassen and Gushee also mention some other Old Testament examples; see their *Kingdom Ethics*, 200.

of human life, including abortion, euthanasia, capital punishment, and war. (This view is sometimes called the "seamless garment" argument.) Jim Wallis takes this position in his book *God's Politics*.[28] Joseph Cardinal Bernardin of Chicago was an advocate of this view, stating, "The spectrum of life cuts across the issues of genetics, abortion, capital punishment, modern warfare and the care of the terminally ill."[29] Pope John Paul II also advocated this position in his *Evangelium Vitae*, writing,

> This is the context in which to place the problem of the death penalty. On this matter there is a growing tendency, both in the Church and in civil society, to demand that it be applied in a very limited way or even that it be abolished completely. The problem must be viewed in the context of a system of penal justice ever more in line with human dignity and thus, in the end, with God's plan for man and society. The primary purpose of the punishment which society inflicts is "to redress the disorder caused by the offence." Public authority must redress the violation of personal and social rights by imposing on the offender an adequate punishment for the crime, as a condition for the offender to regain the exercise of his or her freedom. In this way authority also fulfills the purpose of defending public order and ensuring people's safety, while at the same time offering the offender an incentive and help to change his or her behaviour and be rehabilitated.
>
> It is clear that, for these purposes to be achieved, the *nature and extent of the punishment* must be carefully evaluated and decided upon, and ought not go to the extreme of executing the offender except in cases of absolute necessity: in other words, when it would not be possible otherwise to defend society. Today however, as a result of steady improvements in the organization of the penal system, such cases are very rare, if not practically non-existent.[30]

In response, the proper approach to decide a biblical position on a topic is to take *the specific teaching of the Bible about that topic*, rather than fleeing to a vague cloud of generalities (such as "whole life ethic") that can then be used to support most any position the proponent wants.

---

28. Jim Wallis, *God's Politics*, 300, 303–6. Wallis does not discuss any passages from the Bible in support of his view, but just his vague, general principle of a "consistent ethic of life."

29. Joseph Cardinal Bernardin: quoted in R. Kenneth Overberg, "A Consistent Ethic of Life," *Catholic Update*, St. Anthony's Press, 2009.

30. John Paul II, "*Evangelium vitae*: On the Value and Inviolability of Human Life," Paragraph 56 (March 25, 1995). www.vatican.va/edocs/ENG0141/_Index.htm.

As I have argued above, the specific texts pertaining to abortion and euthanasia teach against these things, but the specific texts that pertain to capital punishment support it.

Another argument against the "whole life ethic" is the fact that in Ezekiel 13:19 God says, "You have profaned me among my people …," and then he condemns both "putting to death souls who should not die and *keeping alive souls who should not live*" (emphasis added). ("Souls" here is used to mean "people.") Therefore the true biblical ethic is not "protect all human life in every case," but rather "protect the innocent and also punish the guilty, in proportion to the crime they have committed."

Rather than a "whole life ethic," Christians should adopt a "whole Bible ethic" and be faithful to the teaching of the entire Bible on this subject as well as on others.

b. Objections to the death penalty based on results and fairness

Most arguments about capital punishment *apart from* the teachings of the Bible have to do with the results of using or abolishing the death penalty. Those who argue against the death penalty say that (a) it does not deter crime; (b) innocent victims might be put to death; (c) violence by government provokes more violence in society; (d) it is unfairly administered, so that the poor and some ethnic minorities are much more likely to receive the death penalty; and (e) capital punishment historically has been used in cruel and oppressive ways, even by Christians.

In response, proponents of the death penalty argue the following:

(1) Is the death penalty a deterrent to murder? When overall statistics are examined, there is *a fairly clear inverse relationship* between the number of executions of murderers and the number of murders in the United States. When the number of executions goes down, the number of murders goes up, but when executions increase, murders drop. This is seen on the next page in the chart by two professors at Pepperdine University.[31]

Some studies have shown that for each murderer executed, as many as fourteen to eighteen additional murders are deterred.[32]

---

31. Roy D. Adler and Michael Summers, "Capital Punishment Works," *Wall Street Journal* (Nov. 2, 2007). http://online.wsj.com/article/SB119397079767680173.html.

32. Testimony of David B. Muhlausen, Ph.D., "The Death Penalty Deters Crime and Saves Lives," Heritage Foundation (Aug. 28, 2007). www.heritage.org/Research/Crime/tst082807a. cfm: citing Paul R. Zimmerman, "State Executions, Deterrence, and the Incidence of Murder," *Journal of Applied Ecomonics* 7:1 (May 2004), 909–41.

This deterrence effect has been recognized even by researchers who oppose capital punishment. "I personally am opposed to the death penalty," said H. Naci Mocan, an economist at Louisiana State University and an author of a study finding that each execution saves five lives. "But my research shows that there is a deterrent effect."[33]

Similarly, anti-death penalty proponents Cass Sunstein of the University of Chicago and Adrian Vermeule of Harvard University wrote, "Capital punishment may well save lives." They added, "Those who object to capital punishment, and who do so in the name of protecting life, must come to terms with the possibility that the failure to inflict capital punishment will fail to protect life."[34]

This shows the inadequacy of the arguments from authors such as Wallis, who claims it is part of a "consistent ethic of life" to be against capital punishment.[35] My response is to say that when we support capital punishment, we show that we place *the highest possible value on human life*: for when it is wrongfully taken, society requires the greatest punishment, forfeiting the life of the murderer. These studies also show that Wallis is incorrect when he writes that "there is no real evidence that [capital punishment] deters murder; it just satisfies revenge."[36] (He quotes no data to support this.)

In addition, there is an argument from common sense: If a criminal knows he will possibly be put to death, will he be more likely or less

33. H. Naci Mocan: quoted in Adam Liptak, "Does Death Penalty Save Lives? A New Debate," *New York Times* (Nov. 18, 2007). www.nytimes.com/2007/11/18/us/18deter.html?ei=5124&en=fe19d37a68eea8b4&ex=1353042000&partner=delicious&exprod=delicious&pagewanted=all.

34. Cass Sunstein and Adrian Vermeule, "Is Capital Punishment Morally Required? The Relevance of Life-Life Tradeoffs," 58 *Stanford Law Review* 703 (2005): quoted in Liptak, "Does Death Penalty Save Lives?"

35. See Wallis, *God's Politics*, 300, 303.

36. Ibid., 303.

likely to commit murder than if he knows he cannot be put to death? He will be less likely.

The current legal system in the United States allows appeals to drag on for a decade or more, so we have not been able to see in recent years a reliable evaluation of the deterrent effect if the death penalty were carried out more quickly when someone has clearly been determined to be guilty and reasonable appeals have been exhausted. The deterrent effect would no doubt be much greater than it is today. The Bible says, "Because the sentence against an evil deed is not executed speedily, the heart of the children of man is fully set to do evil" (Eccl. 8:11).

(2) Are innocent people put to death? With regard to the possibility of innocent victims being put to death, there has been (to my knowledge) *no known example* of an innocent person put to death in the United States since the resumption of the death penalty in 1976. A number of innocent death-row prisoners have been *released* due to DNA testing,[37] but that does not prove that any people have wrongfully been executed. Of course, the death penalty should be carried out only when guilt is established with extremely high standards of proof, but that is done in many murder convictions.

What is the result of failing to carry out the death penalty in the case of premeditated murder? Life imprisonment is also a cruel kind of punishment and is extremely expensive. Moreover, giving a murderer life in prison or a long-term sentence may lead to his committing other murders in prison or after he escapes or is pardoned. For example, in 1981 Glen Stewart Godwin was sentenced to twenty-five years in prison for the stabbing death of a drug runner and pilot named Kim Robert LeValley. Godwin stabbed LeValley twenty-six times. He escaped from Folsom (California) Prison and fled to Mexico, where he began a new life as a drug dealer. He was arrested there and killed a member of a Mexican drug cartel while in prison. Soon afterward, he broke out of prison again and (as of 2008) has remained a refugee from justice, with a $100,000 reward offered by the US Federal Bureau of Investigation (FBI) for information leading to his arrest.[38]

The fact remains that God gave the requirement for the death penalty in Genesis 9:6 at the beginning of human society after the flood, when methods of collecting evidence and the certainty of proof were far less

---

37. One example is Nicholas James Yarris, who was exonerated by DNA evidence in 2003 for the rape and murder of a suburban Philadelphia woman and was removed from death row. See Cindi Lash, "DNA Exonerates Death Row Inmate," *Pittsburgh Post-Gazette* (Dec. 10, 2003). www.post-gazette.com/localnews/20031210yarris1210p1.asp.

38. Melissa Underwood, "Glen Stewart Godwin Wanted for Murder, Escape From Prison," *Fox News* (Jan. 28, 2008). www.foxnews.com/story/0,2933,326034,00.html.

reliable than they are today. Yet God still gave the command to fallible human beings, not requiring that they be omniscient to carry it out, but only expecting that they act responsibly and seek to avoid further injustice as they carried it out. Among the people of Israel, a failure to carry out the death penalty when God had commanded it was to "pollute the land" and "defile" it before God, for justice had not been done (see Num. 35:32–34).

(3) *Does all violence beget more violence?* The idea that "violence" by government (in capital punishment) "begets more violence" is simply wrong. It is contrary to the teachings of Genesis 9:5–6, Romans 13:4, and 1 Peter 3:12–13. In fact, exactly the opposite is true: Capital punishment actually has a deterrent effect and saves many innocent lives, as several studies have shown (see discussion above).

(4) *Are there racial or economic disparities in the death penalty?* If capital punishment is unfairly or disproportionately carried out among certain segments of a population *when compared with the number of murders committed by that segment of the population*, then the necessary legal steps should be taken to correct that imbalance. But that is not an argument against the death penalty in general. It is merely an argument that demonstrates that it should be carried out fairly, among rich and poor alike, and among members of every ethnic group, when crimes worthy of capital punishment have been committed. There should be no discrimination based on a person's social status or economic class or racial background.

(5) *Has the death penalty been abused in past history?* It is true that capital punishment has sometimes in history been used with horrible excess and for far lesser crimes than murder. There are tragic examples in the history of the church where people were put to death because of what the church considered to be the propagation of false doctrine. But these executions are *abuses* that should not be defended by anyone today; such abuses are not arguments against the rightful use of the death penalty.

5. Recommendations about laws and policies

In light of the previous discussion, I would make two specific recommendations:

a. *Governments should institute the death penalty for cases of premeditated murder.* The reasons for this have been discussed above (pp. 75–78).

b. *Societies and governments should use the normal decision-making processes established by their governments to decide whether any crimes other than murder are so similarly horrible that they are worthy of capital punishment.* Some factors relevant to that determination have been discussed above (pp. 81–82).

6. The importance of this issue

The issue of capital punishment is important for four reasons: (1) God in both the Old Testament and the New Testament teaches that governments should carry out this punishment at least for the crime of murder; (2) it satisfies a deep human sense that just punishment is required when a murder has been committed; (3) it satisfies God's requirement for just punishment that he expects societies to carry out in such cases; (4) it acts as an important deterrent to the horrible crime of murder, especially in cases where the execution is carried out fairly and swiftly and with adequate safeguards against punishing innocent people.

7. For further reading

Bibliography on capital punishment:

Davis, *Evangelical Ethics,* 203–18; Feinberg and Feinberg, *Ethics for a Brave New World,* 127–48; Frame, *The Doctrine of the Christian Life,* 701–4; H. Wayne House and John Howard Yoder, eds., *The Death Penalty Debate: Two Opposing Views of Capital Punishment* (Waco, TX: Word, 1991); Erik Owens, John Carlson, and Eric Elshtian, eds., *Religion and the Death Penalty: A Call for Reckoning* (Grand Rapids: Eerdmans, 2004); Rae, *Moral Choices,* 209–24; Glen H. Stassen and David P. Gushee, *Kingdom Ethics* (Downers Grove, IL: InterVarsity Press, 2003), 194–214.

C. SELF-DEFENSE AND OWNERSHIP OF GUNS

The political question regarding gun ownership is this:

> Should governments prohibit private citizens from owning some or all kinds of guns?

1. The relevant biblical teaching

The biblical teaching that is relevant to the question of gun-control laws has to do, first, with the question of self-defense. Is it right to defend ourselves from physical attacks, and is it right ever to use a weapon in such self-defense? If self-defense is morally right, then the question of gun ownership is primarily a question of whether that is an appropriate kind of weapon to use for self-defense.

a. Is it right to defend ourselves and others from physical attacks when we are able to do so?

Sometimes people think that Jesus prohibited all self-defense when he told his disciples that they should turn the other cheek:

> "You have heard that it was said, 'An eye for an eye and a tooth for a tooth.' But I say to you, do not resist the one who is evil. But if anyone slaps you on the right cheek, turn to him the other also" (Matt. 5:38–39).

But Jesus is not prohibiting self-defense here. He is prohibiting individuals from taking personal vengeance simply to "get even" with another person. The verb "slaps" is the Greek term *rhapizô*, which refers to a sharp slap given in insult (a right-handed person would use the back of the hand to slap someone "on the right cheek").[39] So the point is not to hit back when someone hits you as an insult. But the idea of a violent attack to do bodily harm or even murder someone is not in view here.

Other passages of Scripture seem to show that it is right to try to avoid being harmed by a violent attacker. When King Saul threw a spear at David, David "eluded Saul, so that he struck the spear into the wall," and David fled from him (1 Sam. 19:10).

When King Aretas attempted to capture him in Damascus, Paul escaped by being let down in a basket through an opening in the wall (2 Cor. 11:32–33). Jesus also escaped from an angry crowd at Nazareth that was trying to throw him off a cliff (see Luke 4:29–30), and on another occasion Jesus hid himself in the temple and then escaped from hostile Jews who were seeking to harm him (see John 8:59; 10:39).

In none of these cases did the person who was attacked "turn the other cheek"—that is, David did not hand the spear back to Saul and say, "Try again!"

In the very context of Matthew 5:38–39, several of Jesus' other statements give *examples* of how Christ-like conduct will look, but they are *not absolute commands* to be obeyed in every situation. For example, "Give to the one who begs from you, and do not refuse the one who would borrow from you" (Matt. 5:42, just three verses after the verse on turning the other cheek) cannot be obeyed in *every* situation, or a persistent beggar could bankrupt any Christian or any church just by asking.

In another passage Jesus seemed to encourage his disciples to have swords for self-defense:

---

39. In rabbinic literature there is a parallel to this expression: see Mishnah, *Baba Kamma* 8.6.

He said to them, "But now let the one who has a moneybag take it, and likewise a knapsack. And let the one who has no sword sell his cloak and buy one. For I tell you that this Scripture must be fulfilled in me: 'And he was numbered with the transgressors.' For what is written about me has its fulfillment." And they said, "*Look, Lord, here are two swords.*" And he said to them, "It is enough" (Luke 22:36–38).

People commonly carried swords at that time for protection against robbers, and apparently at least two of Jesus' disciples, who had been with him for three years, were still carrying swords and Jesus had not forbidden this. Although some interpreters understand Jesus to be speaking about "swords" in a metaphorical way (meaning the disciples should be armed spiritually to fight spiritual enemies), this is not a persuasive interpretation, because in this very context the *moneybag* and *knapsack* and *sandals* (see vv. 35–36) are all literal, and *the swords that they showed him* were literal swords. The fact that Jesus was going to be crucified meant an increasing danger of people attacking the disciples as well. When Jesus says, "It is enough," it is immediately in response to the disciples showing him "two swords," so "enough" is best understood to mean "enough swords."

In attempting to argue that this verse does not justify carrying a sword, some interpreters have said that Jesus means, "It is enough of this talk about swords." But that would make little sense, for Jesus himself was the one who first brought up the topic of a sword, and the disciples had simply answered him by showing him swords and making a very brief comment. He would not rebuke them ("Enough of this talk!") for merely answering him with one short sentence. When Jesus says, "It is enough," he means that two swords are enough, and this is an expression of approval of what they have just said and done. There is no hint of a rebuke. But that means that *Jesus is encouraging his disciples to carry a sword for self-defense*, and even to "buy one" (v. 36) if they do not have one.

Another argument in favor of self-defense is that God wants us to care for the health of our bodies, not to encourage actions that would harm them (see 1 Cor. 6:19–20).

Yet another argument is that failing to oppose a violent attack will often lead to even more harm and more wrongdoing. Therefore acting in love *both* toward the attacker *and* toward one's self would include seeking to stop the attack before harm is done.

It is true that later in Luke 22 Jesus rebuked Peter for cutting off the right ear of the servant of the high priest (with a literal sword—see Luke 22:50; John 18:10), but this was because he did not want his disciples to attempt to stop his crucifixion or to try to start a military uprising against Rome. This is also the meaning of Matthew 26:52: "All who take the sword will perish by the sword." Jesus did not want Peter to try to advance the kingdom of God by force. But in the very same verse, Jesus did not tell Peter to throw away his sword, but to keep it, for he said, "Put your sword back into its place" (Matt. 26:52). (See further discussion of this verse on p. 85).

b. Is it right for a person to use a weapon for self-defense?

The verses discussed above (both Luke 22:36–38 and Matt. 26:52) give significant support for the idea that Jesus wanted his disciples to have an effective weapon to use in self-defense. Most of the time, merely carrying a sword would deter a criminal, who would not want to risk being harmed himself. The sword would also enable a person to defend someone else such as a woman or a child or an elderly person who might be under attack from someone stronger.

Another reason for carrying a weapon such as a sword is that it could overcome great inequalities in size or strength between an attacker and a victim. One of Jesus' disciples might be smaller or weaker, but if reasonably skilled in the use of a sword, he still could provide an effective defense against an attacker, who would not want to risk being harmed himself.

A third reason why people carried swords is that although the Roman officials and local police were able to enforce the peace in general, there simply would never be enough of them to be on the spot whenever a crime was being committed. The sword would provide protection against violent crime whenever a policeman or soldier was not in sight.

c. Is it right to use a gun for self-defense?

If the Bible authorizes the idea of self-defense in general, and if Jesus encouraged his disciples to carry a sword to protect themselves, then it seems to me that it is also morally right for a person to be able to use *other kinds of weapons* for self-defense. Today that would include the use of a gun (where the nation or state allows this) or the use of other weapons such as pepper spray that would deter an attacker.

One significant reason why people will choose a gun as a weapon for self-defense is that a gun is a great equalizer that offsets huge differences in physical strength. An eighty-year-old woman with a gun, living alone in her home at night, or a frail seventy-year-old shopkeeper in a high-crime area, would have an effective means of defense against a twenty-five-year-old, 280-pound athletic male intruder. No other kind of weapon would give a person that ability.

In the vast majority of cases, merely brandishing a handgun will cause an attacker to flee (the literature cited below contains references to hundreds of such stories), and in the next most common event, the intruder is wounded and disabled, the attack is thwarted, and the attacker fully recovers and stands trial. The requirement to act in love toward our neighbors, including even the intruder, implies that the least amount of force required to stop the attack should be used, resulting in the least amount of physical harm to the intruder himself.

2. In nations where there is already widespread possession of guns, the laws should allow private citizens to own guns for self-defense

From several personal conversations, I am aware that the attitudes of Christians regarding gun ownership tend to differ quite widely depending on the nation in which they live. For example, in the United Kingdom, private gun ownership has been quite rare for several generations, and current laws make it almost impossible for most private citizens to own a gun. Most policemen in the United Kingdom do not carry guns either. (Britain's Home Office says being unarmed is part of the "character of the police" there.)[40] The nationwide prohibition on gun ownership seems to have been so effective that a relatively small percentage of crimes are committed by criminals with guns. In such a situation, the long traditions of the nation, the generally law-abiding nature of its population, and the widespread popular disapproval of allowing any private ownership of guns all made it unlikely that any change in the law to allow gun ownership would gain enough support to be approved in the United Kingdom. I can understand the viewpoint of British Christians who would be opposed to any change in the current laws.

On the other hand, things are not as peaceful as they might seem. The recent situation is such that, surprisingly, the rate of violent crime (with or without guns) per capita in the United Kingdom is now about twice as large as the rate in the United States.[41] And gun crime itself is also increasing. In September 2009 it was reported that in the previous twelve months London saw a 17% rise in gun offenses, up from 1,484 to 1,737.[42]

---

40. "For Some Bobbies, a Gun Comes with the Job," Associated Press (Oct. 23, 2009). www.cnbc.com/id/33448132.

41. John Lott Jr., "Banning Guns in the U.K. Has Backfired," *Wall Street Journal Europe* (Sept. 3, 2004), reprinted by American Enterprise Institute for Public Policy Research. www. aei.org/article/21136.

42. "For Some Bobbies, a Gun Comes with the Job," Associated Press.

Bob Ayers, a London-based former US intelligence officer, said, "In the past the police were authority figures dealing primarily with people who respected the police. However, as terrorism and crime increases in the United Kingdom, the traditional icon of the Bobby on the beat is becoming incapable of dealing with terrorists and violent crime."[43]

Sometimes people have a popular perception of higher rates of violent crime in the United States, but these attitudes generally come not from official statistics but from anecdotal evidence stemming from a few highly publicized violent crimes as well as from movies and television shows that hardly paint a fair picture of the nation as a whole.

In the United States, official statistics estimate that 35% of American households own guns, but some people estimate that the actual number may be as high as 50% because government statistics count only documented ownership, not ownership that is not recorded on any government database. Some states and cities have enacted fairly strict restrictions on gun ownership, but the overall statistical pattern seems to be that where more strict laws *against gun ownership* are enacted, the rates of violent crime go up rather than down![44] A. L. Kellerman, writing in the *American Journal of Public Health*, said, "Gun control laws encourage the substitution of other weapons, which may be also quite dangerous if used by a criminal. In fact, such substitution may be even more dangerous like shoulder weapons, or increase the possibility of injury as knives."[45] This makes sense for two reasons: (a) If a law prohibiting guns is enacted in a city, the law-abiding citizens will tend to turn in their guns at a much higher rate than criminals, and (b) if the law-abiding citizens outnumber the criminals in the society, then taking away guns will mostly take away guns from law-abiding citizens who have been using them to prevent crimes from happening.

3. Do gun-control laws reduce gun crime?

My conclusion from reading statistics from a number of studies is that, in general, increasingly strict gun-control laws have not been shown to reduce gun crime, and in several places they seem to have led to an increase in crime. Some significant examples are seen in the experience of New Jersey, Hawaii, and Washington, DC:

---

43. Ibid.
44. A. L. Kellerman, "Firearm Related Violence: What We Don't Know Is Killing Us," *American Journal of Public Health* 84 (1994): 541–42.
45. Ibid.

New Jersey adopted what was described as the "most stringent gun law in America" in 1966, and two years later the homicide rate had increased 46% and the reported robbery rate had doubled.

After Hawaii adopted a series of increasingly restrictive measures on guns, its murder rate tripled from 2.4 per 100,000 in 1968 to 7.2 in 1977.

The District of Columbia enacted one of the most restrictive gun-control laws in the country, and the murder rate has increased 134% at the same time that the national murder rate decreased by 2%.[46]

A major study of the impact of gun-control laws by Florida State University criminologist Gary Kleck showed that in general they had no significant effect on decreasing rates of violent crime or suicide.[47]

A 2003 review of published studies on gun control released by the Centers for Disease Control and Prevention *could not find any statistically significant decrease in crime that came from such laws.*[48]

As a result of a massive study of state gun-control laws, author John Lott concluded that allowing citizens to carry concealed weapons clearly leads to a reduction in crime. This is because a potential criminal will not know whether a possible victim is carrying a gun or not, and this is a significant deterrence to crime. Rather than studying individual examples, Lott compared FBI crime statistics from all 3,054 counties in the United States. He found that:

- Concealed handgun laws reduced murder by 8.5%, rape by 5%, and severe assault by 7%.
- If right-to-carry laws prevailed throughout the country, there would be 1,600 fewer murders, 4,200 fewer rapes, and 60,000 fewer severe assaults over a fifteen-year period.[49]

Some people may imagine that most of the guns found in the United States will eventually be used to commit a crime. But it is interesting to compare the total number of guns with the total number of murders

---

46. "Myth No. 2: Gun Control Laws Reduce Crime," National Center for Policy Analysis. www.ncoa.org/pub/st/st176/s176c.html.

47. Gary Kleck and E. Britt Patterson, "The impact of gun control and gun ownership levels on violence rates." *Journal of Quantitative Criminology* 9:3, 249–87.

48. "First Reports Evaluating the Effectiveness of Strategies for Preventing Violence: Firearms Laws," *Morbidity and Mortality Review,* Centers for Disease Control (Oct. 3, 2003). www.cdc.gov/mmwr/preview/mmwrhtml/rr5214a2.htm.

49. John R. Lott, *More Guns, Less Crime* (Chicago: University of Chicago Press, 1998, 2000), 76–77.

committed using a gun. For the nine-year period 1988–97 there were 233,251 homicides in the United States, of which 68% were committed using guns.[50] That means there were 158,611 homicides with guns over the course of nine years, or an average of 17,623 homicides per year.

How does that number compare with the total number of guns available in the United States? In 1993 there were approximately 223 *million* guns available.[51] This averages out to 12,654 guns for every murder committed with a gun. In other words, for every gun that is used for murder in the United States, there are 12,653 guns that are *not* used in a murder. And many of those guns, in fact, are used to prevent murders.

Nor do guns lead to a higher incidence of suicide. Studies of the relationship between gun ownership and total suicide rates have shown that if gun ownership is restricted, of course the number of suicides *using guns* is diminished, but the total number of suicides apparently is unchanged, because about the same number of people will commit suicide by other means. Gary Kleck writes,

> … one reason that few suicides could be prevented by removing guns was that people who use guns in suicide typically have a more serious and persistent desire to kill themselves than suicide attempters using other methods. If denied guns, some or all of this group would substitute other methods and kill themselves anyway.[52]

Citing the US National Center for Health Statistics, Kleck reported that 57 percent of gun deaths in 1998 were suicides, and "most gun suicides would probably occur even if a gun was not available."[53] Contrary to popular myth, possession of a gun does not increase, but rather decreases, a person's likelihood of being injured in a crime. Studies by Kleck found that victims of a crime or attempted crime who defend themselves with a gun are in fact less likely to be injured or to lose property than victims who did not defend themselves, or attempted to defend themselves without a gun.[54] Kleck argues also that there is no evidence

---

50. National Center for Injury Prevention and Control, Centers for Disease Control and Prevention, "Injury, mortality statistics." www.wonder,cdc.gov/mortICD9J.shtml.

51. John R. Lott, *More Guns, Less Crime* (Chicago: University of Chicago Press, 1998, 2000), 76–77.

52. Gary Kleck, *Armed* (Amherst, NY: Prometheus Books, 2001), 182.

53. Ibid., 317: citing US National Center for Health Statistics, *Deaths: Final Data for 1998* (Washington DC: U.S. Government Printing Office), 71.

54. Ibid., 296, citing Albert J. Reiss and Jeffrey A. Roth, "Firearms and Violence," *Understanding and Preventing Violence* (Washington, DC: National Academy Press, 1993), 266.

that using a gun for self-protection means that the attacker will take the gun away and use it against the victim.[55]

Some argue that ownership of a gun increases the likelihood of domestic violence. But the statistics used in this argument need to be examined carefully, because in many instances of gun violence occurring within a home that owns a gun, the situation involved either a case of self-defense by a weaker, abused victim against a much stronger abuser (and no criminal charges were brought), or else a gun was brought into the home by the criminal (in a violent area, and thus the gun that was already in the home was not used in the crime).

Statistics about the number of "children" killed by guns each year also need to be understood in light of who are the people counted as "children." Many of the aggregate statistics cited include deaths of *gang members up to the age of anywhere from eighteen to twenty-one*, depending on the state, where these persons are legally still considered "children" and not "adults." Actual numbers of fatal gun accidents involving *children age zero to fourteen* in the United States have shown a steady decline from 530 children per year in 1970 to 227 per year in 1991. Even these are tragic numbers, but they need to be understood in light of other statistics, such as more than 300 child deaths per year involving bicycles.[56] And all of these statistics need to be understood in light of the estimated 2.1 million crimes that are prevented every year through private ownership of guns.[57]

4. The current legal situation in the United States and the Second Amendment

For many years a legal battle raged in the United States over the meaning of the Second Amendment to the Constitution, which says this:

> A well-regulated Militia, being necessary to the security of a free State, the right of the people to keep and bear Arms, shall not be infringed.

What is meant by "the right of the people to keep and bear Arms"? Does it refer to an *individual* right belonging to the citizens of the United States generally? Or should it be restricted (as some have argued) to those who have weapons as part of their membership in a military force or "a

---

55. Ibid., 301.

56. Statistics taken from David B. Kopel, *Guns: Who Should Have Them?* (Amherst, NY: Prometheus Books, 1995), 311–13.

57. Don B. Kates Jr., "Gun Control: Separating Reality from Symbolism," *Journal of Contemporary Law* (1994), 353–79.

well-regulated Militia," which is mentioned in the first few words of the amendment? If the second interpretation is correct, then the amendment would only protect a right to own guns for people who belong to a branch of the military or to some kind of police force.

In a landmark decision announced June 26, 2008, the Supreme Court (by a five-to-four majority) held the following:

(1) "The Second Amendment protects an individual right to possess a firearm unconnected with service with a militia, and to use that arm for traditionally lawful purposes, such as self-defense within the home."[58]

So why does the amendment mention "a well-regulated Militia"? The Court's opinion noted that it was due to the fact that individual states feared that a standing army under the leadership of the federal government might seek to take control over the entire nation, and a prelude to this would be the federal government attempting to disarm the people of the individual states. The meaning of "Militia" at the time of the writing of the Constitution was "all males physically capable of acting in concert for the common defense."[59] The phrase therefore did not refer to the actual military forces organized by the government such as the army or navy (as is evident in Article 1, Section 8 of the Constitution, where "the militia" is distinguished from "armies" and "a navy" and also from that part of the militia "as may be employed in the service of the United States"). A "militia" meant armed citizens.

(2) This does not mean that the Second Amendment *only* protects the right of people to own firearms for the purposes of defending themselves against the tyranny of a powerful federal government, but simply means that that purpose is the one that led to its being put into the Constitution. In the majority opinion, Justice Scalia wrote:

> It is therefore entirely sensible that the Second Amendment's prefatory clause announces the purpose for which the right was codified: to prevent elimination of the militia. The prefatory clause does not suggest that preserving the militia was the only reason Americans valued the ancient right; most undoubtedly thought it even more important for self-defense and hunting. But the threat that the new Federal Government would destroy the citizens' militia by taking away their arms was the reason

---

58. *District of Columbia v. Heller*, 554 U.S. __ (2008), 2 (syllabus Sect. 1, Item a). www.supremecourtus.gov/opinions/07pdf/07–290.pdf.

59. Ibid., 22, sec. 2a.

that right—unlike some other English rights—was codified in a written Constitution.[60]

In other words, the reason the Second Amendment was added to the Constitution was to provide another protection against tyranny—to make it harder for any potential dictator or would-be king to take control of the entire nation against the will of the people. Stated another way, it was one outworking of the idea that a separation of powers is the best protection against government misuse of power, for it meant that the federal government could never become the only entity that had all the guns in the nation and thus all the effective power.

(3) The Second Amendment did not confer a new right but simply protected an ancient and basic human right: the right of self-defense. The majority opinion states:

> The Second Amendment was not intended to lay down a "novel principl[e]" but rather codified a right "inherited from our English ancestors," *Robertson v. Baldwin*, 165 US 275,281 (1897)."[61]

Scalia also noted that the central human right to self-defense, far from peripheral to the amendment, was the fundamental right underlying the amendment itself: "Self-defense had little to do with the right's *codification*; it was the *central component* of the right itself."[62]

Justice Scalia's extensive opinion traces the meanings of terms as they were used at the time of the adoption of the Constitution, and the history of interpretation of the Second Amendment, showing the correctness of this opinion. This was an argument based on the "original public meaning" of the words of the Constitution. In particular, the usage of the phrase "the people" elsewhere in the Constitution shows that it was meant to apply to *individual citizens* of the United States, not to organizations such as an organized state or federal military force. (Notice that the First Amendment speaks of "the right of *the people* peaceably to assemble," and the Fourth Amendment speaks of "The right of *the people* to be secure in their persons, houses, papers, and effects.")

(4) The requirement that any guns kept in a home be kept locked and unloaded "makes it impossible for citizens to use arms for the core lawful purpose of self-defense and is hence unconstitutional."[63]

---

60. Ibid., 25, sec. 3.
61. Ibid., 26, sec. 3.
62. Ibid., 26, sec. 3.
63. Ibid., 3 (syllabus, item 3).

(5) This decision does not invalidate most existing laws that prohibit felons and the mentally ill from possessing firearms, or forbid the carrying of firearms "in sensitive places such as schools and government buildings," or other sorts of reasonable conditions and qualifications on the sale and possession of arms. Nor does it invalidate laws that prohibit "dangerous and unusual weapons."[64] This means that existing laws that restrict the sale of machine guns for private use, for example, are still allowed under the Constitution.

5. Objections

The primary objections against allowing gun ownership are arguments from *results*. That is, people argue that allowing gun ownership leads to more injuries and deaths from guns. These arguments have been included in the discussion of the results of gun-control laws (see sec. 3 above, pp. 98–101).

A second kind of objection comes from those who also oppose capital punishment and all use of "violence" in general. I have addressed these objections in the discussion of objections to capital punishment earlier in this chapter (see pp. 89–92).

6. Recommendations about laws and policies

a. Laws should guarantee that citizens have the right to possess some kind of effective means of self-defense

The right to self-defense should be seen as a fundamental human right, and governments should protect that right. This is especially important for women, for the elderly, and for any others who might be less able to defend themselves from an attack or who might appear to be more vulnerable to an attack, but it is a right that should be available to all citizens.

Protecting this right will also tend to reduce crime in any segment of society, because potential attackers will be unable to know who will have an effective weapon to use in self-defense.

Tragic mass murders in which a lone gunman can hold at bay an entire restaurant or church full of people, for example, and begin killing one after the other are much less likely to happen in states where a large number of people carry concealed weapons and would act to stop such a person.

---

64. Ibid., 2 (syllabus, sec. 2).

John Lott reports an example of a lone shooter—Peter Odighizuwa—who opened fire and killed two administrators and a student at Appalachian Law School in Virginia in 2002. Odighizuwa might have killed many more students except that two male students, Mikael Gross and Tracy Bridges, ran to their cars, got their guns, and came back pointing their guns at the shooter, who then threw his gun down and the attack was stopped. But worldwide media coverage, due to a bias against reporting any good use of guns, almost uniformly failed to even mention that Gross and Bridges used guns to subdue the shooter, as they clearly specified in their interviews with reporters.[65]

In December 2007 a gunman killed one person and wounded four others when he opened fire at New Life Church in Colorado Springs, Colorado, but was stopped from killing others when a church security officer shot and killed him. CNN reported that Chief Richard Myers called the Colorado Springs church security staffer "a courageous security staff member who probably saved many lives."[66]

b. In the United States, the right of the citizens to own guns for the purpose of self-defense should be protected by the laws

A gun is the most effective means of defense in all kinds of threatening situations, especially against attackers who may be stronger or more numerous. Protection of the right to own a gun is especially important in areas of higher crime or more frequent violence.

Unfortunately, it is precisely in areas where the right to self-defense is most needed that some gun-control laws have been most restrictive. And when stricter gun-control laws are introduced in a state or city, the incidence of violent crime and murders tends to increase rather than decrease.[67] This is because most of the guns that are taken away by these laws, or rendered ineffective by laws stating that they have to be unloaded and locked up, are taken away from law-abiding citizens who believe they should conform to the new laws. But criminals who have been using guns or want to use guns to commit crimes are the least likely to turn them in. There is truth in the popular slogan, "If guns are outlawed, only outlaws will have guns."

---

65. John Lott, *The Bias against Guns* (Chicago: Regnery, 2003), 24–25.

66. "Gunman Killed After Opening Fire at Church," *CNN.com* (Dec. 9, 2007). www.cnn.com/2007/US/12/09/church.shooting/index.html.

67. See "Myth No. 2: Gun Control Laws Reduce Crime," and Lott, *The Bias against Guns*, 50–96, 135–38.

c. Governments should place reasonable restrictions on gun ownership

It is appropriate for governments to prohibit convicted felons and the mentally ill from owning or possessing guns. It is also appropriate to prohibit the possession of guns in certain sensitive places, such as in courtrooms or on airplanes. (But we must remember that both of these situations are highly controlled areas with very low possibility of a violent attack by one person against another, and in the extremely rare occasions where an attack occurs, it is immediately subdued by the authorities present. Thus these situations are different from life in the general public where citizens have much more freedom.)

Other reasonable restrictions would include the prohibition of private ownership of certain types of weapons not needed for personal self-defense—for example, weapons such as a machine gun or an antitank rocket launcher or an antiaircraft missile launcher that would only be needed in military conflict.

To guarantee compliance with such restrictions, a background check would seem appropriate when someone wants to buy a gun. But it should not become so difficult that it actually becomes a means of preventing gun ownership by legitimate, law-abiding citizens. (In the United States, a background check requires a Social Security number, and some states also require a driver's license, and the necessary approval can usually be obtained within about two minutes by a sales clerk working at a gun store.)[68]

d. What about countries other than the United States?

Strict gun-control laws do not prevent criminal violence in such countries but probably result in an increase in violence. (Brazil and Jamaica[69] are two such examples.)

In countries where there exist almost no guns in the hands of either private citizens or criminals, and where police control and societal customs are strong enough that there is little risk of a citizen being physically attacked by someone else, citizens may decide it is best to leave the situation as it is rather than try to import guns when other means of self-defense and protection are functioning quite well. But if the number of physical attacks increases dramatically, then the laws need to allow responsible, law-abiding private citizens to obtain some effec-

---

68. "Guide to National Instant Check System," www.nraila.org/Issues/FactSheets/Read.aspx?id=82.

69. David B. Kopel, *The Samurai, the Mountie, and the Cowboy—Should America Adopt the Gun Controls of Other Democracies?* (Amherst, NY: Prometheus Books, 1992), 257–77.

tive weapon for use in self-defense. And the most effective weapon in such cases—especially for potential victims who are older, smaller, or weaker, or potentially outnumbered—is some kind of handgun.

e. But should an individual Christian own a gun?

This entire discussion does not address the question of whether individual Christians will decide that it is *wise* to own a gun themselves. There is room for Christians to differ about this question and for individuals to decide what is best in their own situation. Many Christians will live in areas where they think the need for any weapon of self-defense is so small that it is outweighed by the negative considerations of the cost and the potential danger of a gun being found and misused by a child or used in an accidental way. Those are matters of individual preference and personal decision.

7. The importance of this issue

In the United States, the gun-control issue is important for several reasons:

First, because it upholds the meaning of the Second Amendment to the Constitution as it was originally intended.

Second, and more fundamentally, because it effectively protects a basic human right, the right of self-defense.

Third, because the right of citizens to bear arms is a significant protection against tyranny. It is a protection against an oppressive, dictatorial regime taking control of the nation against the will of the vast majority of its citizens.

Fourth, because study after study has shown that where private citizens have the right to possess guns for self-defense, that is a significant deterrent to violent crime.

8. For further reading

Frame, *The Doctrine of Christian Life*, 692–93; Gary Kleck and Don B. Kates, *Armed: New Perspectives on Gun Control* (Amherst, NY: Prometheus, 2001); John R. Lott Jr., *More Guns, Less Crime* (Chicago: University of Chicago Press, 1998); John R. Lott Jr., *The Bias Against Guns: Why Almost Everything You've Heard about Gun-Control Is Wrong* (Washington, DC: Regnery, 2003); Stassen and Gushee, *Kingdom Ethics*, 189–91 (opposed to allowing gun ownership).

Chapter 4

MARRIAGE

Should government define and regulate marriage? And how should marriage be defined?

A. BIBLICAL TEACHING: MARRIAGE IS ONLY BETWEEN ONE MAN AND ONE WOMAN

Not surprisingly, the Bible contains clear and explicit teachings about marriage. Many of these teachings are relevant to our consideration of governmental laws and policies about marriage.

1. God created marriage at the beginning of the human race as a lifelong union between one man and one woman

In the first chapters of the Bible we read that God created Adam and Eve and told them that together they should bear children:

> So God created man in his own image, in the image of God he created him; male and female he created them. And God blessed them. And God said to them, "Be fruitful and multiply and fill the earth and subdue it ..." (Gen. 1:27–28).

But were Adam and Eve actually a married couple? Yes, because the next chapter calls them "the man and his wife" (Gen. 2:25).

The Bible actually views the relationship between Adam and Eve as *the pattern for all marriages to follow on the earth.* This is clear from the more detailed description of their creation that comes in chapter 2. We read that "the LORD God caused a deep sleep to fall upon the man, and while he slept took one of his ribs and closed up its place with flesh," and then, "The rib that the LORD God had taken from the man he made into a woman and brought her to the man" (vv. 21–22). At that point Adam exclaimed with great joy,

> "This at last is bone of my bones
> and flesh of my flesh;
> she shall be called Woman,
> because she was taken out of Man" (v. 23).

The very next sentence uses this union between Adam and Eve as the pattern for marriages generally, for it says,

> Therefore a man shall *leave his father and his mother* and *hold fast to his wife*, and they shall become one flesh (v. 24).

The phrase "a man shall leave his father and his mother" pictures a situation in which the man departs from the household of which he was a part, and it implies that a new household is being established. The phrase "hold fast to his wife" indicates that this new relationship, between a man and his wife, is the basis of the new household that is established. Therefore marriage in general is defined here as a union between "a man" and "his wife."

This is also Jesus' understanding of Genesis 1–2 when responding to a question from the Pharisees about divorce:

> Pharisees came up to him and tested him by asking, "Is it lawful to divorce one's wife for any cause?" He answered, "Have you not read that he who created them from the beginning made them male and female, and said, 'Therefore a man shall leave his father and his mother and hold fast to his wife, and the two shall become one flesh'? So they are no longer two but one flesh. What therefore God has joined together, let not man separate" (Matt. 19:3–6).

Jesus understands that the essence of marriage was established when God "created them from the beginning" and "made them male and female" and also said that "a man shall ... hold fast to his wife, and they shall become one flesh" (vv. 4–5). He also affirms that marriage is therefore an institution God creates between a man and a woman, because he calls marriage a relationship between two people whom "God has joined together" (v. 6).

Jesus also affirms that God intended marriage to be a lifelong relationship, not a mere temporary agreement, for he specifies, "What therefore God has joined together, let not man separate" (v. 6). This perspective is given further emphasis when the Pharisees ask him in response, "Why then did Moses command one to give a certificate of divorce and to send her away?" (v. 7). Jesus answered,

> "Because of your hardness of heart Moses allowed you to divorce your wife, but from the beginning it was not so" (v. 8).

In other words, God's purpose in marriage from the beginning was *a lifelong, committed, faithful relationship between one man and one woman* (though because of sin, God would later allow for some divorce).

In addition, it is clear that sexual faithfulness to one's partner is an essential component of marriage, for adultery is regularly viewed as a sin. In fact, the command "You shall not commit adultery" (Exod. 20:14) is one of the Ten Commandments, and it is reaffirmed several times in the New Testament (see Matt. 19:18; Rom. 2:22; 13:9; James 2:11).

2. God's definition of marriage was not for the Jewish people only, but was intended to apply to all people in all societies for all time

This establishment of marriage is not like a number of laws in the Old Testament that were intended only for the Jewish people and only for a particular time in their history, such as the laws about the sacrifices of animals and clean and unclean foods. All of those laws came after the exodus of the people of Israel from Egypt (see Exod. 1–15). These laws were given in Exodus 20–40 and in Leviticus, Numbers, and Deuteronomy.

But the basic material about marriage comes *from the beginning of the human race*, at the time when Adam and Eve were created. It comes even before there was any evil or sin in the world (which came in Genesis 3). That is why Jesus says that these truths about marriage come "from the beginning" (Matt. 19:4) and they belong to the essence of God's creating us as "male and female."

Therefore this understanding of marriage as the lifelong union between one man and one woman is intended by God to be understood as the correct definition of marriage for all people on the earth, for all cultures and societies, and for all periods of history until the beginning of the new heaven and new earth.[1]

---

1. In Matthew 22:30 Jesus indicates that a significant change will occur after the final resurrection of believers: "For in the resurrection they neither marry nor are given in marriage, but are like angels in heaven." But that does not affect the legal or moral definition of marriage in this present age.

Thus God can bring judgment, for example, on the gentile (non-Jewish) cities of Sodom and Gomorrah because of their widespread practice of homosexual conduct (see Gen. 19:1–28, especially 19:5; also Jude 7). He can bring judgment against Pharaoh, King of Egypt, if he commits adultery with someone else's wife (see Gen. 12:17–20). The book of Proverbs, which contains much wisdom not merely for the people of Israel in the Old Testament but for the conduct of life generally, gives frequent warnings against adultery (see 2:16–19; 5:1–23; 6:20–35; 7:4–27; 23:27–28).

In the New Testament, John the Baptist rebuked Herod Antipas, an Idumean and not part of the people of Israel, for wrongfully committing incest by taking his brother's wife (Mark 6:17–18). Paul can say that Gentiles, who do not have the Jewish laws, are still guilty of violating God's moral standards regarding sexual conduct (see Rom. 1:26–27; 1 Cor. 5:9–10, 13; 6:9; cf. 1 Peter 4:3–5). The great city called "Babylon," which is the center of earthly rebellion against God, is judged in the end of the book of Revelation for many sins, and among them is "sexual immorality" (Rev. 18:3, 9). And those outside the heavenly city in Revelation 21 include "the sexually immoral" (v. 8).

Therefore, from Genesis to Revelation—from the beginning of the Bible to the end—God has established moral standards regarding the nature and conduct of marriage, and he repeatedly indicates that he will hold *all people on the earth* accountable for disobedience to those standards.

Further evidence of this is seen in Leviticus 18, which states that the Canaanites were morally responsible before God for many kinds of sexual sin (specified in vv. 6–23): "For the people of the land, who were before you, did all of these abominations, so that the land became unclean" (v. 27). God held these Canaanites accountable for violating his standards regarding marriage, even though they did not have the written laws of Israel and were not part of the Jewish people. Yet they had God's moral standards written on their hearts, and they had their own consciences that bore witness to those standards, and therefore God rightly held them accountable (see Rom. 2:14–15).

For Christians who are thinking about what kind of definition of marriage a civil government should adopt, these passages indicate that *the definition of marriage as established by God in the Bible* (a lifelong union between one man and one woman) *should be the standard adopted by all governments*. (This does not mean that all divorce should be prohibited: Because of the advent of sin in the world, later teaching in the Bible specified some conditions under which God allowed for divorce to break the lifelong commitment of marriage; see section D.) This legal standard for marriage should apply to all people, not merely to Christians or those who personally happen to agree with the Bible's standards.

3. Marriage between a man and a woman is the most fundamental institution in any society

The establishment of marriage in Genesis 1–2 comes before the establishment of any other institution in human society. It comes immediately after the creation of man and woman.

It is significant that God establishes marriage before there is any establishment of cities, nations, courts of law, or any human laws. It certainly comes before any national government, state government, or city government. It comes before any establishment of schools and universities, or businesses and corporations, or churches and other nonprofit organizations. It comes before the establishment of *any institution* in any human society. And it is foundational to the establishment of any society.

Human societies have long recognized the need for some kind of normalization of a dependable, ongoing, faithful marriage relationship between men and women. So far as I know, every human nation on earth, every society of any size or permanence at all, has recognized and protected the institution of heterosexual marriage. (Though some have had polygamy as a recognized form of marriage, it is still heterosexual marriage.)

British anthropologist J. D. Unwin reached this conclusion after conducting exhaustive research to investigate the assertions made by Sigmund Freud. Unwin discovered that Freud's call for the liberation of sexual behavior had grave consequences for society. In his research Unwin chronicled the historical decline of eighty-six different cultures and found that "strict marital monogamy" was central to social energy and growth. Indeed, no society flourished for more than three generations without it. Unwin wrote, "In human records there is no instance of a society retaining its energy after a complete new generation has inherited a tradition which does not insist on prenuptial and postnuptial continence" (by which he meant abstinence from sex outside of marriage).[2]

---

2. Joseph Daniel Unwin, *Sex and Culture* (London: Oxford University Press, 1934); *Sexual Regulations and Cultural Behavior* (London: Oxford University Press, 1935); and *Hopousia: Or the Sexual and Economic Foundations of a New Society* (London: George Allen and Unwin, 1940), cited by Daniel R. Heimbach, "Deconstructing the Family," The Howard Center for Family, Religion, and Society, *The Religion and Society Report* 22:7 (Oct./Nov. 2005). www.profam.org/pub/rs/rs_2207.htm#endfn57.

B. INCEST, ADULTERY, AND HOMOSEXUALITY ARE PROHIBITED IN BIBLICAL ETHICS

When the moral standards regarding marriage are explained in more detail in other parts of the Old Testament, certain types of relationships are excluded from being accepted as valid marriages. Incest is prohibited in Leviticus 18:1–18; 20:11–20; Deuteronomy 22:30; and 1 Corinthians 5:1–2. And of course, adultery was regularly prohibited (Exod. 20:14), which would also prohibit marrying someone who was already married to someone else.

More specific biblical teaching on the question of homosexuality is found in the following passages:

> You shall not lie with a male as with a woman; it is an abomination (Lev. 18:22).

> If a man lies with a male as with a woman, both of them have committed an abomination; they shall surely be put to death; their blood is upon them (Lev. 20:13).

> For this reason God gave them up to dishonorable passions. For their women exchanged natural relations for those that are contrary to nature [Greek *para physin*]; and the men likewise gave up natural relations with women and were consumed with passion for one another, men committing shameless acts with men and receiving in themselves the due penalty for their error (Rom. 1:26–27).

> Or do you not know that the unrighteous will not inherit the kingdom of God? Do not be deceived: neither the sexually immoral, nor idolaters, nor adulterers, *nor men who practice homosexuality*, nor thieves, nor the greedy, nor drunkards, nor revilers, nor swindlers will inherit the kingdom of God. And such were some of you. But you were washed, you were sanctified, you were justified in the name of the Lord Jesus Christ and by the Spirit of our God (1 Cor. 6:9–11).

> Understanding this, that the law is not laid down for the just but for the lawless and disobedient, for the ungodly and sinners, for the unholy and profane, for those who strike their fathers and mothers, for murderers, the sexually immoral, *men who practice homosexuality*, enslavers, liars, perjurers, and whatever else is contrary to sound doctrine (1 Tim. 1:9–10).

Some pro-homosexual interpreters have objected that these passages do not refer to all kinds of homosexual conduct but only to some specific kind of homosexuality, such as homosexual conduct between men and underage boys, or homosexual prostitution (where money is exchanged), or unfaithful homosexual relationships, or "unnatural" homosexual conduct by people who do not naturally have homosexual desires (as opposed to homosexual conduct by people who are said to be naturally homosexual or "born gay").

However, *none of these biblical passages makes any such distinction* or says anything indicating that it is only talking about certain types of homosexual conduct. And when no such distinction is made in the words or context of the passages, it is not a correct process of interpretation simply to claim that the passages have limited scope anyway. In other words, *the words themselves* as they are written apply to *all kinds* of homosexual conduct, so it is incorrect to say that they do not.

In addition, several ancient writers before or near the time of the New Testament viewed all homosexual conduct as wrong and used language very similar to Paul's language in Romans, 1 Corinthians, and 1 Timothy. The Greek philosopher Plato (c. 429–347 BC) wrote:

> When male unites with female for procreation, the pleasure experienced is held to be due to nature, but contrary to nature [Greek *para physin*, the same phrase used in Rom. 1:26] when male mates with male or female with female, and … those … guilty of such enormities were impelled by their slavery to pleasure.[3]

The Jewish philosopher Philo (c. 30 BC–c. AD 45), in writing about Lev. 18:22 and 20:13, condemned homosexual behavior. Philo wrote: "Much graver than the above is another evil, which has ramped its way into the cities, namely pederasty"[4] (the Greek term *paiderasteuô*, used here, refers to sexual activity between grown men and adolescent boys). Philo says this is a pleasure that is "contrary to nature" (*para physin*, the same phrase Paul used in Rom. 1:26), and says it is "worthy of death."[5]

In another place, Philo speaks of homosexual conduct in general in his writing *On Abraham*, where he says the homosexual conduct in Sodom was "corrupting the whole of mankind," so that God, in raining fire from heaven and destroying the city, "abominated and extinguished this unnatural and forbidden intercourse."[6]

---

3. Plato, *Laws* 1.636C.
4. Philo, *Special Laws* 3:37.
5. Ibid., 3.38–39.
6. Philo, *On Abraham*, 136–37.

The Jewish historian Josephus (AD 37–c. 100) wrote that the people of Elis and Thebes, in their homosexual conduct, practiced an "unnatural [*para physin*, the same expression found in Rom. 1:26] vice," and in that context, he referred to "the practice of sodomy" (homosexual conduct) as "the monstrous and unnatural [*para physin* again] pleasures in which they … indulged."[7]

The Greek historian Plutarch (c. AD 50–c. 120) referred to homosexual conduct between men as "contrary to nature" [*para physin*] and "indecent."[8]

These quotations show that when the New Testament writers condemned homosexual conduct, they were using the same terminology that was commonly used in other Greek literature to condemn all homosexual conduct as something "contrary to nature" and morally wrong. The words of the New Testament do not allow these prohibitions to be limited, as homosexual advocates claim, to some narrowly defined particular type of homosexual conduct.

The conclusion, then, is that the Bible views homosexual conduct as morally wrong in all cases, something contrary to God's moral standards.

C. WHAT ABOUT POLYGAMY IN THE OLD TESTAMENT?

There are a number of examples of polygamy in the Old Testament. Does having more than one wife reflect God's pattern for marriage?

The answer is that God *temporarily allowed* polygamy to occur without giving explicit commands against it, even though it did not conform to his original purpose for marriage as indicated in Genesis 1–2. But we get some hints from the narrative passages, because in every example where a man has more than one wife, the situation leads to significant difficulty in the marriage relationship, and readers are left to draw their own conclusions from this. A helpful summary of the biblical material on polygamy is found in the ESV *Study Bible*:

> Why did God allow polygamy in the Old Testament? Nowhere in the Bible did God ever command polygamy or tell anyone to marry more than one wife. Rather, God temporarily allowed polygamy to occur (he did not give any general prohibition against it) without giving it any explicit moral approval. Nevertheless, in the OT narratives, whenever a man has two

---

7. Josephus, *Against Apion* 2.273–75.
8. Plutarch, *Moralia, Dialogue on Love*, 751.D-E.

or more wives, it seems to lead to trouble (see Gen. 16; 29–31; 1 Sam. 1; 1 Kings 11; note also the prohibition in Deuteronomy 17:17). In addition, polygamy is horribly dehumanizing for women, for it does not treat them as equal in value to their husbands, and therefore it does not recognize that they share fully in the high status of being created "in the image of God" (Gen. 1:27), and of being worthy of honor as "heirs with you of the grace of life" (1 Pet. 3:7). The requirement "husband of one wife" (1 Tim. 3:2) would exclude polygamists from being elders.... This restriction would provide a pattern that would generally lead to the abolition of polygamy in a church in a generation or two.[9]

D. DIVORCE

In the laws that Moses gave to Israel it was assumed that divorce would occur in some cases, though it is difficult to determine exactly what constituted a valid reason for divorce, and subsequent rabbinic discussion varied widely in its interpretations. The passages that assumed that some divorce will occur are found in Deuteronomy 24:1–4 and also Leviticus 21:7, 14 and Numbers 30:9.

In the New Testament, the most common understanding among Protestant interpreters since the time of the Reformation has been that Jesus allowed divorce for the physical act of adultery and also allowed remarriage in such cases:

> "And I say to you: whoever divorces his wife, *except for sexual immorality*, and marries another, commits adultery" (Matt. 19:9).

The implication is that if a man divorces his wife for sexual immorality and marries another, this action does not constitute adultery and it is not sin.

In addition, Paul allowed divorce in a case where an unbelieving spouse has disserted a believing partner:

> But if the unbelieving partner separates, let it be so. In such cases the brother or sister is not enslaved. God has called you to peace (1 Cor. 7:15).

There have been other interpretations of these passages. Some have held that Jesus allowed divorce but not remarriage. Others have held that

---

9. ESV *Study Bible*, p. 2544.

even in the case of adultery, divorce was not allowed, in part because Jesus' words, "except for sexual immorality" (Matt. 19:9), are found in Matthew 5:32 but not in Mark 10:11 or Luke 16:18. But my own understanding of these passages, and the understanding of the majority of evangelical interpreters, is that the Bible allows (but does not require) divorce in the case of adultery or desertion, and it also allows remarriage to another person in such cases. Remarriage in these cases is not sin in God's sight.

What laws should governments make regarding divorce? If we believe that God intended marriage to be a lifelong commitment except in cases of serious defilement of the marriage, then laws should protect marriage by protecting spouses from both abandonment and harm. Protection from abandonment would include measures such as mandatory counseling and significant mandatory waiting periods prior to divorce, and especially the elimination of no-fault divorce, which makes divorce far too easy and trivializes the "commitment" that is made when a marriage begins. In no-fault divorce, the spouse seeking the divorce is not required to show any wrongdoing on the part of the other spouse, so a person can get a divorce simply because he or she no longer wants to be married. (Prior to no-fault divorce, the person seeking divorce had to prove that the spouse had committed a wrong that seriously violated the marriage, such as adultery, abuse, or abandonment. Thus there were far fewer divorces for more trivial reasons or just because one person wanted out of the marriage.) The first no-fault divorce law in the United States took effect January 1, 1970, in California, and all other states except new York eventually adopted no-fault divorce laws, resulting in more frequent divorce throughout the country.

Laws to protect a spouse from harm would include serious penalties (such as mandatory jail time and rehabilitation) for spouses who commit physical abuse (the perpetrator is usually, but not always, the husband) and also more strict reinforcement of the obligations of financial support. To protect a spouse whose marriage has been deeply harmed or defiled, divorce should certainly be allowed in the case of adultery or desertion.

E. CIVIL GOVERNMENTS SHOULD DEFINE MARRIAGE FOR ALL CITIZENS

1. Defining and regulating marriage fits the purposes of government according to the Bible

Among the most important purposes of civil government, according to the Bible, are (1) to restrain evil, (2) to bring good to society, and (3) to bring order to society. On all three of these grounds, a Christian should conclude that it is right for government to define and regulate marriage.

First, marriage restrains evil by promoting sexual faithfulness between a man and a woman, by establishing a legally binding commitment for parents to care for their children, by establishing a legally binding commitment for spouses to be financially responsible for and to care for one another, and by providing a legal protection to keep women from being exploited by men who might otherwise enjoy a sexual relationship for a time and then abandon a woman and any children she may have borne from that union.

Second, marriage brings good to society in multiple ways — in promoting social stability,[10] economic well-being,[11] educational and economic benefits for children,[12] the transmission of moral and cultural values to the next generation, and a stable social unit for interactions within society.[13] (These benefits are explained more fully in section F.)

Third, the establishment of marriage brings order to society so that the general public will know who is married and who is not. Marital status can be established as a matter of public record, so that in various ways the society as a whole can honor and protect individual marriages and can know who is responsible for the care and protection and training of children, and for the care of spouses who have medical or financial or other needs. In this way, defining and regulating marriage gives stability and order to a society. It is an extremely important social good that government should encourage and protect.

2. Defining and regulating marriages is morally right

The definition of marriage as a lifelong faithful union between one man and one woman, as found in the Bible, provides a moral standard in

10. James S. Coleman, "Social Capital in the Creation of Human Capital," *American Journal of Sociology* (1988), 94: S–95–S120: cited in Testimony of Barbara Dafoe Whitehead, Co-Director, National Marriage Project, Rutgers, the State University of New Jersey, before the Committee on Health, Education, Labor, and Pensions, Subcommittee on Children and Families, US Senate (April 24, 2008). http://marriage.rutgers.edu/Publications/Pub%20 Whitehead%20Testimony%20Apr%2004.htm.

11. Mary Parke, "Are Married Parents Really Better for Children?" *Center for Law and Social Policy* (May 2003), 7. www.clasp.org: cited in ibid.

12. Parke, 2–3; Robert I. Lerman, "Marriage and the Economic Well-Being of Families with Children: A Review of the Literature" (2002), www.urban.org/expert. cfm?ID=RobertLerman; and *Why Marriage Matters: Twenty-One Conclusions from the Social Sciences* (New York: Institute, 2002), www.marriagemovement.org: cited in ibid.

13. Coleman, "Social Capital in the Creation of Human Capital."

which God tells us what is right to do. Defining and regulating and protecting marriage as this kind of institution is thus something that is morally right in God's eyes. It is not merely something that brings benefits to society, but also something that a society *should* do, according to God's own definition of right and wrong as given in the Bible.

F. ARGUMENTS FROM REASON AND EXPERIENCE APART FROM THE BIBLE

1. Governments should define and establish marriage because no other institution can do that for an entire society

Only a civil government is able to define a standard of what constitutes a marriage for a whole nation or whole society. No churches or denominations could do this, because they only speak for their own members. No voluntary societies could do this, because they don't include all the people in the society.

If no definition of marriage is given to an entire society, then chaos and much oppression of women and children will result. Stanley Kurtz of the Hudson Institute writes,

> In setting up the institution of marriage, society offers special support and encouragement to the men and women who together make children. Because marriage is deeply implicated in the interests of children, it is a matter of public concern. Children are helpless. They depend upon adults. Over and above their parents, children depend upon society to create institutions that keep them from chaos. Children cannot articulate their needs. Children cannot vote. Yet children *are* society. They are us, and they are our future. That is why society has the right to give special support and encouragement to an institution that is necessary to the well being of children — even if that means special benefits for some, and not for others. The dependence intrinsic to human childhood is why unadulterated libertarianism can never work.[14]

Without a governmentally established standard of what constitutes marriage, the result will be a proliferation of children born in relationships of incest and polygamy as well as many temporary relationships without

---

14. Stanley Kurtz, "Deathblow to Marriage" (Feb. 5, 2004). www.nationalreview.com/kurtz/kurtz200402050842.asp.

commitment, and many children born with no one having a legal obligation to care for them.

The consensus from nations all over the world from all of history is that the society as a whole, through its governing authorities, needs to define and regulate marriage for all its citizens. Aristotle said that the first duty of wise legislators is to define and regulate marriage. He wrote:

> Since the legislator should begin by considering how the frames of the children whom he is rearing may be as good as possible, his first care will be about marriage—at what age should his citizens marry, and who are fit to marry?[15]

Some people may argue that governments today no longer need to define marriage at all, but this is just saying that we can now hope to act contrary to the entire course of all societies in world history for all time.[16] Such a prospect does not encourage optimism for success.

Maggie Gallagher says,

> The purpose of marriage law is inherently normative, to create and to force others to recognize a certain kind of union: permanent, faithful, co-residential, and sexual couplings.[17]

2. Government should encourage and reward marriage between one man and one woman because it gives benefits to society that no other relationship or institution can give

Because marriage provides society with unique and immensely valuable benefits, society has an interest in protecting and encouraging marriage. This was the fundamental question at stake in the Mormon polygamy controversy in the United States from about 1845 to 1895. Although Utah territory, which was dominated by Mormons, applied for statehood seven times, beginning in 1849, Congress did not permit it to become a state until 1896, after Utah finally agreed to insert a ban on

15. Aristotle, "Politica," in William David Ross, ed., *The Works of Aristotle* 10: 1334–35: cited in Lynn D. Wardle, "Is Preference for Marriage in Law Justified?" World Family Policy Forum (1999). www.worldfamilypolicy.org/New%20Page/forum/1999/wardle.pdf. Lynn Wardle is a professor of law at Brigham Young University. Also see www.fordham.edu/halsall/ancient/aristotle-politics1.html.

16. Even if there were short-lived periods of some societies where anarchy regarding marriage prevailed, such a situation would be inherently unstable and would soon result in some standardization of marriage or the dissolution of the society.

17. Maggie Gallagher, "(How) Will Gay Marriage Weaken Marriage as a Social Institution: A Reply to Andrew Koppelman," *University of St. Thomas Law Review*, 2:1 (Fall 2004), 43.

polygamy in the state constitution.[18] Thus Congress imposed on a state (as a condition of its becoming a state) *a national standard for marriage* that excluded polygamous relationships.

In responding to a challenge to this idea, the US Supreme Court in *Murphy v. Ramsey* (1885) said that "the idea of the family, as consisting in and springing from the union for life of one man and one woman" is "the sure foundation of all that is stable and noble in our civilization."[19]

In brief, the history of marriage laws in the United States shows that society has a strong interest in protecting and encouraging marriage between one man and one woman because of the great benefits that this institution gives to society in multiple ways, benefits that no other relationship or institution can give.

These benefits can be summarized in several points:

a. Marriage provides a better environment for having babies than any other relationship or institution. Providing a good environment for having babies is important because all societies need babies in order to survive beyond the lifetimes of the adults now living.

When we compare the environment provided by marriage during the pregnancy and birth of a baby with the environment provided by a cohabiting couple with no legal commitment to marriage, or with the environment provided by a temporary sexual liaison with no ongoing relationship, or with the environment provided by a homosexual couple that lacks either a mother or a father, or with the environment provided by a single mother who bears a child through *in vitro* fertilization or surrogate motherhood, it is evident that the environment provided by a married couple provides for the baby far greater security and provides the baby with both a mother and a father who are committed to provide and care for it.

In addition, the environment is better for the mother, because marriage provides a far better guarantee that the baby's father will not abandon her to care for the child alone. And the environment provided by marriage is better for the father because it provides a strong legal and societal expectation that he will stay around and act responsibly with regard to the responsibilities formally associated with fatherhood.

---

18. "Utah's Struggle for Statehood," UtahPolicy.org (July 2, 2009), www.utahpolicy.com/featured_article/utahs-struggle-statehood; and Edward Leo Lyman, *Political Deliverance: The Mormon Quest for Utah Statehood* (1986); Henry J. Wolfinger, "A Reexamination of the Woodruff Manifesto in Light of Utah Constitutional History," *Utah Historical Quarterly* 39 (Fall 1971); and Gustive Q. Larson, *The Americanization of Utah for Statehood* (1971): cited in http://historytogo.utah.gov/utah_chapters/statehood_and_the_progressive_era/struggleforstatehood.html.

19. *Murphy v. Ramsey* (114 U.S. 45, 1885). http://supreme.justia.com/us/114/15/case.html.

All of these benefits provide an argument that society should encourage and reward marriage between a man and a woman. All societies need babies to survive, and marriage is the best environment for having babies. Societies should *encourage* an institution that provides this best kind of environment for raising babies.

b. *Married couples raise and nurture children far better than any other human relationship or institution.* The benefits that a married couple brings to their children are numerous:

(1) Children who live with their own two married parents have significantly higher educational achievement.[20]

(2) Children who live with their own two married parents are much more likely to enjoy a better economic standard in their adult lives and are much less likely to end up in poverty.[21]

(3) Children who live with their own two married parents have much better physical health and emotional health.[22]

(4) Children who live with their own two married parents are far less likely to commit crimes,[23] are less likely to engage in alcohol and substance abuse,[24] and are more likely to live according to higher standards of integrity and moral principles.[25]

---

20. Mary Parke, "Are Married Parents Really Better for Children?" *Center for Law and Policy* (May 2003), 2–3: cited in Testimony of Barbara Dafoe Whitehead, Co-Director, National Marriage Project, Rutgers, the State University of New Jersey, before the Committee on Health, Education, Labor, and Pensions, Subcommittee on Children and Families, US Senate (April 24, 2008). http://marriage.rutgers.edu/Publications/Pub%20Whitehead%20Testimony%20Apr%2004.htm.

21. Robert I. Lerman, "How Do Marriage, Cohabitation, and Single Parenthood Affect the Material Hardships of Families With Children?" (July 2002), and Robert I. Lerman, "Married and Unmarried Parenthood and Economic Well-Being: A Dynamic Analysis of a Recent Cohort" (July 2002). www.urban.org/expert.cfm?ID=RobertILerman: cited in ibid.

22. Frank F. Furstenburg and Andrew Cherlin, *Divided Families: What Happens to Children When Parents Part* (Cambridge, MA: Harvard University Press, 1991), 56; and Paul R. Amato, "Children's Adjustment to Divorce: Theories, Hypothesis, and Empirical Support," *Journal of Marriage and the Family* 23 (1993): cited in Wardle, "Is Preference for Marriage in Law Justified?"

23. Cynthia Harper and Sarah McClanahan, "Father Absence and Youth Incarceration," *Journal of Research on Adolescence* 14 (2004): 369–97.

24. "Family Matters: Substance Abuse and the American Family," The National Center on Addiction and Substance Abuse at Columbia University (March 2005), 17. www.casacolumbia.org/absolutenm/articlefiles/380-Family%20Matters.pdf.; and Robert L. Flewelling and Karl E. Bauman, "Family Structure as a Predictor of Initial Substance Abuse and Sexual Intercourse in Adolescence," *Journal of Marriage and the Family* 52 (1990): 171–81.

25. Furstenburg and Cherlin, op. cit.; and Amato, op. cit.: cited in Wardle, "Is Preference for Marriage in Law Justified?"

(5) Children who live with their own two married parents are less likely to experience physical abuse and are more likely to live in homes that provide support, protection, and stability for them.[26]

(6) Children who live with their own two married parents are more likely to establish stable families in the next generation.[27]

c. *Marriage provides a guarantee of lifelong companionship and care far better than any other human relationship or institution.*[28]

d. *Marriage leads to a higher economic standard and diminished likelihood of ending up in poverty for men and women.*[29]

e. *Marriage provides women with protection against domestic violence and abandonment far better than any other human relationship or institution.*[30]

f. *Marriage encourages men to socially beneficial pursuits far better than any other human relationship or institution.*[31]

g. *Men and women in general have an innate instinct that values sexual faithfulness in intimate relationships, and marriage provides a societal encouragement of such faithfulness far better than any other relationship or institution.*[32]

h. *Marriage provides greater protection against sexually transmitted diseases than any other relationship or institution.*[33]

---

26. Patrick F. Fagan, Ph.D., "The Child Abuse Crisis: The Disintegration of Marriage, Family, and the American Community," *Heritage Foundation, Backgrounder #1115* (May 15, 1997), www.heritage.org/Research/Family/BG1115.cfm; and E. Thompson, T. L. Hanson, and S. S. McLanahan, "Family Structure and Child Well-Being: Economic Resources versus Parental Behaviors," *Social Forces* 73: 221–42: cited in "The Verdict on Cohabitation vs. Marriage," www.marriageandfamilies.byu.edu/issues/2001/January/cohabitation.htm.

27. Patrick F. Fagan, Ph.D., "How Broken Families Rob Children of Their Chances for Future Prosperity," *Heritage Foundation, Backgrounder #1283* (June 11, 1999). www.heritage.org/Research/Family/BG1283.cfm.

28. Linda J. Waite and Maggie Gallagher, "The Case for Marriage: Why Married People Are Happier, Healthier, and Better Off Financially" (New York: Doubleday, 2000): cited in "The Verdict on Cohabitation vs. Marriage," www.marriageandfamilies.byu.edu/issues/2001/January/cohabitation.htm.

29. David J. Eggebeen and Daniel T. Lichter, "Race, Family Structure, and Changing Poverty Among American Children," *American Social Review* 56: 801, 806: cited in Wardle, "Is Preference for Marriage in Law Justified?"

30. Patrick F. Fagan, Ph.D., and Kirk A. Johnson, Ph.D., "Marriage: The Safest Place for Women and Children," *Heritage Foundation, Backgrounder #1535* (April 10, 2002). www.heritage.org/Research/Family/BG1535.cfm.

31. Linda Waite, "Does Marriage Matter?" *Demographics* 32 (1995): 483: cited in Wardle, "Is Preference for Marriage in Law Justified?"

32. Robert T. Michael, John H. Gagnon, Edward O. Laumann, and Gina Kolata, *Sex in America: A Definitive Survey* (Boston: Little Brown, 1994), 105: cited in "What's Happening to Marriage?" *State of our Unions 2009*, Rutgers University National Marriage Project. http://marriage.rutgers.edu/Publications/pubwhatshappening.htm#2.

33. Fagan and Johnson, "Marriage: The Safest Place for Women and Children."

i. The biological design of men's and women's bodies argues that sexual intimacy is designed to be enjoyed between only one man and one woman.

For all of these reasons, marriage is the basic building block of any stable society, and it is essential to the continuation of a healthy, stable society. All of these reasons argue that it is right that governments *encourage* and *reward* marriage between one man and one woman. This institution gives immeasurable benefits to a society that no other relationship or institution can provide. Therefore society has a high interest in protecting and encouraging marriage through its laws.

But if the benefits that the laws now give to married couples are *also* given to other arrangements (such as polygamous marriages or same-sex marriages, or heterosexual relationships that lack the long-term commitment of marriage), then to that degree, marriage is not given these *special* benefits. To that degree, marriage between one man and one woman is *not encouraged by the government more than these other relationships.* To that degree, then, government no longer gives *special incentives* encouraging men and women to marry. And to that degree, society will begin to lose the benefits gained from giving special advantages to the relationship of marriage between one man and one woman.

Moreover, if the benefits that society now gives to marriage are also given to same-sex couples, then society is *encouraging* the *harmful consequences* to children and to men and women that are the opposite of these benefits that come from same-sex monogamous marriage. Rather than doing "good" for the nation, such changes in the laws will do harm for the nation. This is the opposite of what God intends government to do.

The damaging consequences of homosexual conduct are rarely mentioned in the mainstream press. However, Jeffrey Satinover, a psychiatrist who is a graduate of MIT, Harvard, and the University of Texas and has lectured at both Yale and Harvard, reports some of the medical harm that is typically associated with male homosexual practice:

- A twenty-five to thirty-year decrease in life expectancy
- Chronic, potentially fatal, liver disease—infectious hepatitis
- Inevitably fatal immune disease including associated cancers
- Frequently fatal rectal cancer
- Multiple bowel and other infectious diseases
- A much higher than usual incidence of suicide[34]

---

34. Jeffrey Satinover, *Homosexuality and the Politics of Truth* (Grand Rapids: Baker, 1996), 51. (This is an excellent book on the medical harm and addictive nature of homosexual conduct and also the ability of homosexuals to change their behavior.)

What is the reason for these medical conditions? Satinover explains that many are due to the common homosexual practice of anal intercourse:

> ... we are designed with a nearly impenetrable barrier between the bloodstream and the extraordinarily toxic and infectious contents of the bowel. Anal intercourse creates a breach in this barrier for the receptive partner, whether or not the insertive partner is wearing a condom. As a result, homosexual men are disproportionately vulnerable to a host of serious and sometimes fatal infections caused by the entry of feces into the bloodstream. These include hepatitis B and the cluster of otherwise rare conditions.[35]

Satinover also points out a significant contrast in the sexual behaviors of heterosexual and homosexual persons. Among heterosexuals, sexual faithfulness was relatively high: "90 percent of heterosexual women and more than 75 percent of heterosexual men have never engaged in extramarital sex." But among homosexual men the picture is far different:

> A 1981 study revealed that only 2 percent of homosexuals were monogamous or semi-monogamous — generously defined as ten or fewer lifetime partners.... a 1978 study found that 43 percent of male homosexuals estimated having sex with five hundred or more different partners.... Seventy-nine percent said that more than half of these partners were strangers.[36]

Such patterns of behavior need to be taken into account when voters decide whether to give societal encouragement and legal benefits to same-sex relationships.

One additional argument in favor of laws defining marriage as one man and one woman is that laws in any society also have a "teaching" function. The kinds of relationships that are approved by the law are more likely to be approved of and followed by the society as a whole. People will reason, "This is according to the law, therefore it must be right." Thus laws that limit marriage to one man and one woman will tend to encourage the society to think that this is the kind of marriage that is right and that should be supported by them and by others.

For all of the foregoing reasons, therefore, I differ with the viewpoint of Jim Wallis. In *God's Politics* he argues that different views on same-sex "marriage" should be allowed within churches. He says,

---

35. Ibid., 67.

36. Ibid., 55. Satinover points out, however, that "Lesbian sexual practices are less risky than gay marriage practices; and lesbians are not nearly so promiscuous as gay men" (52).

The controversies over gay marriage and the ordination of gay bishops, and so on, should not be seen as "faith breakers." The church is going to have to learn to stay together and talk about these things until we find some resolutions together.... One could also argue that gay civil marriage is necessary under "equal protection." One could also argue for church blessings of gay unions. I think all those are strong points, even if the churches are unlikely to change their whole theology and sacrament of marriage itself.[37]

Wallis also speaks of "encouraging healthy, monogamous, and stable same-sex relationships—which religious conservatives should be careful not to pit themselves against, regardless of how such relationships are ultimately defined."[38] Wallis thus fails to uphold and defend the Bible's teaching on marriage for either the laws of society or the policies adopted by churches.

The Manhattan Declaration stands in clear contrast to Jim Wallis's statements. This document, released November 20, 2009, declares:

Because we honor justice and the common good, we will not ... bend to any rule purporting to force us to bless immoral sexual partnerships, treat them as marriages or the equivalent, or refrain from proclaiming the truth, as we know it, about morality and immorality and marriage and the family. We will fully and ungrudgingly render to Caesar what is Casesar's. But under no circumstances will we render to Caesar what is God's.[39]

G. LEGAL ARGUMENTS

1. Appeals courts in the United States have repeatedly held that the State has a legitimate interest in protecting marriage between one man and one woman[40]

The Indiana Court of Appeals in 2005 said this:

The State of Indiana has a legitimate interest in encouraging opposite-sex couples to enter and remain in, as far as possible,

---

37. Jim Wallis, *God's Politics: Why the Right Gets It Wrong and the Left Doesn't Get It* (New York: HarperSanFrancisco, 2005), 334.

38. Ibid., 340.

39. The entire statement is found at http://manhattandeclaration.org/home.aspx.

40. In this section I am indebted to Jordan Lorence of the Alliance Defense Fund for the collection of relevant legal material that is quoted here. Much of it is taken from his unpublished paper "Same-Sex 'Marriage' and Its Relatives" from January 2009, which he provided to me.

the relatively stable institution of marriage for the sake of children who are frequently the natural result of sexual relations between a man and a woman. One commentator has put it succinctly as follows: "The public legal union of a man and woman is designed ... to protect the children that their sexual union (and that type of sexual union alone) regularly produces."[41]

Similarly, the Arizona Court of Appeals said the following in 2003:

Indisputably, the only sexual relationship capable of producing children is one between a man and a woman. The State could reasonably decide that by encouraging opposite-sex couples to marry, thereby assuming legal and financial obligations, the children born from such relationships will have better opportunities to be nurtured and raised by two parents within long-term, committed relationships, which society has traditionally viewed as advantageous for children. Because same-sex couples cannot by themselves procreate, the State could also reasonably decide that sanctioning same-sex marriages would do little to advance the State's interest in ensuring responsible procreation within committed, long-term relationships.[42]

Other appeals courts have reached similar conclusions.[43]

2. No right to polygamous marriages is found in the US Constitution

This was the decision of the United States in *Murphy v. Ramsey*, 114 US15 (1885) (cited above). To allow a "right" to a marriage of one man and two or more women would redefine marriage as it had been understood in all the laws of the United States and the individual states up to that point. Therefore it would not simply be granting a "right" to certain

---

41. *Morrison v. Sadler*, 821 N.E.2d 15, 30–31 (Indiana Court of Appeals, 2005): citing Maggie Gallagher, *What Is Marriage For? The Public Purposes of Marriage Law*, 62 La. L. Rev. 773, 782 (2002).

42. *Standhardt v. Superior Court*, 77 P.3d. 451, 462–63 (Ariz. App. Div. 1 2003).

43. Jordan Lorence, "Same-Sex 'Marriage' and its Relatives" (Jan. 2009), 7–8. Lorence cites the decision of the New Jersey Court of Appeals in *Lewis v. Harris* (2005) and two New York appellate court decisions: *Hernandez v. Robles* (2005) and *Samuels v. New York Department of Health* (2006).

men and women involved in polygamy, but also actually be *changing the definition of marriage itself* for the entire society.

3. No right to "homosexual marriage" is found in the Constitution

To many people it will seem obvious that the US Constitution, which says nothing at all about homosexual marriage, cannot be claimed to support any "right" to homosexual marriage. The US Supreme Court has not ruled on this issue, but several state courts have issued rulings. Most notably the Massachusetts,[44] Connecticut,[45] and Iowa[46] supreme courts have now "found" a right to same-sex marriage in state constitutions that contained absolutely no mention at all of homosexual marriage. The California Supreme Court also created a "right" to same-sex marriage,[47] but that decision was overturned when the voters in November 2008 passed Proposition 8, a constitutional amendment that restored marriage as the union between one man and one woman.[48]

How could various courts "discover" same-sex "marriage" in their state constitutions? Or how could it ever be decreed by any federal court or by the US Supreme Court? Only if it were invented by the judges out of their own imaginations.

Judge Richard Posner, a widely respected judge on the US Court of Appeals for the Seventh Circuit, said this in a public interview:

> Nothing in the Constitution or its history suggests a constitutional right to homosexual marriage. If there is such a right, it will have to be manufactured by the justices out of whole cloth. The exercise of so freewheeling a judicial discretion in the face of adamantly opposed public opinion would be seriously undemocratic. It would be a matter of us judges, us enlightened ones, forcing our sophisticated views on a deeply unwilling population.[49]

---

44. *Goodridge et al. v. Department of Public Health* SJC–08860, Supreme Judicial Court of Massachusetts (Nov. 18, 2003).

45. *Kerrigan v. State of Connecticut,* SC 17716, Connecticut Supreme Court (Oct. 28, 2008).

46. *Varnum v. Brien,* No. 07–1499, Iowa Supreme Court (April 3, 2009).

47. *In re: Marriage Cases,* S147999, California Supreme Court (May 15, 2008).

48. Jessica Garrison, Cara Mia DiMassa, and Richard C. Paddock, "Voters Approve Proposition 8 Banning Same-Sex Marriages," *Los Angeles Times* (Nov. 5, 2008). www.latimes.com/news/local/la-me-gaymarriage5-2008nov05,0,1545381.story.

49. Richard Posner, "Wedding Bell Blues," *The New Republic Online* (Dec. 22, 2003).

Three states—Maine,[50] New Hampshire,[51] and Vermont[52]—have passed laws legalizing same-sex "marriage," and one state, New Jersey, has created "civil unions" that are the legal equivalent of marriage.[53] But on November 3, 2009, the people of Maine overruled the legislature and governor by enacting Question 1, restoring the definition of marriage as one man and woman in the state.[54]

4. Restricting marriage to one man and woman does not violate anyone's fundamental rights

Sometimes advocates for same-sex marriage argue that the right to marry is a fundamental human right and that this is being denied to them as homosexuals.

But the answer is that when the law defines marriage as between one man and one woman, *it does not prohibit any homosexual person from marrying*. They would just have to marry in the same way that everyone else in society has to marry—namely, they would have to marry someone of the opposite sex. This right is extended *equally* to all unmarried adults in the society.

Yet, when homosexuals claim that they want to marry *another person of the same sex*, they are not simply claiming the right to marry that is available to everybody else in society. Rather, they are claiming *a new right* that had not previously been available to anyone in this society—namely, the right to marry someone *of the same sex*. Such a right has been denied to everyone in the society prior to this time, so it is not discriminating against them to say that this kind of right is denied to them.

This would be somewhat analogous to a man claiming that he wanted to marry his sister and that the law was wrongfully denying him a basic human right that everybody else had, the right to marry. But that would be an invalid argument. No man in this society has the legal right to

50. "Baldacci signs same-sex marriage into law," *Portland Press-Herald* (May 6, 2009). http://pressherald.mainetoday.com/story.php?id=254850&ac=PHnws.

51. Eric Moskowitz, "New Hampshire Ties Gay-Marriage Knot," *Boston Globe* (June 4, 2009). www.boston.com/news/local/new_hampshire/articles/2009/06/04/nh_ties_gay_marriage_knot/.

52. "Abby Goodnough, Vermont Legalizes Same-Sex Marriage," *New York Times* (April 7, 2009). www.nytimes.com/2009/04/08/us/08vermont.html.

53. Jeff Zelevansky, "Gay Couples in New Jersey Line Up for Civil Unions," *USA Today* (Feb. 20, 2007). www.usatoday.com/news/nation/2007–02–18-nj-civil-unions_x.htm.

54. Susan Cover "Mainers Vote Down Gay Marriage Law," *Kennebec Journal* (Nov. 4, 2009). http://pressherald.mainetoday.com/story.php?id=293976&ac=PHnws.

marry his sister, and no woman has the legal right to marry her brother. The law prohibits such kinds of marriage. But if no man in a society has the right to marry his sister, then when the law denies him the right to marry his sister, it is not denying him anything that it does not deny to everybody else as well. When he claims that he should have a right to marry his sister, he is really claiming the right *to redefine marriage* according to his own desires and preferences. He is not just claiming a private right for himself, but *is claiming a right to change the definition of marriage that has been adopted by the whole society.* And the law is correct when it denies him the right to do this.

The same arguments would go for a woman who claimed that she should have the right to marry her son, or a man who claimed that he should have the right to marry his daughter. And the same kind of arguments would apply to a man who claimed he should have the right to marry a woman who was already married to someone else. Or to a man who claimed that he should have the right to marry more than one wife at the same time. All these would not simply be claims that an *individual* would make regarding a *private right* that would affect no one else. These are claims to be able to *redefine* the institution of marriage for the whole of a society.

Another argument sometimes raised by same-sex advocates is that laws limiting marriage to one man and one woman are unconstitutional "sex discrimination" because they use gender-based classifications.

However, both the US Supreme Court and various state supreme courts have rejected this argument. According to constitutional law expert Jordan Lorence, the US Supreme Court has held that marriage laws treat men and women equally and the court has ruled that uses of gender classifications in the law are not inherently discriminatory. In addition, Lorence asserts that, based on Supreme Court precedents in *Nguyen v. I.N.S.* and *Nordlinger v. Hahn,* government programs to prevent breast cancer or prostate cancer are not discriminatory and that separate bathrooms for men and women are not "sex discriminatory." As a result, there is no disparate impact on men or women because marriage laws treat men and women the same.[55] In addition, the New York Court of Appeals said:

> By limiting marriage to opposite-sex couples, [the State] is not engaging in sex discrimination. The limitation does not put men and women in different classes, and give one class a benefit not given to the other. Women and Men are treated alike—

---

55. Jordan Lorence, "Same-Sex Marriage and Its Relatives."

they are permitted to marry people of the opposite sex, but not people of their own sex.[56]

The Maryland Court of Appeals and the Washington State Supreme Court have reached the same conclusion: Laws that limit marriage to one man and one woman are not unconstitutional sex discrimination. Lorence quotes from the Maryland court:

> The limitations on marriage effected by Family Law §2–201 do not separate men and women into discrete classes for the purpose of granting to one class of persons benefits at the expense of the other class. Nor does the statute, facially or in its application, place men and women on an uneven playing field. Rather, the statute prohibits equally both men and women from the same conduct.[57]

5. A marriage amendment to the US Constitution would be the most effective way to establish a uniform understanding of marriage once again in the United States

Some people have proposed an amendment to the US Constitution that would limit marriage to one man and woman. As of November 2008, thirty states had approved such amendments to their individual state constitutions.[58]

The wording of the 2004 Federal Marriage Amendment, as introduced in both the US Senate and the US House, was as follows:

> Marriage in the United States shall consist solely of the union of a man and a woman. Neither this Constitution, nor the constitution of any State, shall be construed to require that marriage or the legal incidents thereof be conferred upon any union other than the union of a man and a woman.[59]

In order to amend the Constitution, a two-thirds majority of both houses of Congress is required. The House took a vote on the amendment

---

56. *Hernandez v. Robles*, 7 N.Y. 3d 388, 821 N.Y.S. 2d 770, 855 N.E. 2d 1, 6 (2006).

57. *Conaway v. Deane*, 401 Md. 219, 264, 932 A.2d 571, 598, Md. (2007).

58. The following states have passed constitutional amendments protecting marriage as the union between one man and one woman: Alabama, Alaska, Arizona, Arkansas, California, Colorado, Florida, Georgia, Hawaii, Idaho, Kansas, Kentucky, Louisiana, Michigan, Missouri, Mississippi, Montana, Nebraska, Nevada, North Dakota, Ohio, Oklahoma, Oregon, South Carolina, South Dakota, Tennessee, Texas, Utah, Virginia, and Wisconsin. www.domawatch.org/stateissues/index.html.

59. H.J. Res. 106, introduced September 23, 2004. www.congress.gov/cgi-bin/query/z?c108:H.J.RES.106.

on September 30, 2004. The result was 227 yea votes (55%) to 186 nay votes (45 percent).[60] Republicans voted 191-to–27 *for* the amendment; Democrats voted 158–36 *against* it.[61] Therefore the amendment failed. A two-thirds majority would have been 290 votes.

The amendment failed in the Senate because of a filibuster by its opponents. On July 14, 2004, there was a cloture motion in the Senate that would have forced a vote on the amendment. It needed 60 votes to pass, but received only 48 yea votes to 50 nay votes, so it was 12 votes short of the supermajority needed to end debate and force the Senate to vote on the amendment. Forty-two Democrats voted against the amendment, compared with eight Republicans.[62] Therefore there is not now strong enough support for such an amendment to pass by two-thirds majority in both houses of Congress. And even if it were to pass Congress, it would then have to be ratified by the legislatures of three-fourths (thirty-eight) of the states.

But political sentiment in the United States can change over time, and it may be that sometime in the future the sentiment of the people of the nation will be strong enough to support such a measure.

The benefits of such an amendment would be that (1) it would prevent the current US Supreme Court and all future US Supreme Courts from redefining marriage as the Massachusetts, Connecticut, and Iowa supreme courts have already done; (2) it would prevent individual state supreme courts from redefining marriages; and (3) it would give a uniform definition of marriage throughout the nation rather than allowing a hodge-podge of definitions to spring up in the various states.

Such an amendment would not wrongfully violate the constitutional separation of powers between the federal government and the state governments, because neither the Congress nor the Constitution itself has ever understood such separation of powers to mean that states could completely redefine marriage in this way. In fact, in the Mormon polygamy controversy, the nation affirmed that the United States has a strong national interest in establishing a uniform definition of marriage for the entire nation. This concern was also reiterated by Congress when it welcomed Arizona into the Union and simultaneously required that the constitution of Arizona similarly prohibit polygamous marriages.[63]

---

60. See www.congress.gov/cgi-bin/bdquery/z?d108:h.j.res.00106.

61. See http://clerk.house.gov/evs/2004/roll484.xml.

62. See www.senate.gov/legislative/LIS/roll_call_lists/roll_call_vote_cfm.cfm?congress=108&session=2&vote=00155.

63. "Modern History of Polygamy," *AZCentral.com* (May 30, 2008). www.azcentral.com/news/articles/2008/05/30/20080530centennial-timeline.html.

6. Is this imposing Christian moral standards on society?

The primary objection brought against the view of marriage that I support in this chapter is that "Christians should not try to impose their moral standards on the rest of society."

The first response is that attempting to *persuade* people that these moral standards are right and beneficial to society is not the same as "imposing" them on others. Everyone in a free society should have the right to attempt to persuade others to agree with his or her views, and that is what I am attempting to do here, arguing that for many reasons this one-man, one-woman standard is best for society.

The second answer is one I discussed in chapters 1 and 2: The Bible presents these standards for marriage not as merely Christian standards but as the standards that come from the one true God, the Creator of the universe. They are the standards by which he will one day hold all people accountable. In that sense, I am arguing here that these moral standards regarding marriage *already are the true standards that apply to the whole society in every nation*, whether or not everyone acknowledges that.

7. Is limiting marriage to one man and one woman an unconstitutional "establishment" of religion?

The proponents of same-sex "marriage" also argue that limiting marriage to one man and one woman is wrong because it is "establishing" a religion, which is contrary to the First Amendment to the Constitution. For example, when the Iowa Supreme Court decided to impose same-sex "marriage" on the state of Iowa (in the case *Varnum v. Brien*, April 3, 2009), it noted that only 28.1% of Iowans supported it.[64] The court then observed that "much of society rejects same-sex marriage due to sincere, deeply ingrained—even fundamental—religious belief." But such views should not be taken into account, said the court, because the Iowa constitution says, "The general assembly shall make no law respecting an establishment of religion."[65] In other words, limiting marriage to one man and one woman would be equivalent to "establishing" a religion.

The same kind of argument was made in California. David Boies, a prominent lawyer challenging Proposition 8 (a California constitutional amendment that limits marriage to one man and one woman), argued that while people may have "genuine religious beliefs" that marriage

---

64. *Varnum v. Brien*, 763 N.W.2d 862 (Iowa Supreme Court, 2009), 64, n. 29.
65. Ibid., 64–65.

should be between a man and a woman, still "the other half of the First Amendment, the Establishment Clause ... says that a majority is not entitled to impose its religious beliefs on a minority."[66] In other words, even though 52% of Californians voted to define marriage as between one man and one woman, they were wrongly "establishing" a religion.

a. Marriage is not a religion.

This "establishing a religion" argument is wrong because marriage is not a religion! When voters define marriage, they are not establishing a *religion*. In the First Amendment—"Congress shall make no law respecting an establishment of *religion*, or prohibiting the free exercise thereof"—the word "religion" refers to the church that people attend and support. "Religion" means being a Baptist or Catholic or Presbyterian or Jew. It does not mean being married. These arguments try to make the word "religion" in the Constitution mean something different from what it has always meant.

b. The reasons for a law are different from the content of the law.

These arguments also make the logical mistake of failing to distinguish the *reasons* for a law from the *content* of the law. There were *religious reasons* behind many of our laws, but these laws do not "establish" a religion. All major religions have teachings against stealing, but laws against stealing do not "establish a religion." All religions have laws against murder, but laws against murder do not "establish a religion." The campaign to abolish slavery in the United States and England was led by many Christians, based on their religious convictions, but laws abolishing slavery do not "establish a religion." The campaign to end racial discrimination and segregation was led by Dr. Martin Luther King Jr., a Baptist pastor, who preached against racial injustice from the Bible. But laws against discrimination and segregation do not "establish a religion."[67]

If this kind of argument were to succeed in court, it could soon be applied against evangelicals and Catholics who make "religious" arguments against abortion. Majority votes to protect unborn children could then be invalidated by saying these voters are "establishing a religion." And by such reasoning, *all the votes of religious citizens* for almost *any*

---

66. "Prop. 8 Defenders Say Plaintiffs Attacked 'Orthodox Religious Beliefs,'" *Wall Street Journal* (online blog, Feb. 10, 2010). http://blogs.wsj.com/law/2010/02/10/prop–8-defenders-accuse-plaintiffs-of-attacking-orthodox-religious-beliefs/tab/print/.

67. See also the discussion of the "exclude religion" view in chapter 1, pp. 15–18.

issue could be found invalid by court decree! This would be the direct opposite of the kind of country the Founding Fathers established, and the direct opposite of what they meant by "free exercise" of religion in the First Amendment.

H. RECOMMENDATIONS ABOUT SPECIFIC LAWS AND POLICIES RELATED TO MARRIAGE

1. Marriage should continue to be defined by government for society as a whole.

I gave arguments in support of this policy in section E above (pp. 117–19).

2. Laws should define marriage as a union between one man and one woman.

This would mean that laws should continue to exclude same-sex marriages and polygamous marriages, just as they have in the past.

3. Laws should make other restrictions on marriages that reflect historical and traditional standards. (These are standards that Christians also think reflect biblical moral standards.)

It is appropriate that marriage be restricted to those who have attained a certain age (eighteen in many states today) and who give their consent to be married. Marriage should also be restricted to those who are not already married, so as to protect the status of marriage as a union between one man and one woman and to prevent adulterous relationships from being considered marriage. Laws should also prohibit polygamous marriages — that is, a man who is already married to one woman would not be allowed to marry another woman at the same time.

In addition, the laws should prohibit incestuous relationships from being considered marriage. Therefore a person could not marry someone of the opposite sex in his or her immediate family, such as a brother or sister or a son or daughter. A person could not marry an aunt or uncle or niece or nephew or first cousin.

Such provisions not only reflect biblical moral standards, but also reflect the historical wisdom that such relationships are harmful rather than helpful to society.

4. Homosexual relationships should not be granted the status of "marriage."

If a society were to grant this status, it would give governmental encouragement and endorsement to a relationship that is contrary to the moral standards of the Bible and detrimental to the raising of children. No Christian should support such a proposal.

5. It is doubtful that domestic partner benefits should be given to homosexual relationships or that they should be normalized in any way as "civil unions."

Regarding "domestic partnership" benefits, the question is whether the society as a whole, through its government, wishes to give encouragement and endorsement to a relationship that is contrary to the moral standards of the Bible. If the members of a society wish to do this, they are of course free to do so, but it is not a proposal that Christians should support. Our standards of what is right and wrong for human conduct, and what is helpful or harmful to individuals and to society, should be taken from the Bible.

Nevertheless, if the majority of a society decides to grant such domestic partner benefits, they should not be limited to homosexual domestic partners, but should apply to *all people living together in long-term relationships where there is mutual commitment and obligation to care and support.* They should also certainly apply to an elderly sister and brother living together and caring for one another, or an adult child living with and caring for an elderly parent. These relationships should be allowed the same privileges and benefits that would be given to homosexual couples living together. And such benefits, if given, should be dependent on the couple making a legal commitment to some measure of obligation for mutual financial support and physical care if needed. Such a provision would guarantee that society receives some benefits in return for granting some privileges or benefits.

Of course, there are various kinds of "benefits" that might be granted. Domestic partner benefits with no significant financial costs to the taxpayers or to consumers are less controversial and would include things such as allowing hospital visitation rights and access to medical records. But other kinds of domestic partner benefits would involve substantial costs to taxpayers or consumers, such as coverage by a partner's health insurance plan at work, the right to a partner's pension plan, significant financial benefits in inheritance laws by which no tax penalty is incurred for inheriting an estate when a spouse dies, and access to a portion of Social Security benefits that have been earned by one spouse during his or her lifetime. Campaigns for this kind of benefit are primarily campaigns for monetary benefits.

The objections to giving such monetary benefits to same-sex relationships are the following: (1) These benefits were originally intended by society to encourage the bearing and raising of children in a heterosexual marriage, which is the only kind of sexual union that can produce children; (2) to give such benefits to homosexual relationships which (by themselves) cannot produce new children becomes a means by which *society encourages other types of relationships* that will not ordinarily produce children and will not raise them in the most beneficial way; (3) such benefits also confer a societal indication of *approval* on the relationships; but Christians should not support policies that give approval to relationships that the Bible disapproves of and considers morally wrong.

It is in fact this symbol of approval by society that is one of the major reasons behind the push by homosexuals to gain domestic partner benefits and ultimately to gain the status of marriage. To the extent that these benefits confer such endorsement and approval, and for that very reason, Christians should oppose and not support such proposals.

For the same reasons, other privileges related to marriage such as the right to adopt children should not be granted to homosexual relationships.

6. Known homosexuals should continue to be prohibited from military service.

Widespread evidence indicates that mixing active homosexual persons with nonhomosexuals in the close quarters required in military service has a significantly detrimental effect on military morale and effectiveness. That alone is sufficient reason for restoring the policy of not allowing known homosexuals to serve in the military.

Campbell University Law Professor William A. Woodruff has stated,

> The American military does not fight an armed enemy sworn to destroy our way of life by showing how enlightened and progressive our popular culture is. The armed forces exist to project combat power as an arm of foreign policy and to protect our vital national interests. Anything, whether it is height, weight, IQ, character, physical fitness, medical condition, or any other condition that detracts from unit cohesion and combat effectiveness, disqualifies an otherwise patriotic American from serving in the military. The military is not popular culture. It is very different and must remain so to defend the freedoms that advance our popular culture.

Woodruff added,

> Those who favor personnel policies grounded in notions of fairness to the individual must be required to demonstrate beyond any doubt that military discipline, unit cohesion, and combat effectiveness will not be diminished one iota by adoption of their preferred policy. Otherwise, it elevates the individual over the mission, and that is the antithesis of military service."[68]

Brian Jones, a retired US Army Ranger, testified to Congress in 2008:

> As a US Army Ranger, I performed long-range patrols in severe cold weather conditions, in teams of 10, with only mission essential items on our backs. No comfort items. The only way to keep from freezing at night was to get as close as possible for body heat—which means skin to skin. On several occasions, in the close quarters that a team lives, any attraction to same sex teammates, real or perceived, would be known and would be a problem. The presence of openly gay men in these situations would elevate tensions and disrupt unit cohesion and morale.[69]

In an open letter to President Obama, more than one thousand flag and general officers of the military wrote:

> Our past experience as military leaders leads us to be greatly concerned about the impact of repeal [of the law] on morale, discipline, unit cohesion, and overall military readiness. We believe that imposing this burden on our men and women in uniform would undermine recruiting and retention, impact leadership at all levels, have adverse effects on the willingness of parents who lend their sons and daughters to military service, and eventually break the All-Volunteer Force.[70]

---

68. William A. Woodruff: quoted in Summary Statement of Elaine Donnelly, President, Center for Military Readiness House Armed Services Committee. Subcommittee on Personnel in Support of Section 654, Title 10, the 1993 Law Stating that Homosexuals Are Not Eligible to Serve in the Military. 2118 Rayburn House Office Building, Washington, DC (July 23, 2008). http://cmrlink.org/fileuploads/HASC072308DonnellyShortStatement.pdf.

69. Statement of Brian Jones, Sergeant Major USA (Ret) CEO, Adventure Training Concepts Subcommittee on Personnel. In Support of Section 654, Title 10, The 1993 Law Stating That Homosexuals Are Not Eligible to Serve in the Military. 2118 Rayburn House Office Building, Washington, DC (July 23, 2008).

70. "Concerns Regarding Recruiting, Retention, and Readiness." www.flagandgeneralofficersforthemilitary.com/.

7. Private organizations such as the Boy Scouts should continue to be allowed to exclude homosexuals from employment as scoutmasters.

The US Supreme Court agreed with this position with its decision in *Boy Scouts of America et al. v. Dale* in 2000. A majority of the court (five-to-four) agreed that the First Amendment right of freedom of association "plainly presupposes a freedom not to associate."[71]

The concluding paragraph of the majority opinion was very explicit in this regard:

> We are not, as we must not be, guided by our views of whether the Boy Scouts' teachings with respect to homosexual conduct are right or wrong; public or judicial disapproval of a tenet of an organization's expression does not justify the State's effort to compel the organization to accept members where such acceptance would derogate from the organization's expressive message. "While the law is free to promote all sorts of conduct in place of harmful behavior, it is not free to interfere with speech for no better reason than promoting an approved message or discouraging a disfavored one, however enlightened either purpose may strike the government." *Hurley*, 515 US, at 579.

8. Should homosexuals be granted the legal status of a protected class?

Certain groups have a special legal status in society, the status of a protected class of persons. This is true, for example, regarding gender and race, so that discriminating on the basis of gender or race is illegal. Should homosexuals also be granted such a special status, so that discrimination on the basis of "sexual orientation" is considered illegal? This is the force of many "gay rights" ordinances and laws in various cities and twenty-one states.[72]

Christians should not support such ordinances, because they also have the force of giving governmental approval and encouragement to a relationship that is contrary to the moral standards of the Bible.

Deciding that homosexuals should *not* be considered a "protected class" in the law simply means they have *the same legal status everyone*

---

71. *Roberts v. United States Jaycees*, 468 U.S. 609, 622 (1984): cited by Chief Justice William Rehnquist, *Boy Scouts of America v. Dale* 530 U.S. 5 (2000).

72. State Nondiscrimination Laws in the US. www.thetaskforce.org/downloads/reports/issue_maps/non_discrimination_7_09_color.pdf.

else does. Homosexual men have the same status and protections as all other men in society. Homosexual or lesbian women have the same status and protections that every other woman has in society. They have these without designating them as a specially protected class in the law.

But if homosexuals are designated as a protected class, then it very quickly becomes against the law for Christians and others with similar moral standards to act in a way consistent with their beliefs. For example, if homosexuals are a protected class, then can a Christian wedding photographer decide not to provide photography services to a homosexual wedding or commitment ceremony? Or can a church refuse to rent an auditorium for the purpose of holding a homosexual marriage or civil union ceremony?

In these and other cases, Christians are being put in the position of *lawbreakers* simply because they do not want to use their facilities or services to endorse a relationship that they consider morally wrong. In this way such gay rights ordinances *violate the freedom of conscience of individuals* in the society. Such ordinances, when they have this effect, are certainly wrong.

9. Should homosexual conduct itself be against the law?

Until 2003, some states had laws that prohibited private homosexual conduct. In fact, such "sodomy laws" existed at one point in many or all states in the United States.[73] In 1986, the US Supreme Court, in *Bowers v. Hardwick*, upheld the right of Georgia to have such a law.[74] In the majority opinion, then-Chief Justice Warren Burger wrote:

> Decisions of individuals relating to homosexual conduct have been subject to state intervention throughout the history of Western civilization. Condemnation of those practices is firmly rooted in Judeo-Christian moral and ethical standards ... To hold that the act of homosexual sodomy is somehow protected as a fundamental right would be to cast aside millennia of moral teaching."[75]

But seventeen years later, in 2003, the Supreme Court explicitly overruled *Bowers v. Hardwick* in the case *Lawrence v. Texas*. In that case, the

---

73. See footnote 6 in *Bowers v. Hardwick*, 478 U.S. 186 (1986). Sodomy laws existed in all of the colonies and subsequent states. The first state repealing its law barring sodomy was Illinois in 1962.

74. *Bowers v. Hardwick* was decided by a 5–4 majority, with Burger, White, Powell, Rehnquist, and O'Connor in the majority and Blackmun, Brennan, Marshall, and Stevens dissenting.

75. *Bowers v. Hardwick*, 478 U.S. 186 (1986) concurring opinion by Chief Justice Warren Burger.

Supreme Court held that consensual sexual activity between same-sex adults is an essential freedom protected by the idea of "due process" in the Fourteenth Amendment.[76]

Sodomy laws (that prohibited private homosexual conduct) were in several ways similar to the laws against fornication that had been on the books in various states for most of the history of the United States, *but had seldom or never been enforced*. And if laws prohibiting private consensual sexual acts between unrelated adults are never enforced, then it seems pointless to have such laws in the first place. As I will argue below in the discussion on laws regarding fornication (see p. 147), there are some actions that are contrary to biblical morality but that nevertheless should not be prohibited or penalized by law. With regard to homosexual conduct, this also seems to be the consensus of a broad majority of American society at this time, probably out of a common realization that attempts at enforcement of such laws would inevitably involve excessive government intrusion into people's private lives.

In any case, since *Lawrence v. Texas*, it is now considered unconstitutional to have laws against sodomy (and probably, by implication, against fornication). I see no reason for Christians to argue that this conclusion should be overturned.

I. PORNOGRAPHY

1. The issue

Should governments restrict the production and distribution of pornography?

2. The relevant biblical teaching

The question of pornography must be analyzed within the broader framework of the Bible's teaching on marriage (see above). The Bible indicates that, for married persons, having sexual intercourse outside of

---

76. In *Lawrence v. Texas*, the majority of six justices included Kennedy, Stevens, Souter, Ginsburg, Breyer, and O'Connor, while the minority of three justices in dissent included Scalia, Rehnquist, and Thomas. All three justices who dissented said they did so, not because they approved of laws against sodomy, but because they argued that it is not the right of the court to decide issues of law based on society's view of sexual morality, because this is a matter that should entirely be decided by the legislative processes in the nation and the states themselves. They argued that there is nothing in the Constitution itself that could provide a basis for the ruling of the majority in *Lawrence v. Texas*. (I think that they were correct in this dissent.)

marriage (that is, committing adultery) is morally wrong. The seventh commandment says, "You shall not commit adultery" (Exod. 20:14).

Having sexual intercourse outside of marriage is also viewed as morally wrong for unmarried persons. This was called "fornication" in older Bible translations and in legal statutes that dealt with this subject, but in more recent Bible translations other terms have been used, most commonly "sexual immorality."[77]

The prohibition against sex between unmarried persons is clear not only from the laws of Moses that penalized such conduct (see Exod. 22:16–17; Deut. 22:13–21), but also from the teachings of Jesus, who pointed out sin in the life of the woman at the well in Samaria by saying to her, "You have had five husbands, and the one you now have is not your husband" (John 4:18). Other verses that use the phrase "sexual immorality" (translating Greek *porneia*) in modern translations (such as Matt. 15:19; Gal. 5:19; Eph. 5:3) also show that sexual intercourse outside of marriage is sin. (See also John 8:41; Acts 15:20; 1 Cor. 6:18; 7:2, 9; 1 Thess. 4:3; note also the imagery in 2 Cor. 11:2.)

With regard to pornography, more can be said: The consistent teaching of the Bible is that God is concerned not merely with human *actions*, but also with the *attitudes of our hearts*. That is clear from the last of the Ten Commandments:

> "You shall not covet your neighbor's house; you shall not covet
> your neighbor's wife, or his male servant, or his female servant,
> or his ox, or his donkey, or anything that is your neighbor's"
> (Exod. 20:17).

The command not to "covet" means not to have a desire to take what belongs to someone else as your own. But the command not to covet "your neighbor's wife" therefore is a command not to *desire* to have her as your own or to have intercourse with her. This is made explicit, for example, in Proverbs 6:25, referring to an adulteress: "Do not desire her beauty in your heart."

Jesus brought out the intent of these Old Testament laws of sexual purity in his teaching on the Sermon on the Mount:

> "You have heard that it was said, 'You shall not commit adul-
> tery.' But I say to you that everyone who looks at a woman with
> lustful intent has already committed adultery with her in his
> heart" (Matt. 5:27–28).

---

77. For example, in the English Standard Version (ESV), the New International Version (NIV), the New English Translation (NET), and the Holman Christian Standard Bible (HCSB).

In fact, one Old Testament prophet shows an example of a relationship between looking at pictures and lusting after what one sees, and then committing sinful actions. Speaking of the city of Jerusalem in a parable of a woman called Oholibah, Ezekiel says the following:

> But she carried her whoring further. She *saw* men portrayed on the wall, the images of the Chaldeans portrayed in vermilion, wearing belts on their waists, with flowing turbans on their heads, all of them having the appearance of officers, a likeness of Babylonians whose native land was Chaldea. When she saw them, she *lusted* after them and *sent* messengers to them in Chaldea. And the Babylonians came to her into the bed of love, and they defiled her with their whoring lust. And after she *was defiled* by them, she turned from them in disgust (Ezek. 23:14–17).

Here Ezekiel traces a progression of sexual sin. Oholibah saw, then she lusted, then she sent for those who were pictured, then she committed adultery with them.

The conclusion from all of these verses is that God's moral standards require that people avoid longing for sexual intercourse with someone apart from being married to that person (a relationship in which the Bible views sexual attraction and intimacy as a wholesome and wonderful gift from God).

The moral question about pornography, then, is the question of whether it is right to create, to distribute, to acquire, and to view photographs or videos, or written material, or audio material *whose primary purpose is to arouse in people sexual desires that are contrary to God's moral standards*. It seems clear that this is not a morally right thing to do and should be considered morally wrong.

3. Arguments from reason and experience apart from the Bible

From the standpoint of an appeal to ordinary common sense, one significant argument is that pornography attracts a person's affections and desires outside of one's marriage and away from one's spouse. A man who uses pornography is robbing his wife of emotional affection that should be hers and is turning his heart away from her and from desiring her affection. It will hinder his sexual relationship within marriage and will create harmful memories that will last for a long time and interfere with his marriage probably for several years to come. In addition, when a man uses pornography, his wife (or girlfriend) will often sense some impurity or moral uncleanness in the man even if she does not discover any facts about what he is doing.

An abundance of evidence from sociological studies is also available, showing the harmful effects of pornography on those who view it and then on those who are subsequently harmed by these people. The harmful results may be summarized in the following points by the National Coalition for the Protection of Children and Families in their report, "The Effects of Pornography and Sexual Messages."[78] The report says that

> research has shown that pornography and its messages are involved in shaping attitudes and encouraging behavior that can harm individual users and their families. Pornography is often viewed in secret, which creates deception within marriages that can lead to divorce in some cases. In addition, pornography promotes the allure of adultery, prostitution and unreal expectations that can result in dangerous promiscuous behavior.[79]

It continues:

> Young people growing up in our already overly sexualized culture are being exposed to sexually explicit material on a daily basis through network television, movies, music and the Internet. Children are being subjected to sexual material and messages before they are mentally prepared to understand or evaluate what they are viewing. In addition, the majority of sex education is taking place in the media, not in the home, church or school.[80]

According to the report, the following false messages are sent by our culture:

- Sex with anyone, under any circumstances, any way it is desired, is beneficial and does not have negative consequences.
- Women have one value — to meet the sexual demands of men.
- Marriage and children are obstacles to sexual fulfillment.
- Everyone is involved in promiscuous sexual activity, infidelity and premarital sex.[81]

---

78. "The Effects of Pornography and Sexual Messages." www.nationalcoalition.org/effects.asp.

79. Ibid.

80. Ibid.

81. Ibid.

The report goes on to deal with the issue of pornography and addiction. It states, "Not only is the pornography industry, as well as the mainstream media, filling consumers' heads with these false beliefs and attitudes, but studies have found that pornography can be highly addictive. In fact, Dr. Victor Cline, an expert on sexual addiction, found that there is a four-step progression among many who consume pornography.

1. **Addiction:** Pornography provides a powerful sexual stimulant or aphrodisiac effect, followed by sexual release, most often through masturbation.
2. **Escalation:** Over time addicts require more explicit and deviant material to meet their sexual "needs."
3. **Desensitization:** What was first perceived as gross, shocking and disturbing, in time becomes common and acceptable.
4. **Acting out sexually:** There is an increasing tendency to act out behaviors viewed in pornography.[82]

The report goes on to say that the National Council on Sexual Addiction Compulsivity estimates that 6 to 8% of Americans are sexual addicts.[83]

As for the negative ramifications of pornography on communities, the report states, "Sexually oriented businesses, such as strip clubs and massage parlors, attract crime to communities. In addition, the general content of pornography supports abuse and the rape myth (that women enjoy forceful sex) and serves as a how-to for sex crimes, primarily the molestation of children." Land Use Studies by the National Law Center for Children and Families show evidence of the correlation of adult businesses and crime. For example, in Phoenix neighborhoods where adult businesses were located, the number of sex offenses was 506% greater than in areas without such businesses. The number of property crimes was 43% greater, and the number of violent crimes 4% greater. Dr. Mary Anne Layden, director of education for the University of Pennsylvania Health System, points out, "I have been treating sexual violence victims and perpetrators for 13 years. I have not treated a single case of sexual violence that did not involve pornography."[84]

Finally, with regard to the child pornography, the report says, "Most will agree on the amount of harm caused by child pornography, which

---

82. Ibid.
83. Ibid.
84. Gow, Haven Bradford, "Child Sex Abuse: America's Dirty Little Secret," MS Voices for Children (March 2000): cited in ibid.

consists of photographs, videos, magazines, books and films that show children engaged in sexual acts, all of which are illegal. All production of these materials is an illegal and permanent record of the abuse or exploitation of children. Material digitally doctored to look like child pornography was also illegal, until a Supreme Court decision in April 2002 that found the 'virtual' child porn law unconstitutional."[85] The report concludes:

> Child and adult pornography is frequently used by pedophiles to lure children. The typical child molester befriends the child, often through Internet chat rooms, and, after building "trust," exposes the child to pornography. This is done in attempt to make the child think that this behavior is acceptable and to lure him or her to participate. The experience of exploitation and abuse becomes a lifelong struggle for the victim and leaves them with the fear that their photos are still out there.[86]

Alan Sears, president and CEO of the Alliance Defense Fund and former director of then-Attorney General Edwin Meese III's Commission on Pornography, adds:

> The sexual union within marriage, between one man and one woman, is meant by the Creator to be an act of supreme love, giving and unity. It's a picture, if you will, of supreme selflessness. Virtually all advocates of secular sexual behavior center on an "it's all about me" philosophy rather than mutual love and care for the other partner.... In years of public speaking since that time, I have repeatedly referred to pornography as the "true hate literature" of our age, because of its hatred and exploitation of the human person, regardless of size, shape, color or gender. It reduces human beings to valueless commodities to be ogled at and disposed of like used tissue.[87]

4. What laws should governments make regarding pornography?

The fact that something is morally wrong according to the Bible does not by itself mean that governments should have laws against it. For

---

85. "The Effects of Pornography and Sexual Messages," op. cit.

86. Ibid.

87. Interview with Alan Sears: "Pornography: The Degrading Behemoth," CitizenLink.org (Aug. 3, 2005). www.citizenlink.org/FOSI/pornography/A000000851.cfm.

instance, there are no laws against private drunkenness or laziness or foolish and wasteful uses of money. For the entire history of the United States, either there were *no laws* against fornication (in the sense of private sexual intercourse between consenting unrelated, unmarried adults of the opposite sex), or else those laws were *never enforced.* Thus, for example, I don't think anyone should support the idea of laws against looking at pornographic material, however a person might obtain it.

But the question of *creating* and *distributing* such material to others is a different question. In that case a person is creating material that (from a biblical point of view) has a harmful effect on the moral standards of the society and specifically on the people who use the pornography and others to whom they relate in intimate ways.

Therefore, since pornography makes people more likely to commit violence against women or children or more likely to commit rape, a strong argument can be made for enacting laws against the production, distribution, and sale of pornographic materials.

5. The definition of pornography

The First Amendment was primarily intended to protect political speech, and not all kinds of speech are protected. Slander, libel, and incitement to riot are not protected, nor is consumer fraud or mail fraud, for example, and courts have rightly recognized this. The courts have also recognized that the First Amendment cannot rightly be used to claim protection for obscene material.

How, then, should pornography be defined? In the 1957 Supreme Court decision *Roth v. United States,* the standard established by the court was "whether to the average person, applying contemporary community standards, the dominant theme of the material taken as whole appeals to the prurient interest." (The word "prurient" means "inordinately interested in matters of sex.") Then, in the 1973 case *Miller v. California* the Supreme Court decided that a work is not considered obscene unless it "lacks serious literary, artistic, political, and scientific value."[88]

These cases still provide a useful standard that can be used effectively in prosecutions of pornographers, provided that juries are allowed to give a common-sense meaning to the word "serious," so that the word is not robbed of its force by misleading jury instructions or undue deference to

---

88. *Miller v. California,* 413 U.S. 15.

testimony by so-called "experts" brought in by lawyers defending pornographers.[89] In addition, most of the problems in the country concerning pornography could be addressed if prosecutors would decide to bring charges only against the production and distribution of *visual images* (photos and videos) and not try to prosecute publications that contain only words, where standards are more blurry and some literary merit is easier to claim.

Therefore the ongoing problem with pornography in the United States is not that laws are inadequate but that prosecutors are not sufficiently willing to bring charges against those who produce and distribute pornography.

Former federal prosecutor Alan Sears claims that "obscenity laws, though far from perfect, are more definite than many other criminal laws successfully and regularly used in the criminal justice system."[90] He notes that the Attorney General's Commission on Pornography, for which he served as director, provided a useful definition of pornography as "sexually explicit material designed primarily for arousal."[91]

Sears also says,

> Pornography includes several classes of material: obscenity, material harmful to minors, child pornography, indecency, and lawful but nonetheless pornographic depictions....
>
> Depending on the type of material, its offensiveness ranges from the "merely immoral" — which depicts women and other persons as a subspecies of humans to be used, to be abused and to amuse — to what I have always called "crime scene photographs," actual depictions of unlawful sexual behavior for profit or exploitation.
>
> I call those who produce material that is unlawful part of a "criminal enterprise," not an "industry."
>
> So, pornography is shamefully large in its scope and, depending on how broadly it is defined, it is a multibillion-dollar enterprise. As large and pervasive as it may be, however, it is not too large to be reigned in and dramatically limited in any community with the will to do so.[92]

---

89. See *United States v. Kilbride*, No. 07–10528, and *United States v. Schaeffer*, No. 07–10534, United States Court of Appeals for the 9th Circuit (2008).

90. Alan E. Sears, "The Legal Case for Restricting Pornography," in *Pornography: Research Advances and Policy Considerations*, ed. Dolf Zillman and Jennings Bryant (Hillsdale, NJ: Lawrence Erlbaum Associates, 1989), 327.

91. Interview with Sears: "Pornography: the Degrading Behemoth."

92. Ibid.

Under the administrations of two Republicans, President Ronald Reagan (1981–1989) and President George H. W. Bush (1989–1993), federal prosecutors were highly successful in prosecuting and winning convictions against numerous pornographers in the United States. Under the leadership of Patrick Trueman, chief of the Child Exploitation and Obscenity Section (CEOS) in the Department of Justice's Criminal Division, there were multiple prosecutions, and the result was "50 individual or corporate convictions of sending obscene advertisements through the mails, and a 'Los Angeles project' that … led to the conviction of 20 out of 50 producers and suppliers of obscene materials targeted in the L.A. area."[93] They also obtained a conviction of Reuben Sturman, reputedly the nation's largest distributor of pornographic material, in 1992.[94]

But once President Clinton took office, Trueman reported, the Democratic administration "all but halted obscenity prosecutions," saying that it would focus instead on child pornography[95] (which effectively meant ignoring adult obscenity prosecution). When George W. Bush became President in 2001, veteran prosecutors saw some return to an emphasis on prosecuting pornographers under Attorney Generals John Ashcroft and Albert Gonzales, but it was not as great as under Reagan's Justice Department or that of George H. W. Bush. An *ABA Journal* article on this topic concludes: " … the real reason Internet obscenity has not been tackled stems from the fact that law enforcement seems not to have the time, resources or inclination to pursue it."[96]

J. THE IMPORTANCE OF LAWS CONCERNING MARRIAGE

It is hard to overstate the importance of laws concerning marriage, as discussed in this chapter. The future of the nation's children depends in large measure on how we define marriage and whether we continue to encourage and protect it. The future lives of millions of men and women in society will be affected by the way in which we define marriage. It is the foundational institution in our society, and it affects everything else.

---

93. Jason Krause, "The End of the Net Porn Wars," *ABA Journal* (Feb. 2008). www.aba-journal.com/magazine/article/the_end_of_the_net_porn_wars, Feb. 7, 2010.
94. Ibid.
95. Ibid.
96. Ibid.

For further reading

Davis, *Evangelical Ethics,* 113–36; James Dobson, *Marriage Under Fire* (Sisters, OR: Multnomah, 2004); Feinberg and Feinberg, *Ethics for a Brave New World,* 185–206; Daniel R. Heimbach, *True Sexual Morality* (Wheaton: Crossway, 2004); Roger Magnuson, *Are Gay Rights Right?* (Portland, OR: Multnomah, 1990); Rae, *Moral Choices,* 270–301; Jeffrey Satinover, *Homosexuality and the Politics of Truth* (Grand Rapids: Baker, 1996); Thomas Schmidt, *Straight and Narrow? Compassion and Clarity in the Homosexuality Debate* (Downers Grove, IL: InterVarsity Press, 1995); Alan Sears and Craig Osten, *The Homosexual Agenda: Exposing the Principal Threat to Religious Freedom Today,* rev. ed. (Nashville: Broadman & Holman, 2003); Linda J. Waite and Maggie Gallagher, *The Case for Marriage: Why Married People Are Happier, Healthier, and Better Off Financially* (New York: Doubleday, 2000).

Chapter 5

THE FAMILY

Should parents or the government have the primary responsibility for training children?

A. GOVERNMENTS SHOULD ENCOURAGE MARRIED COUPLES TO BEAR AND RAISE CHILDREN

From beginning to end, the Bible has a very positive view of bearing and raising children. In fact, the very first recorded command to human beings was the command to bear children:

> So God created man in his own image, in the image of God he created him; male and female he created them. And God blessed them. And God said to them, *"Be fruitful and multiply and fill the earth* and subdue it and have dominion over the fish of the sea and over the birds of the heavens and over every living thing that moves on the earth"* (Gen. 1:27–28).

God was pleased with the man and woman whom he had made. He took delight in them (see Gen. 1:31) and indicated that they were the most wonderful part of his creation, for they alone were said to be "in the image of God." (This means that they were more like God than any other creature, and they represented him on earth.) Therefore we can understand why God wanted to have many more men and women on the earth, for they would also be human beings who would be "in his image" and would represent him and reflect his excellence. Because human beings are such wonderful creations, more human beings would bring more glory to their excellent Creator! This explains why God commanded Adam and Eve to "fill the earth" with God-glorifying human beings, with generation after generation of God's image-bearers spreading over the whole earth.

God's desire for his people to bear more children is seen in several other passages, such as the following:

> Behold, children are a heritage from the LORD, the fruit of the womb a reward (Ps. 127:3).

> Did he not make them one, with a portion of the Spirit in their union? *And what was the one God seeking? Godly offspring.* So guard yourselves in your spirit, and let none of you be faithless to the wife of your youth (Mal. 2:15).

> So I would have younger widows marry, *bear children*, manage their households, and give the adversary no occasion for slander (1 Tim. 5:14; cf. Deut. 28:4; Hosea 1:10).

It is not surprising that the Bible views children in such a positive way. Unless each generation of a society bears and raises at least as many children as themselves, the entire population will dwindle and eventually the society itself will weaken and perhaps go out of existence.

Moreover, people all grow old eventually and become too weak to do productive work and support themselves. Unless there is a new generation of younger workers coming along, the society will become top-heavy with elderly people unable to work. Eventually fewer and fewer young people will be supporting more and more older, retired people, and a society's economy will spiral downward.

This has already happened in Europe. In 2003, researchers found that in the year 2000, the number of children in Europe had declined to the point that assured mathematically that there would be fewer parents than the previous generation. Brian O'Neill, a researcher at the International Institute for Applied Systems Analysis, said,

> The implications of negative momentum are small right now, but they are going to get bigger quickly. If you add another 10 years of low fertility, that decline (by 2100) would be 25 to 40 million. If we have two decades of low fertility, then it would be another 25 to 40 million.[1]

1. Brian O'Neill, researcher at the International Institute for Applied Systems Analysis in Austria: quoted in Bootie Cosgrove-Mather, "European Birth Rate Declines," Associated Press (March 27, 2003). www.cbsnews.com/stories/2003/03/27/world/main546441.sthml.

In America, the crisis will hit with Social Security and Medicare. According to David C. John, a research fellow at the Heritage Foundation,

> As millions of baby boomers approach retirement, the program's annual cash surplus will shrink and then disappear. Then, Social Security will not be able to pay full benefits from its payroll and other tax revenues. It will need to consume ever-growing amounts of general revenue dollars to meet its obligations—money that now pays for everything from environmental programs to highway construction to defense. Eventually, either benefits will have to be slashed or the rest of the government will have to shrink to accommodate Social Security....
>
> The reason that Social Security's deficits are inevitable is fairly simple. Demographics are more predictable than most events. Millions of baby boomers will begin to retire in 2008, when those born in 1946 reach Social Security's early retirement age of 62. From then until 2025, every year will see another crop of baby boomers reach the 62-year-old threshold. Because the baby boomers have not produced enough children to replace themselves, the number of taxpayer workers will shrink....
>
> The future is coming with steady speed. Social Security's annual cash surpluses will begin to fall in 2008.... Over roughly the next ten years, those Social Security surpluses ... will continue to shrink and then disappear completely. Without those surpluses to reduce the size of the federal deficit, Congress will have to raise taxes to bring in billions of dollars of new revenues, cut programs, or let annual deficits climb.... Together, Social Security and Medicare will consume an estimated 60 percent of income taxes collected by 2040.[2]

Every society also needs children to pass on its cultural values and its moral and behavioral standards to succeeding generations. To the extent that a society stops bearing children, to that extent it fails to pass on its distinctive values to those who will live in the future.

But are there already too many people on the earth? There are certainly not too many God-glorifying people, which is what God expects the children of Christian believers to become. And there really are not too many people in general, as recent statistical studies indicate.

---

2. David C. John, "Social Security's Inevitable Future," *Heritage Foundation Web Memo #696* (March 21, 2005). www.heritage.org/Research/SocialSecurity/wm696.cfm.

B. PARENTS, NOT THE GOVERNMENT, SHOULD HAVE THE PRIMARY RESPONSIBILITY FOR TRAINING THEIR CHILDREN

It is remarkable how often the Bible places the responsibility for training children on their parents, not on "society" as a whole and not on the civil government. For example, Moses commanded the people of Israel that they should teach their children, and the language of the verse assumes the setting of a household or family:

> "Hear, O Israel: The LORD our God, the LORD is one. You shall love the LORD your God with all your heart and with all your soul and with all your might. And these words that I command you today shall be on your heart. *You shall teach them diligently to your children*, and shall talk of them when you sit in your house, and when you walk by the way, and when you lie down, and when you rise" (Deut. 6:4–7).

The commands in Proverbs also repeatedly assume that fathers and mothers are training their children:

> Hear, my son, your *father's* instruction, and forsake not your *mother's* teaching (Prov. 1:8).

> Hear, O sons, a *father's* instruction, and be attentive, that you may gain insight (4:1).

> My son, keep your *father's* commandment, and forsake not your *mother's* teaching (6:20).

> A wise son makes a glad *father*, but a foolish son is a sorrow to his *mother* (10:1).

> A wise son hears his *father's* instruction, but a scoffer does not listen to rebuke (13:1).

> A wise son makes a glad *father*, but a foolish man despises his *mother* (15:20).

> Listen to your *father* who gave you life, and do not despise your *mother* when she is old (23:22).

> The words of King Lemuel. An oracle that his *mother* taught him (31:1).

When we turn to the New Testament, instruction of children is also a responsibility given to parents:

Children, obey your parents in the Lord, for this is right. "Honor your father and mother" (this is the first commandment with a promise), "that it may go well with you and that you may live long in the land." *Fathers*, do not provoke your children to anger, but bring them up in the discipline and instruction of the Lord (Eph. 6:1–4).

Children, obey your parents in everything, for this pleases the Lord. *Fathers*, do not provoke your children, lest they become discouraged (Col. 3:20–21).

What is striking about these passages is the complete absence of *any indication* that *government* has the responsibility for training children *or for deciding what children should be taught*. The responsibility for teaching and training children, according to the Bible, falls entirely on their parents. This has significant implications for governmental policy regarding families and children.

First, this consistent pattern implies that *parents, not the government, should have the freedom to decide how best to educate their children*. This is the complete opposite of the policies of communist countries, who take children from their parents at a young age and seek to indoctrinate them with communist propaganda that in many cases is contrary to the convictions of the parents, particularly Christian parents. And it is completely opposite to the policy of the government of Germany today, which will actually take children from their parents by force in order to compel them to attend state-run schools, even when the parents object to the immoral and anti-Christian values taught in those schools.

In September 2006 the European Court of Human Rights outlawed homeschooling in Germany, and homeschooling families have been threatened with state seizure of their children and imprisonment. The Court of Human Rights ruled that Germany had not violated the human rights of parents when the government forbade them from educating their children at home because of religious reasons.[3]

Attorney Benjamin Bull of the Alliance Defense Fund, which provided funding in the legal effort to defend the rights of home-school families in Germany, said: "The decision by the European Court of Human Rights opens the door to continued prosecution and should

---

3. *Konrad v. Germany*, European Court of Human Rights (Sept. 18, 2006). www.telladf. org/UserDocs/KonradDecision.pdf.

highlight to Americans the extreme dangers of allowing international law to be authoritative in our own court systems."[4]

In June 2008 two parents, Juergen and Rosemarie Dudek, were sentenced to three months in prison for homeschooling their children. Wolfgang Drautz, general counsel for the Federal Republic of Germany, said the government "has a legitimate interest in countering the rise of parallel societies that are based on religion."[5]

In May 2009, Alliance Defense Fund attorneys appealed to the European Court of Human Rights the conviction of two parents who chose to educate their child at home on sexuality rather than have her participate in a four-day "sexual education" course that taught values that conflicted with the family's Christian faith. The couple were fined for exercising their parental rights.[6]

The threat has now reached American shores. In July 2009 a ten-year-old home-schooled student in New Hampshire was ordered by a judge to attend public school because the girl "appeared to reflect her mother's rigidity on questions of faith" and the girl's best interests "would be best served in a public school setting" and "different points of view at a time when she must begin to critically evaluate multiple systems of belief ... in order to select, as a young adult, which of those systems will best suit her own needs."[7] The judge issued this order even though the "marital master" who evaluated the young lady said she was "well-liked, social, and interactive with her peers, academically promising, [and] has more than kept up with the academic requirements of the ... public school system."[8]

But if the Bible teaches that it is the responsibility of parents and not of government to train children, then should Christians give support to the idea of government-supported public schools? I think such schools can be supported by reasoning that the public schools are simply helping the parents fulfill their task of training their children. But parents should never begin to think that the public school system is replacing the parents as the party *primarily responsible* for training children. If we

---

4. "ADF: Homeschooling Outlawed in Germany: Americans Should Be on Guard," *ADF Press Release* (Sept. 27, 2006). www.telladf.org/news/pressrelease.aspx?cid=3864.

5. Bob Unruh, "Parents Sent to Jail for Homeschooling," *WorldNetDaily.com* (June 18, 2008). www.worldnetdaily.com/index.php?pageId=67413.

6. "ADF attorneys file second appeal involving German 'sex education' program," *ADF Press Release* (May 19, 2009). www.telladf.org/news/pressrelease.aspx?cid=4954.

7. *In the Matter of Kurowski and Kurowski,* court order issued by Judge Lucinda V. Sandler, Family Division of the Judicial Court for Belknap County, Laconia, New Hampshire (July 14, 2009). www.telladf.org/UserDocs/KurowskiOrder.pdf.

8. Ibid.

understand public schools to be *helping parents* in their task, then the schools will be subject to and responsive to the concerns of the majority of parents in any district (rather than simply being run by educational "experts" who regularly override the desires and convictions of parents regarding their children's education).

C. A SCHOOL VOUCHER SYSTEM SHOULD BE ADOPTED BY EVERY SCHOOL DISTRICT

In the United States today I think the most beneficial change to our schooling system would be a system of school vouchers provided by the local government to pay for the education of children in each family. Parents could use these vouchers to pay for the cost of any public or private school they would choose for their children (including church-related schools).

This policy would have a number of benefits:

(1) It would restore much more parental influence in the training of children, a policy that would be consistent with the biblical teaching that parents have the primary responsibility for training their children.

(2) It would establish healthy competition in the educational system, with the result that the schools that give children the best training would gradually gain more and more students, and underperforming schools would either have to improve or they would have to close because they had no students. This would be far superior to the current government-run monopoly on the use of tax money for schools—a system that, on average, takes more and more money and produces fewer and fewer good results (when compared with other nations) year after year. In a 2001 study, Washington, DC, for instance, had the third highest per-capita expenditure per student, yet was last in achievement, and Delaware had the eighth-highest spending but landed in the bottom third with regard to results.[9]

Jay Greene, the author of "Education Myths," said, "If money were the solution, the problem would already be solved.... We've doubled the per pupil spending, adjusting for inflation, over the last 30 years, and yet the schools aren't better."[10]

---

9. Kirk A. Johnson, "Why More Money Will Not Solve America's Education Crisis," *Heritage Foundation Backgrounder #1448* (June 11, 2001). www.heritage.org/Research/Education/BG1448.cfm.

10. Jay Greene: quoted in John Stossel, "Stupid in America," *ABC News 20/20* (Jan. 13, 2006). http://abcnews.go.com/2020/print?id=2383857.

The results of this spending? In a 2006 study of educational achievement, the United States ranked twenty-first out of thirty countries in science, and twenty-fifth out of thirty in math.[11] In a recent survey of Oklahoma public school students, only one in four could identify George Washington as the first President of the United States.[12]

Meanwhile, in a September 2009 report on the difference between charter school students in New York City Public Schools compared with regular public school students, researchers found that by the third grade, the average charter school student was 5.3 points ahead on state English exams, compared with their peers in public schools, and 5.8 points ahead in math.[13]

(3) It would allow parents to send children to schools that supported their own moral and behavioral values.

(4) Children would be better educated. After the city of Milwaukee launched its school voucher program over the protests of the National Education Association (NEA), Caroline Hoxby of Harvard University performed a survey of the results. Comparing schools where at least 66% of students were eligible for vouchers with schools where fewer students were eligible, she found that in just one year schools with the most students eligible for vouchers made gains greater than those of other Milwaukee public schools. The schools with the voucher-eligible students went up 3 percentile points in math, 3 points in language, 5 points in science, and 3 points in social studies.[14]

According to Greg Forster, a research fellow at the Friedman Foundation for Educational Choice, every empirical study conducted in Milwaukee, Florida, Ohio, Texas, Maine, and Vermont showed that where vouchers were available, these programs improved public schools.[15]

---

11. The Programme for International Student Assessment (PISA). www.pisa.oecd.org/dataoecd/15/13/39725224.pdf. Also see http://international-education.suite101.com/article.cfm/us_students_left_behind.

12. "75 Percent of Oklahoma High School Students Can't Name the First President of the U.S." *News9.com* (Sept. 16, 2009). www.news9.com/global/story.asp?s=11141949.

13. Caroline M. Hoxby, Sonali Murarka, and Jenny Kang, "How New York City's Charter Schools Affect Achievement, August 2009 Report." Second report in series (Cambridge, MA: New York City Charter Schools Evaluation Project, September 2009).www.nber.org/~schools/charterschoolseval/how_NYC_charter_schools_affect_achievement_sept2009.pdf.

14. Caroline M. Hoxby, "Rising Tide," *Education Next,* Winter 2001: cited in Greg Forster, Ph.D., "A Win-Win Solution: The Empirical Evidence on How Vouchers Affect Public Schools," *School Choice Issues In Depth* (Jan. 2009), 16. www.friedmanfoundation.org/downloadFile.do?id=357.

15. Forster, "A Win-Win Solution," 16–21.

The reason that the NEA (the largest teachers union) so vehemently opposes even small, localized experiments in using vouchers is that it knows that privately run schools *will do a much better job of educating children* if only they can compete on an equal basis for the tax dollars that are supporting the public schools.[16]

A common objection to the use of school vouchers is that parents will use them to send children to church-related schools and thus the government will be supporting training in a certain religion.

But this objection is not persuasive: (a) It is not the *government* that is supporting such church-related schools, but the *parents* of the children, because they are making the choice of where to send them. This principle has been upheld in a number of court decisions. In 2002 the US Supreme Court, in *Zelman v. Simmons-Harris,* decided that a limited school voucher program in Cleveland, Ohio, for children in woefully underperforming schools was allowed under the US Constitution. The voucher program in Cleveland was only available to parents whose children were trapped in failing schools. Only three of the twenty-seven inner-city schools met minimal academic standards. Parents were allowed to take the $2,250-a-year voucher and place their children in the school of their choice, including faith-based schools.

The court ruled that the program was not in violation of the Establishment Clause of the First Amendment to the US Constitution. The program passed a five-part test to determine its constitutionality. The test, called the Private Choice Test, asked the program to meet the following criteria:

1. The program must have a valid secular purpose,
2. Aid must go to parents and not the schools,
3. A broad class of beneficiaries must be covered,
4. The program must be neutral with respect to religion, and
5. There must be adequate nonreligious options.

The court, in a five-to-four decision written by Chief Justice William Rehnquist, decided that the program met all these criteria.[17] As long as other voucher programs meet this criteria, the "freedom of religion" objection to school vouchers is effectively removed.

To use an analogy, if I get a tax-refund check from the government and then decide to give the money to my church, the government is not supporting my church. It is *my money,* and I am using it to support

---

16. Ibid.
17. *Zelman v. Simmons-Harris*, 536 U.S. 639 (2002).

my church. Similarly, if the government gives a voucher to parents with the restriction it must be used for the education of children, then parents should have complete freedom to purchase education at any kind of school, so long as it meets certain requirements of academic quality.

(b) Sometimes people think this objection is based on the First Amendment to the Constitution, which guarantees religious freedom. But this objection misunderstands the First Amendment. The First Amendment was only intended to prohibit *the governmental establishment of one certain church* or religion as the official state church. It was never intended to prevent all government support for everything that is done by a church. In addition, the vouchers are not restricted to be used at only one particular denominational school or religiously oriented school, but can be used at any kind of school that the parents choose.

(c) The goal of civil government with regard to education should be to produce educated citizens for the next generation. If that is being done through a voucher system, then the government's goal is being accomplished. The goal of government should not be *to prevent children from obtaining education* in a school that also teaches religious values. It should be no part of the government's purpose to *prevent* children from receiving religious training.

The primary barrier to adopting a school voucher system is the massive political influence of the NEA and the support of this union by the Democratic Party. In 2007 a statewide voucher system was established in Utah, but the NEA mounted a massive political campaign, spent $3.2 million, and defeated the program in a state referendum.[18] If even one state could adopt such a system and the public could see its success for a few years, parents around the nation would demand a similar program.

One striking example of Democratic opposition at the national level to school vouchers was seen in 2009 in Washington, DC. This city voted 92.9% for President Obama in the 2008 election,[19] and it is historically a Democratic stronghold. It also has an unusually high poverty level of 23%.[20] Yet the city established a very successful voucher program in a desperate attempt to improve the city's failing schools. However, the US Congress has governing authority over the District of Columbia, and when the new Democratic majority in both the House and Senate took office in January 2009, they cut off future funding for this voucher

---

18. "Utah Voters Defeat Measure to Create U.S. First Statewide School Voucher Program," Associated Press (Nov. 7, 2007). www.foxnews.com/story/0,2933,308936,00.html.

19. See www.usatoday.com/news/politics/election2008/dc.htm.

20. District of Columbia: Poverty Rate by Race/Ethnicity, states (2006–2007), US (2007), StateHealthFacts.org. www.statehealthfacts.org/profileind.jsp?ind=14&cat=1&rgn=10.

program. The Senate vote was 58–39 to kill the voucher program in the Omnibus Appropriations Act.[21] Only two Democrats voted to keep the funding, while 36 Republicans and 1 independent voted to keep the voucher program alive.[22]

The Democratic mayor and other local political leaders vigorously protested these cuts, but Congress turned a blind eye. (Many Democratic members of Congress as well as President Obama choose to send their own children to private schools rather than the Washington public schools, but they would not allow this choice for poor parents in that same district.)

Where there is no voucher system, other plans can also significantly expand parental choice in education. For example, some states have established a system of tax credits for tuition payments to any public or private schools, a system that has an effect similar to that of vouchers.

Scholars Abigail and Stephan Thernstrom have devoted years of their lives to researching the state of education in the United States and especially the racial gaps in educational achievement. They report the glaring and tragic failure of American schools to educate children, especially black and Hispanic children:

> Another generation of black children is drifting through school without acquiring essential skills and knowledge. Hispanic children are not faring much better, and for neither group is there a comforting trend in the direction of progress....
>
> How do we actually know how much students are learning? The best evidence comes from the National Assessment of Educational Progress (NAEP).... The NAEP results consistently show a frightening gap between the basic academic skills of the average African-American or Latino student and those of the typical white or Asian American. By twelfth grade, on average, black students are four years behind those who are white or Asian. Hispanics don't do much better....
>
> Imagine that you are an employer considering two job applicants, one with a high school diploma, the other a dropout at

21. Elizabeth Hillgrove, "Senate Kills GOP's D.C. Vouchers Bid," *Washington Times* (March 11, 2009). www.washingtontimes.com/news/2009/mar/11/senate-kills-gops-dc-vouchers-bid/.

22. The two Democratic senators were Robert Byrd of West Virginia and Mark Warner of Virginia. The independent was Joseph Lieberman of Connecticut. See "Federally-Funded Private and Religious School Vouchers." http://action.aclu.org/site/VoteCenter?page=voteInfo&voteId=9110.

the end of eighth grade.... an employer will seldom find the choice between the two candidates difficult. The employer hiring the typical black high school graduate (or the college that admits the average black student) is, in effect, choosing a youngster who has made it only through eighth grade. He or she will have a high school diploma, but not the skills that should come with it.... blacks nearing the end of their high school education perform a little worse than white eighth-graders in both reading and U.S. history, and a lot worse in math and geography.... Hispanics do only a little better than African Americans.[23]

The Thernstroms illustrate this with a shocking graph of skill levels:[24]

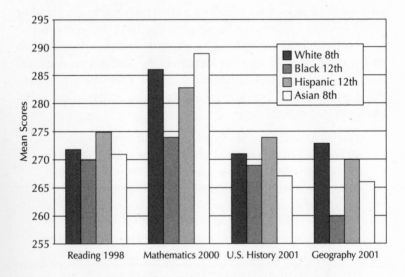

Sources: National Assessment for Educational Progress Data Tool

This is a national tragedy of immense proportions. Lack of educational skills perpetuates a permanent economic "underclass" in our society, for education is the primary determinant of earning capacity for life. But the responsibility for this tragedy lies squarely with the failed public school system and the NEA that uses its monopoly power over tax-supported schools to prevent real school choice.

---

23. Abigail Thernstrom and Stephan Thernstrom, *No Excuses: Closing the Racial Gap in Learning* (New York: Simon & Schuster, 2003), 11–15.
24. Ibid., 13.

Throwing more money at the same failed schools will not solve the problem, the Thernstroms point out, because the teachers unions have such a stranglehold on public schools that poor teachers cannot be fired and the best teachers cannot be given enough incentives to excel or to stay in teaching as a career. The Thernstroms write,

> Big-city superintendents, as well as principals, operate in a straitjacket.... the enormous power of teachers unions stops almost all real change in its tracks.... It is no accident that the revolutionary schools we describe in Chapters 3 and 4 [where they detail several examples of high-performing schools in low-income areas] are outside the traditional public system.[25]

Later they continue the same theme:

> We have described some wonderful public schools where youngsters living in distressed communities throve. But it is no accident that none of them is a traditional public school. They are charter schools.... The principals in these charter schools have real power — over their budgets, their discipline policies, and their staffing.... But no entire urban school district has been able to achieve results comparable to those we found in the best charter schools, and we doubt that any ever will without fundamental reform in the structure of public education.[26]
>
> The job of unions is to protect the interests of teachers. The job of schools is to educate the students. Many well-meaning reformers ... fail to understand the difference between the two objectives.... What's good for unions is not necessarily good for kids.... When there's a vacancy, the most senior applicant gets the position.... Quality is irrelevant.... Getting rid of an unwanted teacher, however, can be an expensive nightmare.... tenured teachers who can't teach, can't control a class, and behave in manifestly unacceptable ways are in the system as long as they want to stay, with rare exceptions.[27]

As for a solution, the Thernstroms emphasize the importance of providing parents with *the ability to choose which schools their children attend*, which would introduce the necessary element of competition, leading to better-quality schools. The Thernstroms write in their conclusion,

---

25. Ibid., 7.
26. Ibid., 249.
27. Ibid., 259–61.

Vouchers are a matter of basic equity. The term "middle class" is slippery, but here's one good definition: Middle-class parents are people who can choose where their children go to school by choosing where they live. Choice should not be a class-based privilege.... The racial gap is thus the most important civil rights issue of our time. If Americans care about racial equality ... they must demand more than the current reform movement is offering—standards, tests, some consequences for educational failure, and limited public school choice.[28]

What do the Thernstroms say is a real solution, one that will go beyond these current "reforms" that have had such limited success? These two experts, who know more than perhaps anyone else in America about the shameful racial gap in education, say *the entire system must be reformed, with genuine educational choice* made available to lower-income parents, indeed to all parents. Their final conclusion is this:

The nation's system of education must be fundamentally altered, with real educational choice as part of the package.[29]

I am convinced that care about racial reconciliation in our country, care for all our country's children, and care for the future of our country requires no less than such fundamental, total reform of our educational system.

D. DISCIPLINE OF CHILDREN AND SPANKING

The biblical passages cited earlier give strong support to the idea that parents have the primary responsibility for training their children. Other passages indicate that "discipline" will be a part of that process:

Fathers, do not provoke your children to anger, but bring them up in the *discipline* and instruction of the Lord (Eph. 6:4).

Besides this, we have had earthly fathers *who disciplined us* and we respected them. Shall we not much more be subject to the Father of spirits and live?... *For the moment all discipline seems painful* rather than pleasant, but later it yields the peaceful fruit of righteousness to those who have been trained by it (Heb. 12:9, 11).

---

28. Ibid., 273–74.
29. Ibid., 274.

In some European countries and elsewhere, laws now prohibit parents from spanking their children ("corporal punishment") as part of the disciplinary process. Australia, Sweden, Finland, Norway, Austria, Cyprus, Denmark, Latvia, Croatia, Bulgaria, Germany, Israel, Iceland, Romania, Ukraine, and Hungary have all outlawed corporal punishment.[30] (In Sweden, in spite of such a law, it is interesting that assaults by adults against children between the ages of one and six had increased fourfold between 1984 and 1994.)[31] Similar laws have been considered in parts of the United States as well—Massachusetts[32] and California,[33] for example—but they have not been adopted.

One antispanking crusader named Jordan Riak proposed "no-spanking zones" that would stigmatize parents.[34] He wrote in 1997:

> Whether any child, on any pretext, in any circumstance, should be subjected to physical battery, and whether such treatment is beneficial to the child, should have ceased long ago to be matters for serious debate. The fact is that the deliberate traumatization of a child by a caretaker is destructive to that child.... Some of our citizens cling to an anachronistic notion that children are chattels and that their owners have a right, or are even dutybound, to control their property by violent means and may assign that right to others, such as teachers. The Proverbs of King Solomon have been cited, on occasion as their authority.... My hunch is that the fundamentalists' fondness for Old Testament authority is driven by a need for self-exculpation over their mistreatment of children.[35]

The testimony of the Bible is clear, however, that effective discipline of children will at times include the infliction of some kind of physical pain, not to bring actual physical damage to the child's body, but to emphasize the significantly wrong or dangerous character of the behavior that led

30. World Corporal Punishment Research, www.corpun.com/rules.htm.

31. "Kriminalistatistk vid SCB," 115 81 Stockholm, vol. 5 (1995): cited in John S. Lyons and Robert E. Lazelere, "Where Is Evidence That Non-Abusive Punishment Increases Aggression?" Presented at the XXVI International Congress of Pyschology (Aug. 18, 1996). http://faculty.biola.edu/paulp/sweden.html.

32. "Should Spanking Your Child Be Illegal?" *ABCNews.com* (Nov. 28, 2007). http://abc-news.go.com/GMA/story?id=3924024.

33. Nancy Vogel, "A Spanking Ban: Are We Going to Get It?" *Los Angeles Times* (Jan. 20, 2007). http://articles.latimes.com/2007/jan/20/local/me-spanking20.

34. Jordan Riak: quoted in Edward Wong, "No-Spanking Zone Sought in Oakland," *Los Angeles Times* (Jan. 24, 1999), A10.

35. Jordan Riak, "Spanking and Hitting Are Perilous," *The Brown University Child and Adolescent Behavior Letter,* 13:9 (Sept. 1997), 1.

to the discipline. Such use of "the rod" (probably a wooden stick of some sort) to strike a child is viewed as the responsibility of a parent and an indication of the parent's love for a child (a love that strongly desires right behavior in the child). That is the point of the following verses:

> Whoever *spares the rod* [Hebrew *shebet*, here a rod or stick of wood] hates his son, but he who loves him is diligent to discipline him (Prov. 13:24).

> Folly is bound up in the heart of a child, but *the rod of discipline* drives it far from him (22:15).

This verse indicates that imposing physical punishment (in a wise and nonexcessive manner) is a help in overcoming the tendency to do wrong in every child's heart.

> Do not withhold discipline from a child; *if you strike him with a rod*, he will not die. If you strike him with the rod, you will save his soul from Sheol (Prov. 23:13–14).

> *The rod* and reproof give wisdom, but a child left to himself brings shame to his mother (29:15).

Related verses compare the discipline of earthly parents with the discipline of God himself and also show the benefit of such discipline in the life of a child:

> My son, do not despise the LORD's discipline or be weary of his reproof, for the LORD reproves him whom he loves, as a father the son in whom he delights (Prov. 3:11–12; see also Heb. 12:6).

> Discipline your son, for there is hope; do not set your heart on putting him to death (19:18).

> Discipline your son, and he will give you rest; he will give delight to your heart (29:17).

The laws already in place in the United States are sufficient to guard against genuine physical abuse of children and bring appropriate punishment where that occurs. But such laws should not be expanded to rule out the use of such physical discipline as spanking a child. A biblically based system of values understands that when spanking is administered wisely and with restraint, it is beneficial, not harmful, in the raising of children. Yet the Bible also cautions that parents should not be so demanding that they cause frustration and despair in their children: "Fathers, do not provoke your children, lest they become discouraged" (Col. 3:21).

From time to time the news media report various new scholarly studies claiming to "prove" that spanking does no good or is psychologically harmful to children. But these studies seldom if ever distinguish wise, nonabusive spanking that causes temporary pain but no physical harm from more violent beatings that bring serious bruising or other physical harm to children; they also fail to distinguish wise, restrained parental spanking from unjustified rage and actual physical abuse coming from drunken or pathologically abusive parents. Thus the studies are skewed and give distorted results.

Dr. Murray Straus of the University of New Hampshire is one of the most outspoken voices calling for the banishment of corporal punishment and has from time to time issued skewed and distorted studies to try to advance his agenda. Straus over the years has tried to link corporal punishment to lower IQs in children[36] and to antisocial behavior.[37]

In response to one of Straus's studies, even *Time* magazine, hardly an advocate for corporal punishment, wrote about the flawed methodology:

> The problem has to do with who was in the study. Straus and company culled their information from telephone interviews conducted by the U.S. Bureau of Labor Statistics beginning in 1979 with 807 mothers of children ages 6 to 9. They were then asked how many times they had spanked their children in the past week and what the kids' behavior was like — did they lie, cheat, act up in school? Then the bureau polled the same group two years later. Sure enough, the kids who had been spanked had become increasingly anti-social.
>
> But when you look a little closer at the findings, they start to seem a little murky. To begin with, observes Dr. Den Trumbull, a Montgomery, Alabama pediatrician … the mothers ranged in age from 14 to 21. That is hardly a slice of American motherhood. Moreover, those who spanked did so on average twice a week. These factors, says Trumbull, plus the fact that some of the kids were as old as nine, "are markers of a dysfunctional family in my mind, and in the minds of most psychologists and pediatricians."
>
> Trumbull also observed that limiting the study to 6 to 9 year olds skewed the results; by then the kids can understand the consequences of their actions. For them frequent physical punishment is likely to be humiliating and traumatic — and might well lead to worse behavior down the line.

---

36. "Want Smarter Kids? Don't Spank Them," *Reuters* (Aug. 3, 1999), and "Children who are spanked have lower IQs, new research finds," www.physorg.com/pdf173077612.pdf.

37. Murray A. Straus, Ph.D.; David B. Sugarman, Ph.D.; Jean Giles-Sims, Ph.D., Archives of Pediatric and Adolescent Medicine, vol. 151 (Aug. 1997), 761–67.

> Trouble is, while spanking is down, child abuse is up. It appears that well-meaning professionals have been using the wrong whipping boy—and Straus' study offers little reason to change that assessment.[38]

In 1993, a group of American pediatricians presented a review of all articles on corporal punishment to the American Academy of Pediatrics. Their results found that of the 132 studies that supposedly documented negative effects of corporal punishment on children, only 24 had any empirical data. All the others were either editorials, commentaries, opinions, or reviews. And of the 24 valid studies, 23 had ambiguous wording and broad definitions that skewed the results. They found that physical punishment was defined to include anything from mild spanking to beating a child with a hair brush or electrical cord to pouring boiling water on the child. They concluded that the studies failed to "entirely answer the real scientific issue—does occasional spanking aid or harm the development of a child's ability to learn?"[39]

Christians should be suspicious of supposedly conclusive "expert studies" that result in telling parents that they should not do exactly what the Bible tells them to do.

Of course, opponents of spanking can always bring up extreme examples of abuse and of harsh distortion of biblical standards. Christians shouldn't advocate such actions either, but should instead oppose them. It must be kept in mind, however, that the *abuse* of something (such as spanking of children) does not prove that *the action itself* is wrong. Anything good can be abused or used wrongfully.

Gene Edward Veith, provost at Patrick Henry College and former executive director of the Cranach Institute at Concordia Theological Seminary, wrote in *World* magazine that *not* spanking children is actually a form of child abuse:

> Not only the ACLU but also many educators, child psychologists, and even parents subscribe to the "expressive" theory of mental health. According to this model, human beings, deep down, are basically good. They simply need to express their feelings they have inside. Obstacles to this expression—such as "society rules," "oppressive" authority figures, and "judgmental" belief systems—cause repression and thus mental unhappi-

38. Michael D. Lemonick, "Spare the Rod? Maybe," *Time* (Aug. 25, 1997).

39. Dr. David Larson, "Is Mild Spanking Abusive or Helpful for Young Children?" Physicians Research Forum Research Summary (1993).

ness and twisted behavior. Under this worldview, any attempt to control or punish or suppress the feelings of a child is construed as cruel. And disciplining a child becomes next to impossible.... For all the attempts to discipline children through "positive reinforcement" and such non-painful methods as "time outs" and guilt trips, young people are learning that since adults will not exert force against them, they can pretty much ignore those in authority ... allowing children to grow up without discipline—however kindly it appears on the surface—is child abuse, an expression of our culture's hatred for children.[40]

We should not be surprised that many non-Christians will seek to argue against spanking. Many of them do not think that there is a tendency toward evil in human hearts, including the hearts of children. But this is contrary to a Christian worldview, which holds that there is a tendency to evil (as well as a competing tendency to do good, by common grace) in every child's heart. Therefore a non-Christian worldview is less likely to think that children should be disciplined for the wrong that they do. Moreover, many people's non-Christian worldview does not believe that superior physical force should be necessary to restrain evil, but a Christian view understands that some of the evil in people's hearts is so irrational that it cannot be restrained by reasoning but only by force. When applied to the discipline of children, the Christian worldview understands that there is sometimes a need for a spanking and that this quickly overcomes willful or irrational wrongdoing in a way that hours of pleading and reasoning will not accomplish, and it helps build a more righteous character in the child.

Another deeper reason underlying the opposition to physical punishment of children may be, in at least some cases, opposition to the very idea of *parental authority* over children (because of a dislike of all authority) or opposition to the idea that parents can know better than children what is right and wrong (because of a belief that nobody can know right or wrong for anyone else). In a number of cases this opposition to all spanking may be strengthened by a deep spiritual influence (an evil influence) that seeks to undermine God's plan for the family and for the restraint of evil in children's lives.

40. Gene Edward Veith, "Hating Our Children," *World* (June 12, 1999). www.worldmag.com/articles/2936.

Chapter 6

FREEDOM OF SPEECH

A. BIBLICAL TEACHING

Several arguments from earlier chapters provide the biblical basis for a government to protect freedom of speech in a nation.

1. To prevent the abuse of power by government

Because of the tendency to sin that is in the heart of every human being (Rom. 3:23), when rulers obtain government power, there is always a temptation for them to use that power not for the good of the people but for the benefit of the ruler himself or his friends or family. Thus government power tends to corrupt people (1 Sam. 8:11–17; 2 Sam. 11:1–27). But if a society safeguards freedom of speech, that tends to restrain government officials, because it makes them more accountable to the people. Freedom of speech allows people to speak out and criticize the government when they think it is doing something wrong.

2. To enable government to be chosen by the people

There are significant reasons to hold that the Bible gives support to the idea that government should be chosen by the people themselves, which in practice means some kind of democracy (note the assumptions behind Gen. 1:27; Exod. 4:29–31; 2 Sam. 2:4; Rom. 13:4).

If there is freedom of speech in a nation, then people are able to express their own ideas about what kind of government policy should be adopted and what candidates should be elected to office. Therefore freedom of speech in a society is necessary to protect the idea of democracy itself. Without freedom of speech (and freedom of the press), rulers could suppress any criticism of their actions and prohibit opposing candidates or any critics from being able to express their views in public. Then a true democracy would cease to exist in that society.

3. To protect human liberty

Governments should also safeguard human liberty, which the Bible views as a highly valued privilege in the sight of God (Exod. 20:2; Lev. 25:10; Deut. 30:19; Isa. 61:1). But one significant part of human liberty is the ability to express our ideas freely and attempt to persuade others of those ideas. Therefore this is another reason for governments to protect freedom of speech (and freedom of the press).

4. To protect religious speech

When freedom of speech in general is protected in a society, religious speech in particular will also be protected. This should be a very important value for Christians to defend, because it enables them to speak the Gospel message freely in public (and so obey Matt. 28:19–20) without fear of censorship or punishment.

5. To protect the ability of individuals to think and decide issues for themselves

The Bible places a high value on respecting human freedom of choice (Deut. 30:19; Josh. 24:15; Matt. 11:28; Rev. 22:17). But protecting peoples' ability to think and decide issues freely for themselves means that they must be able to have access to arguments on all sides of an issue. This can only happen if freedom of speech is permitted in a society and if all the different viewpoints on an issue are able to be freely expressed.

B. THE UNITED STATES CONSTITUTION

The founders of the United States realized that freedom of speech (along with its closely related idea of freedom of the press) is such an important protection that it was included in the First Amendment:

> Congress shall make no law respecting an establishment of religion, or prohibiting the free exercise thereof; *or abridging the freedom of speech, or of the press*, or the right of the people peace-

ably to assemble, and to petition the Government for a redress of grievances.[1]

This amendment was important as a means of guarding against excessive power in the federal government, one of the primary goals of the framers of the Constitution as they sought to prevent the kind of abuse of government that they had experienced from Great Britain.

This amendment was also a significant part of protecting human liberty, for the preface of the Constitution said that one of the purposes of the government and the Constitution was to "secure the blessings of liberty to ourselves and our posterity." Several years earlier, in the Declaration of Independence, the founders had listed "liberty" among the "certain unalienable rights" that had been given to each person "by their Creator." Therefore, protecting freedom of speech and freedom of the press was important because they were crucial components in protecting human liberty.

With this background, we can now consider some specific topics related to freedom of speech.

C. RESTRICTIONS ON FREEDOM OF SPEECH

Should any restrictions be placed on freedom of speech (and, similarly, on freedom of the press)?

For many years there have been four commonly accepted categories of speech that are still illegal and are not protected by the First Amendment. The first category is defamation—that is, speech that is false and wrongfully harms the reputation of another person. Laws against libel and slander fall under this category. The second category is incitement to riot—that is, it is illegal to shout, "Fire!" in a crowded theater, which would promote a panic and directly cause immediate harm to many people. The third and fourth categories are obscenity and child pornography.[2]

D. CAMPAIGN FINANCE RESTRICTIONS

1. The goal

The stated goals of legal restrictions on financial contributions to political campaigns are usually said to be (a) removing the corrupting influ-

---

1. Amendment 1, United States Constitution. www.law.cornell.edu/constitution/constitution.billofrights.html.

2. Henry Cohen, "Child Pornography: Constitutional Principles and Federal Statutes," *CRS Report for Congress* (Oct. 15, 2003). www.firstamendmentcenter.org/pdf/CRS.childporn1.pdf.

ence of money from politics, and (b) giving every citizen an equal voice in political discussions.

But law professor Bradley Smith, who is also a former chairman of the Federal Election Commission and served on the FEC from 2000 to 2005, looks back at the historical record and sees a much more partisan goal:

> Campaign-finance reform is creating an intrusive regulatory regime on all levels of government. Its proponents, mostly on the left, have chiefly used it to bolster their own political fortunes and to undermine limited, constitutional government.... From the mid–1960s on, opinion polls showed steady erosion in public support for big government and liberalism.... By 1970, Democrats feared—with reason—that their longstanding electoral majority was in jeopardy.
>
> To help prevent that outcome, the Democrats passed the Federal Election Campaign Act (FECA) in 1971 (and amended it three years later), which would, they hoped, strike at the heart of Republican political power—while leaving untouched their own sources of influence, such as union-organized volunteers. The law tightly limited both political contributions and any expenditure that might "influence" an election....
>
> Campaign-finance reform neatly accomplishes Democrats' goal of muffling political speech on the right.[3]

Smith also points out that when supporters of such laws talk about removing "corrupting influences" from politics and giving every person an equal voice, they leave alone "important sources of influence—including academia, and Hollywood, both tilting to the left."[4] Then he points out that "the press" is also untouched by these restrictions.

2. The real effects of campaign finance restrictions

The real effect of campaign finance restriction laws, therefore, is not to "level the playing field" and give every person an equal voice. It is simply to remove much of the influence of private citizens who want to use their own contributions to support candidates they believe in. But if this kind of influence of average citizens is restricted by these laws, then where does the remaining influence in politics come from? That is, is

---

3. Bradley Smith, "The Speech Police," *Wall Street Journal* (Jan. 27, 2007), A13.
4. Ibid.

there any *advantage* that the restrictions give *to other groups*? Yes, there certainly is, for some remaining groups are not affected by these laws and therefore gain influence.

Here are the real beneficiaries of campaign finance restriction laws:

(1) *Incumbents* benefit, because they already have the huge advantage of name recognition.

(2) *The press* gains influence, because if there are spending limits on campaign advertising, then people will mostly get their information about candidates from what the press writes and broadcasts. And it is unquestionable that the majority of the press (both newspaper and TV) in the United States favors more liberal candidates. A May 2004 survey conducted by the Pew Research Center for the People in the Press of 547 journalists, including 247 in the national media, found the following:

- Five times more national journalists identify themselves as "liberal" (34%) than "conservative" (just 7%).
- The percentage of national reporters saying they are liberal has increased, from 22% in 1995 to 34% in 2004. The percentage of self-identified conservatives remains low, rising from 4% in 1995 to 7% in 2004.
- Liberals also outnumber conservatives in local newsrooms; 23% of the local journalists they questioned say they are liberals, while about half as many (12%) call themselves conservative.
- Fully 91% of those who work at national news organizations say it is *not* necessary to believe in God to be moral; 78% of local journalists agree.[5]

(3) *Labor unions* gain influence, because they are not subject to these finance restrictions, and they provide large amounts of funding and volunteer labor for more liberal candidates. In 2008, the Service Employees International Union spent $27 million through what are called "527 organizations" (more on that later) to elect candidates sympathetic to labor unions.[6]

(4) *Hollywood movies* gain influence, and they lean reliably to the left. One example is Michael Moore's *Fahrenheit 9/11*, which was a virulently anti-Bush movie. But because it was a movie, it was exempt from Federal Election Commission regulation. By contrast, there was

---

5. "How Journalists See Journalists in 2004," *Pew Research Center for the People and the Press*, 24. http://people-press.org/reports/pdf/214.pdf.

6. "Top 50 Federally Focused Organizations," Center for Responsive Politics. www.opensecrets.org/527s/527cmtes.php?level=C&cycle=2008.

an alternative movie that responded to much of what Michael Moore publicized in *Fahrenheit 9/11,* and that was produced by a conservative group called Citizens United. But when they tried to release the film, the FEC objected, saying it had to submit to the campaign finance regulation laws. This was because it was not produced by a Hollywood film studio that is "normally in the movie business."[7] (However, Citizens United won their case when they appealed this matter to the US Supreme Court. In a 5–4 decision in the case *Citizens United v. FEC,* announced January 21, 2010, the court overturned parts of the McCain-Feingold bill and declared that corporations and unions could purchase political ads [but not contribute directly to candidates] at any point in an election cycle. I see this decision, which also grants more freedom to nonprofit corporations, as a significant victory for freedom of speech in the United States.)

(5) *University faculty members* gain influence, and they have significant impact on young voters who are in or have recently graduated from universities. But university faculty members overwhelmingly tilt leftward in their political convictions. A 2005 poll of college and university faculty headed by Robert Lichter, a professor at George Mason University, found that 72% of the faculty described themselves as liberal, compared with only 15% who called themselves conservative. Some 50% said they were Democrats, compared with only 11% who said they were Republicans; 51% said that they rarely or never attended church. Lichter said, "What's most striking is how few conservatives there are in any field. There was no field we studied in which there were more conservatives than liberals or more Republicans than Democrats. It's a very homogenous environment, not just in the places you'd expect to be dominated by liberals."[8]

(6) *Super-wealthy candidates* benefit, because the campaign finance laws still allow a candidate to contribute unlimited amounts of money to his own campaign. Therefore these laws have not "kept the money out of politics," but they have made it much more difficult for an ordinary citizen of modest means to enter a campaign on his own when an opponent can simply chip in millions or even tens of millions of dollars of his own money and far outspend any opponent of moderate means.

This is one reason why there are numerous multimillionaires now in prominent political offices in the United States. A report in November

---

7. Smith, "Speech Police," A13.

8. Howard Kurtz, "College Faculties a Most Liberal Lot, Study Finds," *Washington Post* (March 29, 2005). www.washingtonpost.com/wp-dyn/articles/A8427–2005Mar28.html.

2009 said there are now 237 millionaires in Congress![9] This includes many Democrats such as Herbert Kohl of Wisconsin (worth about $214.5 million through Kohl's discount clothing stores) and Senator John Kerry of Massachusetts (worth about $208.8 million and married to Theresa Heinz Kerry of the Heinz food fortune). House Speaker Nancy Pelosi was the twenty-second-wealthiest person in Congress ($31.4 million). There are also some wealthy Republicans, such as Darrell Issa of California ($251 million) and Vernon Buchanan of Florida ($142 million), but in 2008, eight of the ten wealthiest members of Congress were Democrats.[10]

Another effect of these campaign finance laws has been to make it much more difficult for ordinary citizens to run for office or even participate in a campaign. Former FEC Chairman Bradley Smith quotes several examples from a file of numerous letters he received from ordinary citizens who, without intending to violate any law, were tripped up by complex reporting requirements for campaign finances and were facing fines for doing what they thought was simply carrying out their civic duty of participating in a political campaign.

For example, when four men made a homemade sign that said "VOTE REPUBLICAN: NOT AL GORE SOCIALISM" and put it on the side of a trailer next to a Texas highway, the FEC spent nearly *eighteen months* investigating them for improper documentation![11] An experienced CPA who had served as an unpaid campaign treasurer on a volunteer basis, but who was being fined more than $7,000 for improper reporting, wrote to the FEC, "No job I have ever undertaken caused me more stress than this one. I was frightened and concerned every day that I would do something wrong."[12] Rather than enabling *ordinary citizens* to participate in the political process, these laws are frightening people away from participating in politics in any way. They are chilling and destroying ordinary freedom of speech in the nation.

Finally, the real effect of these laws has *not* been to keep money out of politics. Hundreds of millions of dollars are still spent, first,

---

9. "Congressmen Lose Big Bucks in 2008, But Still Rank Among Nation's Richest," Center for Responsive Politics (Nov. 4, 2008). www.opensecrets.org/news/2009/11/congressmen-lose-big-bucks-in.html.

10. For a list, see the website of the Center for Responsive Politics at www.opensecrets.org/pfds/overview.php?type=W&year=2008 (accessed Nov. 10, 2009). The website cautions that the public disclosure forms required of members of Congress only list assets in broad ranges of value, so these estimates are approximate.

11. Ibid.

12. Ibid.

because wealthy candidates contribute their own money to their campaigns, and second, because a loophole was discovered in the law by which so-called "527 organizations" could raise unlimited amounts of money and spend unlimited amounts of money to influence elections so long as they don't coordinate the activities with any specific candidate or party. For example, in the 2003–4 election campaign, currency speculator George Soros was reported to have donated more than $23.5 million to 527 organizations (such as MoveOn.org) that were dedicated to preventing the reelection of George W. Bush as President and Republicans to Congress.[13] If such a man can spend over $23 million to influence an election, then of what use are the current laws that place a $2,400 annual limit on personal contributions to a candidate? Soros contributed *10,000 times* that much! Our campaign finance laws greatly hinder ordinary citizens from giving more support to their candidate, but they simply have not been able to keep money out of politics.

3. Campaign finance laws have become a booby-trapped minefield that can destroy innocent people

Because the campaign finance laws have become so complex and confusing, it is remarkably easy for citizens and candidates who intend nothing wrong to find themselves accused of campaign finance violations.

A former commissioner on the Federal Election Commission, Hans A. von Spakovsky, explains:

> The Federal Election Campaign Act (FECA), enacted in 1972, is 244 pages of restrictions and requirements. The regulations issued by the FEC are an additional 568 pages. The Federal Register is filled with 1,278 pages of explanations and justifications from the FEC for its regulation. The FEC has issued almost 1,800 advisory opinions since 1975, trying to explain to a confused regulated community the meaning of various provisions of FECA. The law and the regulations are a Byzantine labyrinth that burdens the ability to participate in political debate and federal elections.[14]

---

13. "Going Out on Top," Center for Responsive Politics (Aug. 9, 2005). www.opensecrets.org/capital_eye/inside.php?ID=179.

14. Hans A. von Spakovsky, "What's Wrong with 'Hillary: the Movie'?" *Wall Street Journal* (Aug. 29, 2009), A13.

4. Restricting campaign contributions is restricting freedom of speech

In light of the preceding information, it seems clear that the United States should simply recognize that *restricting contributions to political campaigns is restricting freedom of speech* and is actually contrary to the First Amendment. In modern society it is impossible to get a message out to enough people to win an election unless you have the money to buy advertising on TV, on the Internet, and through print media and mailings. Simply saying that I have freedom of speech to knock on doors in my neighborhood is not sufficient, because it would be impossible for me or any other candidate to reach enough voters to get a message out effectively in the time available for any political campaign today other than at a very small, local level.

This is why eight former commissioners on the Federal Election Commission filed a brief that urged the Supreme Court to overrule two of its previous decisions and declare that the McCain-Feingold campaign finance law of 2002 is unconstitutional. One of these commissioners writes:

> It's clear to us that the D.C. Court's decision should be over-turned on First Amendment grounds and McCain-Feingold ruled unconstitutional....[15]

The eight former commissioners argue that current campaign finance restrictions

> fundamentally violate the First Amendment and have chilled political speech.... The law and its accompanying regulations are so complex and so confusing that ordinary citizens, and even specialists, have a hard time understanding what's legally permissible and what's not.[16]

5. What is the solution?

It seems to me that the solution would be to abolish all these restrictions on campaign financing except for a requirement that all donations above a certain amount ($500? or $1,000?) be publicly reported, so that the public is aware of where the funding and the influence is coming from for various political advertisements.

15. Ibid.
16. Ibid.

Some may object that abolishing these finance restrictions will enable various people to "buy" elections. But they fail to realize that *unlimited amounts of money can already be spent by super-wealthy candidates on their own campaigns* (note all the millionaires in Congress). Still, while millions of dollars can help, sometimes wealthy candidates are defeated. On November 3, 2009, for example, Jon Corzine was defeated in his reelection attempt as governor of New Jersey, even though he had spent massive amounts of his own money to attempt to win the election. (Corzine was a former chairman and co-CEO of the investment firm Goldman Sachs.) Over the years he had spent $130 million in his bids for higher office, and in October 2009 alone, he "lent" his campaign $4.7 million dollars.[17] Also, Mitt Romney, who has an estimated net worth between $100 and $200 million, was unable to win the Republican presidential nomination, though he spent $42 million in his loss to John McCain.[18] In 1992 and 1996, Texas billionaire Ross Perot spent $63.5 million on his independent bids for President,[19] and Steve Forbes spent $38 million on his 1996 run for President. Both failed to win.[20]

E. CAMPUS "HATE SPEECH" CODES AND OTHER RESTRICTIONS OF FREE SPEECH ON COLLEGE CAMPUSES

In the past twenty years many colleges and universities in the United States (and even governments in other countries) have enacted policies that restrict freedom of speech in various ways. The Foundation for Individual Rights in Education (FIRE) has reported that 253 public universities have "speech code" policies that can be used to severely restrict free speech, including religious speech. This is 97% of all public universities![21] Whereas previous restrictions of freedom of speech were only because some speech could cause immediate harm to other people (such as slander or inciting to riot), these new "hate speech" regulations attempted to restrict speech that would cause "offense" to someone else.

---

17. Bill Pascoe, "Corzine's Self-Funded Campaign: Will Taxpayers Get Stuck with the Tab?" *CQ Politics* (Oct. 30, 2009). http://blogs.cqpolitics.com/in_the_right/2009/10/corzine.html.

18. "Romney Put in $42 Million of His Own Fortune," *Boston Globe* (Feb. 20, 2008). www.boston.com/news/politics/politicalintelligence/2008/02/romney_put_in_4.html.

19. Ibid.

20. Ibid.

21. "FIRE's Spotlight on Speech Codes 2009," Foundation for Individual Rights in Education (2009), 4.

Therefore new rules have been adopted that prohibit or penalize speech that would offend people because of their race, gender, religion, disability, national origin, or "sexual orientation."

Various kinds of restrictions on the speech of Christians and others with conservative moral views have often been the result.

1. Censoring the Gospel and expressions of Christian moral values

Because of such "hate speech" codes, sometimes students have been penalized for expressing belief in the Gospel of Jesus Christ or attempting to share their faith with others. In other cases, Christians have been penalized for expressing Christian moral values, such as a conviction that homosexual conduct is contrary to Scripture or supporting California's Proposition 8, which defined marriage as between one man and one woman.

The good news is that in numerous cases Christian legal organizations such as the Alliance Defense Fund (ADF) have had remarkable success in challenging these policies, claiming that they are an unconstitutional violation of the First Amendment's guarantees of freedom of speech. They have launched a special litigation effort to defend the God-given First Amendment freedoms of students at public universities (www.speakupmovement.org). As of November 2009, they have never lost a case litigated to conclusion against these unconstitutional policies. For example:

- Georgia Tech University enacted a speech code that prohibited "acts of intolerance," engaged in viewpoint discrimination by defunding religious student groups, and fostered a state-approved religious view of homosexual behavior by informing students to shun religious groups that do not affirm homosexual behavior. A federal court ruled that the speech code be replaced, and it later found that the program denigrating religions that do not approve of homosexual behavior was unconstitutional.[22]
- After ADF attorneys filed suit, officials at Savannah State University in Georgia quickly settled with a student group that had been dismissed from campus for engaging in "harassment," because they shared their faith with other students, and "hazing," because they engaged in the biblical practice of footwashing. The group was restored to campus.[23]

---

22. *Sklar v. Georgia Tech.*
23. *Commissioned II Love v. Scott.*

- ADF attorneys in the state of Washington filed a lawsuit against officials of Community Colleges of Spokane and Spokane Falls Community College for violating the constitutional rights of pro-life students. SFCC officials threatened Beth Sheeran and members of a Christian student group with disciplinary measures, including expulsion, if they chose to hold a pro-life event on campus to share information with other students, because the message was "discriminatory" and did not include a pro-abortion viewpoint. The school eventually settled.[24]

But the bad news is that such legal challenges are necessary at all in the United States, with its historic legacy of freedom of speech. There are thousands of students who never know they can file a legal challenge, but just quietly submit to these misguided restrictions on their speech.

2. Discrimination against Christian organizations

In a number of cases, Christian organizations such as InterVarsity Christian Fellowship or the Christian Legal Society have been prohibited from meeting on university campuses or being recognized as a legitimate university organization along with other organizations. In other cases these groups have been pressured to accept leaders who do not affirm their beliefs, and if they refuse, they are denied the right to meet on campus or use campus facilities to promote their meetings.

ADF has been involved in numerous legal cases involving these so-called "nondiscrimination" policies, which are used only to discriminate against Christians! Here are some examples:

- Rutgers University used a "nondiscrimination" statement to require an InterVarsity Christian Fellowship to accept leaders who reject the group's Christian beliefs. After an ADF attorney filed suit, the school quickly dropped their effort.[25] Conservative commentator Laura Ingraham said, "One can only imagine if a group of devout Christians tried to join a Rutgers lesbian student group. The Christians would probably be brought up on disciplinary charges, accused of violating Rutgers' 'principle of community.'"[26] Alan

---

24. *Sheeran v. Shea.*

25. "Rutgers University settles case fully in favor of the Rutgers InterVarsity Multi-Ethnic Christian Fellowship," *ADF Press Release* (April 2, 2003). www.alliancedefensefund.org/news/pressrelease.aspx?cid=2931.

26. Laura Ingraham, "Universities Throwing Christians to the Lions," *Laura Ingraham E-Blast* (Jan. 6, 2003).

Kors of FIRE commented that "if an evangelical Christian who believed homosexuality to be a sin tried to become president of the university's Bisexual, Gay, and Lesbian Alliance ... the administration would have led candlelight vigils on behalf of diversity and free expression."[27]

- Christian Legal Society chapters at Arizona State University,[28] Ohio State University,[29] and Southern Illinois University,[30] to name just a few, have had to file lawsuits with the help of ADF attorneys to successfully preserve their ability to reserve leadership positions for Christians.

- Officials at the University of North Carolina at Chapel Hill tried to force a Christian fraternity to open up its leadership to individuals who reject Christianity. ADF attorneys filed suit, and the school backed down.[31]

One recent high-profile case at the Supreme Court had the potential for a landmark ruling that would resolve such cases for the entire nation. The case *Christian Legal Society v. Martinez* involved a Christian Legal Society chapter that had been denied recognized student organization status at Hastings College of Law in San Francisco because it refused to agree to allow non-Christians to become officers and voting members. It also required its officers and voting members to refrain from unrepentant sexual conduct outside of marriage between one man and one woman. I was one of the authors of an *amicus curiae* ("friend of the court") brief in which evangelical scholars in Bible and theology argued that the CLS standards were necessary to their deeply held core religious beliefs and flowed directly and properly from their belief in the Bible as the inspired Word of God.[32] (Unfortunately, the Christian Legal Society lost this case in a 5-4 decision on June 28, 2010.)

27. John Leo, "Playing the Bias Card," *U.S. News and World Report* (Jan. 13, 2003).

28. "ADF and CLS Reach Settlement Agreement with Arizona State University," *ADF Press Release* (Sept. 5, 2005). www.alliancedefensefund.org/news/pressrelease.aspx?cid=3520.

29. "Ohio State University throws in the towel, agrees to change non-discrimination policy," *ADF Press Release* (Oct. 4, 2004). www.alliancedefensefund.org/news/pressrelease. aspx?cid=2811.

30. "Southern Illinois University settles lawsuit with Christian Legal Society, will recognize chapter," *ADF Press Release* (May 22, 2007). www.alliancedefensefund.org/news/press-release.aspx?cid=4126.

31. "Federal court to UNC-Chapel Hill: Suspend your policy," *ADF Press Release* (March 5, 2005). www.alliancedefensefund.org/news/pressrelease.aspx?cid=3358.

32. See Evangelical Scholars brief at www.abanet.org/publiced/preview/briefs/ pdfs/09 – 10/08 – 1371_PetitionerAmCuEvangelicalScholarsand2Grps.pdf.

Other examples of discrimination against Christian groups on public university campuses are related to student fees. The University of Virginia denied a Christian newspaper equal access to student fees because of its "Christian perspective" even though it funded other student publications. The case, *Rosenberger v. Rector and Visitors of the University of Virginia*, eventually went all the way to the US Supreme Court, which ruled that the university had acted unconstitutionally when it denied the paper the same funding that all other groups received.[33] (This was a 5–4 decision announced June 29, 1995, with Rehnquist, Kennedy, O'Connor, Scalia, and Thomas in the majority and Souter, Stevens, Ginsburg, and Breyer in dissent.) This case set a legal precedent that has been used to reverse hundreds of unconstitutional actions denying Christians equal access to public facilities and funding.

These cases and many others demonstrate that the Alliance Defense Fund and other Christian legal groups have had remarkable success in protecting the rights of these organizations to have campus access equal to that of any other student organization.

3. Conclusion

Almost uniformly, such "hate speech" codes constitute a wrongful restriction of freedom of speech. For the twenty years or so that such speech codes were allowed to operate freely on American campuses, they no doubt contributed to a remarkable muzzling of conservative moral and religious ideas (and probably conservative political ideas as well). Therefore they effectively indoctrinated students in more liberal moral, political, and religious values. This was done in many state universities with the funding provided by taxpayer dollars, yet the policies were promoting views explicitly *contrary* to the views of large numbers of citizens paying those taxes and supporting those universities, and *contrary* to the views of parents who were paying thousands of dollars in tuition for their children to attend those universities. Some extensive documentation of this effect has been produced in printed form and on DVD.[34]

---

33. Summary of *Rosenberger v. Rector and Visitors of the University of Virginia*, Alliance Defense Fund. www.alliancedefensefund.org/news/story.aspx?cid=2583.

34. See the film *Indoctrinate U*, written by Evan Coyne Malloney, which is available for purchase on Amazon.com, but I have not been able to find it available on Netflix—which is remarkable considering the thousands of DVDs they carry. Another documentation of such bias in universities is *One-Party Classroom: How Radical Professors at America's Top Colleges Indoctrinate Students and Undermine Our Democracy*, by David Horowitz and Jacob Laskin (New York: Crown Forum, 2009).

Such "hate speech" codes are wrong, both because they violate the biblical value of freedom of speech, which is grounded in a number of values mentioned in the first section of this chapter, and because, in the United States, they are violations of a basic constitutional right, the freedom of speech.

If the principle of freedom of speech does not protect speech that other people find offensive or objectionable, then it is not really freedom of speech at all. University campuses should especially be places where a wide diversity of viewpoints can be expressed freely without penalty and without fear of recrimination.

The argument that some speech might cause some people to *feel offended* might be an argument for personally advising the speaker to be more thoughtful in his speech, but it is certainly not an argument that any law or university policy should be used to bring penalties against the speaker.

Nor is it true that expressing *moral opposition* to a certain action *will inevitably lead to violence* against others. For instance, arguing that *abortion* is morally wrong does not *necessarily* or even *probably* lead people to take violent action against those who carry out abortions. Nor does arguing that *homosexual conduct* is morally wrong lead *necessarily* or even *probably* to others taking violent action against homosexuals.

Any speech, in order to be properly restricted by law, needs to *directly cause actual harm* to another person, as inciting to riot in a crowded theater would do. In fact, it is exactly *the free discussion of differences* regarding moral values and principles that is necessary to allow a democracy to work these questions out fairly and reasonably in the political process.

Therefore it should be a cause for thanksgiving—especially by Christians, but also by everyone who values freedom of speech—that legal challenges to these "hate speech" codes have been successful time and again and are beginning to turn back this wrongful policy on American campuses.

Unfortunately, such wrongful restrictions of "hate speech" are still in force in many other nations, sometimes even as a matter of national law. In Sweden, Pastor Ake Green was sentenced to six months in prison for preaching in his church a sermon on sexual behavior, which was deemed to be hate speech. His case eventually went to the Swedish Supreme Court, where he was eventually acquitted, but not before he was told by the prosecutor to "get a new Bible" that does not include sexual issues.[35] The law he was punished under read:

---

35. Firsthand testimony of Benjamin Bull of the Alliance Defense Fund, who assisted with Pastor Green's defense and was present at his trial.

Anyone who, through expression or other form of communication that is spread, *threatens **or** expresses disrespect* for a group of people or other such groups of persons with reference to race, color, national or ethnic origin, confession of faith or sexual orientation, is *sentenced for instigation* against a group of people to prison up to *two years* or, if the crime is minor, to fines. If the crime is major ... *at least six months and up to four years* in jail. In the determination of whether the crime is major, consideration shall be given to whether the message has had an especially *threatening **or** offensive* content and whether the message has been spread to a great number of people in a way that is meant to generate considerable attention.[36]

In the Netherlands, Dutch authorities in 2000 attempted to prosecute Pope John Paul II on discrimination charges after he said that a homosexual advocacy march in Rome was "an offense to Christian values." They eventually realized that the Pope had "global immunity" because of his position as the head of the Vatican state, and therefore they could not pursue legal action against him.[37]

In 2003 the Canadian Parliament passed C–250,[38] which placed severe restrictions on the free speech of churches and ministries. For instance, Janet Epp of the Buckingham Evangelical Fellowship of Canada said, "Pastors are afraid. They're afraid to preach on this subject. Nobody wants the police to come to their door."[39] In addition, Focus on the Family cannot air programs in Canada on the topic of homosexual behavior without facing sanctions from the Canadian Communications Commission.

In December 2007 the Saskatchewan Human Rights Commission's imposition of a "lifetime" ban on a local man's freedom to publicly criticize homosexuality was upheld in its entirety by Saskatchewan Court of Queens Bench. Bill Whatcott was ordered to pay $17,500 (Canadian) to four individuals who complained that their "feelings" and "self-respect" were "injured" by Whatcott's pamphlets that were critical of homosexual behavior.[40]

---

36. "Freedom of Religion on Trial in Sweden." www.akegreen.org.

37. "Dutch Will Not Prosecute Pope for Anti-Gay Remarks," Reuters (July 18, 2000).

38. C–250, Second Session, Thirty-seventh Parliament 51–52 Elizabeth II, 2002–2003, House of Commons of Canada, passed September 17, 2003.

39. "Canada's Anti-Gay Violence Law Worries Some," *Fox News* (May 18, 2004). www.foxnews.com/story/0,2933,120195,00.html.

40. Hilary White, "Catholic Activist 'Banned for Life' from Publicly Criticising Homosexuality," *LifeSiteNews.net* (Dec. 13, 2007). www.lifesite.net/ldn/2007/dec/07121306.html.

Several of these countries do not have the First Amendment protection that we have in the United States. Christians in those countries should oppose such wrongful restrictions on the basic right to freedom of speech in an open and democratic society.

F. THE "FAIRNESS DOCTRINE" AND TALK RADIO

In 1949 the Federal Communications Commission (FCC) introduced a policy called the "Fairness Doctrine," which required that radio stations broadcasting some discussion of controversial issues do so in a way that is honest, equitable, and balanced. In practice this meant that radio stations would often present speakers giving differing views of some political issue or other controversial public matter. But the policy was based on the idea that there were *a limited number of broadcast channels available,* so it was designed to give different sides an opportunity to get their views before the public.

The FCC abolished the Fairness Doctrine in 1987, reasoning that by that time there were so many radio stations and broadcasting channels open that it was no longer necessary to require every station to present differing sides of controversial issues, since that was being done by other stations that held different viewpoints. In this way the FCC was recognizing the principle that radio had become something like newspapers, for which any application of a fairness doctrine would be an obviously unconstitutional restriction of freedom of the press. At the time of the repeal of the Fairness Doctrine, the FCC stated the following:

> The intrusion by government into the content of programming occasioned by enforcement of [the Fairness Doctrine] restricts the journalistic freedom of broadcasters ... [and] actually inhibits the presentation of controversial issues of public concern to the detriment of the public and the degradation of the editorial prerogative of the broadcast journalist.[41]

The actual result of the *abolition* of the Fairness Doctrine has been *the proliferation of conservative talk radio.* Of course, liberal and conservative and Christian radio stations and stations with any other viewpoint are all free to go into business and broadcast as they wish. But as

---

41. John Shu, "Fairness Doctrine," Federalist Society (April 13, 2009). www.fed-soc.org/publications/pubID.1327/pub_detail.asp.

it turned out, conservatives found that there was finally a media outlet (talk radio) that on several stations quite consistently represented their own views (as opposed to the major TV networks or major newspapers), so political conservatives have supported conservative talk radio in overwhelming numbers.

Has this been a good development?

It seems to me that this development has been a wonderful and positive expression of freedom of speech and freedom of the press in the United States. There have been some liberal talk radio stations also, but in general they have not fared nearly as well, nor have many of them been able to attract sufficient advertising dollars to stay in business.

Now some liberal politicians have raised the question, "Should the Fairness Doctrine be reinstituted by the Federal Communications Commission?"

My response is, "Definitely not." If the Fairness Doctrine were reinstituted by the FCC, it would essentially destroy conservative talk radio and would leave American media once again dominated by the liberal journalists who control the major sources of TV and newspaper reporting as well as the government-supported National Public Radio.

How would the Fairness Doctrine destroy talk radio? It would mean that after every hour of Rush Limbaugh's broadcast, the station would have to broadcast an hour of an "alternative viewpoint" by some liberal commentator. And so it would be with every conservative talk show, such as those of Hugh Hewitt, Dennis Prager, Michael Medved, and Sean Hannity. Stations would be allowed to broadcast these conservative commentators only half of the time and would have to broadcast equally liberal commentators the rest of the time. Listeners would never know which viewpoint they were going to hear, and listening audiences would rapidly decline, cutting advertising revenue and making it impossible for these stations to stay in business.

Why would listenership decline? Because *liberal talk shows do not attract many listeners*, as the failure of many liberal radio networks such as Air America has demonstrated. For instance, even liberal *Vanity Fair* magazine reported, "At its height, the network's most popular program, *The Al Franken Show*, was carried by 92 affiliates and had 1.5 million weekly listeners. By contrast, *The Rush Limbaugh Show* is carried by more than 600 affiliates and has somewhere between 14 million and 20 million weekly listeners."[42]

---

42. Matt Pressman, "Whatever Happened to Air America?" *Vanity Fair* (March 12, 2009). www.vanityfair.com/online/politics/2009/03/what-ever-happened-to-air-america.html.

In addition, radio stations would be subject to the large expense of legal fees for responding to regulators from the FCC who are challenging the amount of time given to one issue or another and challenging whether it is "fair" or not. In other words, this would result in *large-scale government regulation of the content* broadcast by radio stations, and thus would be a huge attack against freedom of speech.

Christians who are concerned about freedom of speech as well as any conservatives who are concerned about restricting the right of radio stations to exercise freedom of speech should be concerned about this threat and about any other attempt by liberal politicians to impose creeping new legislation that would further burden conservative stations with *more expenses* and *more restrictions* on the kind of content that they can carry.

Chapter 7

FREEDOM
OF RELIGION

A. BIBLICAL AND CONSTITUTIONAL BACKGROUND

The biblical basis for freedom of religion is found in Jesus' words, "Render to Caesar the things that are Caesar's, and to God the things that are God's" (Matt. 22:21). In this statement Jesus established the principle of a distinct realm of "things that belong to God" that should not be regulated or constrained by the government (or "Caesar"). Although Jesus did not specify what things belong to this realm that is outside of Caesar's control, certainly "the things that belong to God" must include decisions and actions regarding worship and doctrinal beliefs. This means that peoples' *religious convictions and religious activities* should clearly be an area in which government gives citizens complete freedom.

This principle was illustrated in the early history of the church when the governing authorities of the Jewish Sanhedrin attempted to prevent the early apostles from preaching the Gospel. But Peter and the other apostles refused to submit to this governmental restriction on freedom of religion, saying, "We cannot but speak of what we have seen and heard" (Acts 4:20), and then later, "We must obey God rather than men" (Acts 5:29).

Governments should not compel religion, because religious belief, if it is to be genuine, cannot be forced on people against their will. Therefore the government should not try to force compliance with any particular religious belief or practice, or compel people to support any particular religion.

These principles were rightly embodied in the First Amendment to the US Constitution, which says:

> Congress shall make no law respecting an establishment of religion, or prohibiting the exercise thereof....[1]

With this simple statement the Constitution rightly established the proper boundaries for religions and for the state. It protected "free exercise" of religion but then also prohibited the government from making any one religion the "established" religion or the official religion of the government.

But subsequent Supreme Court rulings in the twentieth century significantly distorted the First Amendment from its original meaning. The First Amendment was not understood by anyone in 1787 (when the Constitution was adopted) to prohibit government officials from freely expressing their own religious beliefs in public and particularly at government functions, nor was it understood that way by the entire legal system of the United States for about the next two centuries.

For example, for many years the US Congress allowed Christian worship services to be conducted on Sundays in the Capitol itself. When Thomas Jefferson was President, church services were regularly held there. Jefferson not only attended the service, but made arrangements for the Marine band to play in it. Services were also held in the Supreme Court building. According to the Library of Congress, "Throughout his administration Jefferson permitted church services in executive branch buildings. The Gospel was also preached in the Supreme Court chambers."[2] After the Civil War, the First Congregational Church of Washington held services in the House of Representatives.[3]

Numerous presidential proclamations have made reference to God or even more specific reference to Christian beliefs. For instance, virtually every president since George Washington has issued a proclamation calling for a national Day of Thanksgiving. Washington's first proclamation read:

> WHEREAS it is the duty of all nations to acknowledge the providence of Almighty God, to obey His will, to be grateful for His benefits, and humbly to implore His protection and

---

1. Amendment 1, United States Constitution. www.law.cornell.edu/constitution/constitution.billofrights.html.
2. "The State Becomes the Church: Jefferson and Madison," Part VI: Religion and the Federal Government. www.loc.gov/exhibits/religion/rel06-2.html.
3. Ibid.

favor; and whereas both Houses of Congress have, by their joint committee, requested me "to recommend to the people of the United States a day of public thanksgiving and prayer, to be observed by acknowledging with grateful hearts the many and signal favors of Almighty God, especially by affording them an opportunity peaceably to establish a form of government for their safety and happiness...."[4]

In 1863 the US Senate requested President Abraham Lincoln to "designate and set apart a day for national prayer and humiliation." The request read:

> [S]incerely believing that no people, however great in numbers and resources or however strong in the justice of their cause, can prosper without His favor; and at the same time deploring the national offences which have provoked His righteous judgment, yet encouraged in this day of trouble by the assurances of His word to seek Him for succor according to *His appointed way through Jesus Christ*, the Senate of the United States do hereby request the President of the United States, by his proclamation, to designate and set apart a day for national prayer and humiliation.[5]

Lincoln complied with their request, issuing the following proclamation:

> It has pleased Almighty God to hearken to the supplications and prayers of an afflicted people and to vouchsafe to the Army and the Navy of the United States victories on land and on the sea so signal and so effective as to furnish reasonable grounds for augmented confidence that the Union of these States will be maintained, their Constitution preserved, and their peace and prosperity permanently restored. But these victories have been accorded not without sacrifices of life, limb, health, and liberty, incurred by brave, loyal, and patriotic citizens. Domestic affliction in every part of the country follows in the train of these fearful bereavements. It is meet and right to recognize and confess the presence of the Almighty Father and the power of

4. "Proclamation—Thanksgiving Day 1789" (Oct. 3, 1789). www.wallbuilders.com/libis-suesarticles.asp?id=3584.

5. *Journal of the Senate of the United States of America, Being the Third Session of the Thirty-Seventh Congress* (Washington, DC: Government Printing Office, 1863), 378–79.

His hand equally in these triumphs and in these sorrows: Now, therefore, be it known that I do set apart Thursday, the 6th day of August next, to be observed as a day for national thanksgiving, praise, and prayer, and I invite the people of the United States to assemble on that occasion in their customary places of worship and in the forms approved by their own consciences render the homage due to the Divine Majesty for the wonderful things He has done in the nation's behalf and invoke the influence of His Holy Spirit to subdue the anger which has produced and so long sustained a needless and cruel rebellion, to change the hearts of the insurgents, to guide the counsels of the Government with wisdom adequate to so great a national emergency, and to visit with tender care and consolation throughout the length and breadth of our land all those who, through the vicissitudes of marches, voyages, battles, and sieges, have been brought to suffer in mind, body, or estate, and finally to lead the whole nation through the paths of repentance and submission to the divine will back to the perfect enjoyment of union and fraternal peace.[6]

In 1944 President Franklin Roosevelt went on national radio and offered the following prayer for the soldiers who had landed on the Normandy Beaches to commence D-Day operations:

And so, in this poignant hour, I ask you to join with me in prayer: Almighty God: Our sons, pride of our Nation, this day have set upon a mighty endeavor, a struggle to preserve our Republic, our religion, and our civilization, and to set free a suffering humanity. Lead them straight and true; give strength to their arms, stoutness to their hearts, steadfastness in their faith.... And for us at home—fathers, mothers, children, wives, sisters, and brothers of brave men overseas—whose thoughts and prayers are ever with them—help us, Almighty God, to rededicate ourselves in renewed faith in Thee in this hour of great sacrifice. Many people have urged that I call the Nation into a single day of special prayer. But because the road is long and the desire is great, I ask that our people devote themselves in a continuance of prayer. As we rise to each new day, and again when each day is spent, let words of prayer be on our lips, invoking Thy help to our efforts.... And, O Lord, give

---

6. "Proclamation—Day of Thanksgiving, Praise, and Prayer, August 6, 1863." www.presidency.ucsb.edu/ws/index.php?pid=69897.

us Faith. Give us Faith in Thee; Faith in our sons; Faith in each other; Faith in our united crusade...."[7]

Therefore, recent Supreme Court decisions that have had the effect of *excluding religious expression from the public square* cannot be justified by the original intention or original meaning of the First Amendment. None of the original authors of the Constitution, and none of the national officials first elected under the Constitution, gave any indication that they intended that exclusion to be the meaning of the Constitution, nor did any of the states that approved the Constitution.

Thus the modern concept of "separation of church and state," by which people argue that no government property or government function should contain any religious expression, has no legitimate basis in the original meaning of the Constitution.

What, then, is its basis? This idea of such a strict "separation of church and state" is based on a modern myth that the Constitution legally requires it, whereas those words are found nowhere in the Constitution and nowhere in any subsequent national laws that were passed by Congress. This myth is sustained by endless repetition in the press today, but it finds no legitimate basis in the laws or in the actual Constitution of the United States.

How, then, did this myth of "separation of church and state" acquire its power in our government? The government acquired its power simply because it was imposed on the country by certain decisions of the Supreme Court, especially the decision *Everson v. Board of Education* (1947) and also the decision *Lemon v. Kurtzman* (1971). These decisions have led to numerous other legal controversies as well as to actions such as the prohibition of prayers before high school graduation ceremonies, the removal of crosses or other religious symbols from state seals, the prohibition of the teaching of intelligent design as an alternative to evolution, or (in some places) stopping the teaching of abstinence as part of a sexual-education curriculum.[8]

But if we return to the basic biblical principle that government should allow *freedom of religion* and *freedom of religious expression*, and if we go back to the original meaning of the First Amendment, then we will reach some different conclusions about questions related to freedom of religion in the United States today.

---

7. Franklin Delano Roosevelt, Prayer on D-Day, June 6, 1944. www.presidency.ucsb.edu/ws/index.php?pid=16515.

8. See "Abstinence Scofflaws" at www.villagevoice.com/2002−08−20/news/abstinence-scofflaws/.

B. RELIGIOUS EXPRESSION IN THE PUBLIC SQUARE

Once we base our reasoning on the more sure grounds of biblical teaching and the original meaning of the First Amendment, a proper conclusion is that the government in the United States today should allow much more space in the public square for a wide variety of religious expression. In fact, in some areas this principle still works quite well.

For example, with regard to the armed forces, there is an allocation of chaplains that is in a broad way representative of the many different religious groups in the United States as a whole and in the military services. Until recently, for example, the Navy used a formula dividing its chaplains into thirds: one-third consisting of liturgical Protestant denominations (such as Methodists, Lutherans, Episcopalians, and Presbyterians); another third consisting of Catholics; and a third consisting of nonliturgical Protestant denominations (such as Baptists, evangelicals, Bible churches, and Pentecostals and charismatics) as well as other faiths.[9] Such a system does not constitute an "establishment of religion," because it does not compel anyone to follow a particular religion. But it does give support to *religious practices in general,* because the society has concluded that this makes a positive contribution to the work of the military services and therefore to the public good.

So then, what should a *city council* be able to do? It seems appropriate that some kind of reasonably proportioned representation among various religious groups in the community should be allowed to give opening prayers for city council meetings, with each local council having wide discretion in exactly how they carry this out. Allowing someone to open a city council meeting with prayer is far from *compelling* anyone to *accept* a particular religion, so there should be no question that this is not a violation of the original meaning of the First Amendment.

The Alliance Defense Fund has prepared model constitutional prayer policies for state and local governments in all fifty states.[10] ADF Senior Legal Counsel Mike Johnson says:

> The practice of opening public meetings with prayer is and always has been lawful. The Constitution does not ban citizens or elected officials from invoking divine guidance and bless-

---

9. "Accomodating Faith in the Military," *Pew Forum on Religion and Public Life* (July 3, 2008). http://pewforum.org/events/?EventID=191.

10. "Model Prayer Policies." www.alliancedefensefund.org/adfresources/default.aspx?cid=4134.

ings upon their public work. It's a practice that is part of our nation's religious heritage, and the Constitution does not prevent public officials today from doing the same thing America's founders did.[11] Moreover, such a policy contradicts no other law that has been passed by Congress or by any state.

On the other hand, if a local city council decided it did *not* want to have any opening prayer at its city meetings, then it should be free to enact this as well. Freedom of religion should include the freedom not to participate in any religious activity.

What about *Christmas displays on public property*? These do not *compel* anybody to *believe in or follow* the Christian religion, nor do they compel individuals to *support* the Christian religion. When they are simply a way of giving expression to widely held beliefs in the community, I cannot see any good constitutional or moral reason why they should not be allowed. It would also be appropriate, if there are Jewish people in the community, to allow the placement of appropriate Jewish symbols in the same area during Jewish holidays. The same would be true for Muslim symbols for Muslim holidays if there were a significant number of Muslim believers in the community.

What possible harm could come from that? It would allow communities to give *free expression* to the celebration of various religious beliefs represented in the community. It would allow the "free exercise" of religion in a way that would bring benefit to the entire community.

The Supreme Court has been somewhat more restrictive than allowing the freedom for different kinds of religious displays I am suggesting here, but they have definitely never ruled out religious displays, such as a manger scene at Christmas, in general. Two Supreme Court cases in the 1980s, *Lynch v. Donnelly* (1984) and *County of Allegheny v. ACLU Greater Pittsburgh Chapter* (1989), looked at holiday displays in Rhode Island and Pittsburgh, and the court's rulings resulted from what is now known as the "Three Reindeer Rule." Essentially, public displays of religious symbols are permissible only when the inclusion of other decorations makes it clear that the government is not endorsing a religious message. According to the ADF:

> The "Three Reindeer Rule" used by the courts requires a municipality to place a sufficient number of secular objects in

---

11. "Tangipahoa Parish School Board votes unanimously to adopt ADF model prayer policy," *ADF Press Release* (Aug. 22, 2007). www.alliancedefensefund.org/news/story. aspx?cid=4210.

close enough proximity to the Christmas item (such as a crèche) to render the overall display sufficiently secular. Although the overall display must not convey a message endorsing a particular religion's view, Christmas displays are not banned as some people believe.[12]

What is important is that all religions have the same opportunities that other religions have, or "equal access."

In recent years the American Civil Liberties Union (ACLU) and other secular groups have launched legal attacks on *Ten Commandments displays on public property*. So far, the courts have issued conflicting opinions on the constitutionality of these monuments, with the possibility of another case involving a display in Haskell County, Oklahoma, to be heard soon by the US Supreme Court. However, in 2005 the US Court of Appeals for the 6th Circuit issued a ruling affirming the constitutionality of a Ten Commandments monument in Mercer County, Kentucky, and was critical of the attempts by the ACLU to remove these memorials:

> The ACLU's argument contains three fundamental flaws. First, the ACLU makes repeated reference to "the separation of church and state." This extra-constitutional construct has grown tiresome. The First Amendment does not demand a wall of separation between church and state.... Second, the ACLU focuses on the religiousness of the Ten Commandments. No reasonable person would dispute their sectarian nature, but they also have a secular nature that the ACLU does not address.... Third, the ACLU erroneously—though perhaps intentionally—equates recognition with endorsement. To endorse is necessarily to recognize, but the converse does not follow.
>
> Because nothing in the display, its history, or its implementation supports the notion that Mercer County has selectively endorsed the sectarian elements of the first four Commandments, we fail to see why the reasonable person would interpret the presence of the Ten Commandments as part of the larger "Foundations" display as a governmental endorsement of religion. We will not presume endorsement from the mere display of the Ten Commandments. If the reasonable observer

---

12. "ADF attorneys: U.S. Constitution does not require Christmas to be removed from Mustang holiday play," *ADF Press Release* (Dec. 9, 2004). www.alliancedefensefund.org/news/story.aspx?cid=3254.

perceived all government references to the Deity as endorse-
ments, then many of our Nation's cherished traditions would
be unconstitutional, including the Declaration of Independence and the national motto. Fortunately, the reasonable person is not a hyper-sensitive plaintiff.... Instead, he appreciates
the role religion has played in our governmental institutions,
and finds it historically appropriate and traditionally acceptable for a state to include religious influences, even in the form
of sacred texts, in honoring American legal traditions.[13]

What, then, should be done about the controversial topic of *prayer
in public schools*? Various studies have noted destructive trends in the
nation that began about the time the Supreme Court ruled prayer in
public schools unconstitutional in *Engel v. Vitale* (1962)[14] and *School
District of Abington Township v. Schempp* (1963).[15] Once that happened,
then, by implication, other decisions began to prohibit teachers from
expressing belief in God at all or expressing their belief that there were
moral standards that came from God and should be followed. Once
such changes in the public schools began to take effect, crime and other
destructive forces in society began to increase year after year.

In his book *America: To Pray or Not to Pray?* historian David Barton
documented the negative effects of removing school prayer, by contrast-
ing the top seven leading problems in schools in 1940 with those in 1990.
Here is what he found:

1940	1990
Talking Out of Turn	Drug Abuse
Chewing Gum	Alcohol Abuse
Making Noise	Pregnancy
Running in the Halls	Suicide
Line Cutting	Rape
Dress Code Violations	Robbery
Littering	Assault [16]

---

13. *American Civil Liberties Union of Kentucky v. Mercer County,* No. 03–5142, U.S. Court
of Appeals for the 6th Circuit p.14 (2005). www.telladf.org/UserDocs/ACLUvMCopinion.pdf.

14. *Engel v. Vitale,* 370 U.S. 421, 436, United States Supreme Court (1962).

15. *Abington School District v. Schempp,* 374 U.S. 203, 226–227, United States Supreme
Court (1963).

16. David Barton, *America: To Pray or Not to Pray?* (Aledo, TX: Wallbuilder Press, 1988), 35.

In the book Barton documents the dramatic rise in teen pregnancy rates, teen suicides, and drug abuse since prayer was removed from public schools.[17]

This is a tragic change in our nation, but it makes perfect sense. When children are not allowed to be taught that there is a God or that God has moral standards that they should obey, and when that teaching is *excluded from the classroom* every hour of the day for thirteen of the most formative years of a child's life, then it is little wonder that children grow up with fewer internal moral convictions and an overall pattern of behavior that is increasingly immoral and destructive in society. I realize that schools today still try to teach some "character development" for children—encouraging them to be trustworthy, honest, respectful, tolerant, and such. But merely affirming these qualities—and even cheering loudly for them—provides a far weaker basis for moral conduct than teaching that there is a God who holds us responsible for our conduct.

I see no valid constitutional reason and no valid biblical principle to exclude the use of prayer in public schools or to exclude teaching children that there is a God who watches our conduct and will hold us accountable for our actions. It would be a wonderful benefit for our nation if the Supreme Court could be persuaded that its earlier decisions establishing such a strict "wall of separation" between church and state were not based in any valid way on the Constitution itself and should be overturned. And if some basic ethical standards (approved by a local school district) with divine authorization could once again be taught to children in our schools, it would begin to reverse much of the moral decline seen since the Supreme Court removed God from the classroom in 1962.

To return to the question of prayer in public schools: I would like this to be decided by individual local school districts, which are ultimately responsible to voters in each district. Prayer in school could be solved in various ways that would not involve compelling anyone to believe in any particular religion. For example, school districts could authorize various nonsectarian prayers that could be used by teachers (as was widely done in the United States prior to 1962), or they could ask representatives of various religious groups to open a school day or a school week with prayers, or they could establish a moment of silence where students would be encouraged to pray silently in their own way.

17. Ibid., 23–46 and 57–84.

(Unfortunately—and I think incorrectly—the US Supreme Court in *Wallace v. Jaffree* in 1985 ruled that laws allowing moments of silence of voluntary prayer or meditation were unconstitutional.)[18]

If the Supreme Court were ever to overturn its prohibition of prayer or moments of silence, what would be the harm in allowing local school districts to decide this question as they thought best? It would clearly promote the public good, what the Constitution calls "promote the general welfare." It would not be compelling anyone to believe in any particular religious view. Also, it would teach children that the great majority of people in their community do believe in God and do believe that prayer to him is appropriate. (Even children who did not or whose parents did not believe in God would not be compelled to endorse or support any particular religious viewpoint, but would only be expected to be present while these viewpoints are being expressed, unless parents requested that they be excused.)

Yet today, when the courts operate by a principle that "nobody should be offended" by any religious expression in public, then *freedom of religion and freedom of speech are severely curtailed* in a wrongful way. The government is actually violating the original sense of the Constitution because it is "prohibiting" the "free exercise" of religion! In this way, the will of a tiny minority, sometimes even one person, can be used to frustrate and nullify the wishes of the large majority. And this is done, not in a way of preserving a fundamental human right, but only under the principle that no one should have to feel "offended." There is no constitutional or moral "right" not to feel offended! This is a clearly wrong standard and should be overturned by the courts or outlawed by legislatures and Congress.

In 2009 the so-called "Freedom from Religion Foundation" (FFRF) filed suit against Shirley Dobson, the wife of Focus on the Family founder Dr. James Dobson, and President Obama, in an effort to bring an end to government support for the annual National Day of Prayer, which has been observed by every president since 1952. The FFRF claims that the National Day of Prayer creates a "hostile environment" for non-believers and that it violates the First Amendment.[19] Attorneys with the Alliance Defense Fund are defending Mrs. Dobson in her role as chairman of the National Day of Prayer Task Force, which coordinates the

---

18. *Wallace v. Jaffree*, 472 U.S. 38, 61, United States Supreme Court (1985).

19. *Freedom from Religion Foundation et al. v. President Bush et al.* (now Obama), filed October 3, 2008.

Christian observance of the national prayer day each year. The attorneys are asking the federal court to dismiss the lawsuit.[20]

C. "FAITH-BASED" PROGRAMS

On January 29, 2001, shortly after he became President, George W. Bush established the White House Office of Faith-Based and Community Initiatives (OFBCI). This office was intended to improve the ability of so-called faith-based organizations to obtain federal funding for the social services that they carry out, such as job training, drug rehabilitation, alcoholism rehabilitation, prison ministries, and free housing and food for the poor and homeless. There was much controversy about this initiative, with some Christian conservatives thinking it provided a dangerous precedent for government intrusion into religious activities and many others arguing that it was a wrongful use of government funds to support religious activities.

I will give my own evaluation of such programs here, along with the reasons I find persuasive, but I realize that others, both conservative and liberal, both Republican and Democrat, will decide that they disagree with me on this issue.

In my own judgment, much good can come from government financial assistance to these organizations as they carry out social service functions that "promote the general welfare" of the nation. These activities advance the common good in many ways and actually save tax dollars that would otherwise need to be spent to help the people who are cared for by these religiously based institutions. And these activities help these organizations carry out the work they were set up to do. In addition, there are significant benefits to the people who are helped to learn a new job skill or to overcome drug addiction or to have a changed life that will not see them end up back in prison a few months after being released. *Everybody wins* from such a program—government, the society, the ministry, and the people receiving aid.

Yes, I agree that government funding always carries the danger of increased government control, and both the government and the religious organizations need to continually guard against this. But I do not think that this danger is significant enough to be a reason for the groups to refuse to participate.

---

20. *Freedom from Religion v. Obama,* U.S. District Court for the Western District of Wisconsin.

It is important that government funds be clearly used for the specific social welfare benefit that the organization receives the funds for and not simply to finance the religious worship activities of that organization, for example. Therefore, if a Christian group runs a homeless shelter, they should be able to show through their recordkeeping that the government funds were used directly for the purpose intended—that is, for providing food and shelter for homeless people, not for buying hymnbooks or Bibles and not for paying a Bible teacher to lead Bible studies. (These activities would have to be funded by separate, private contributions.) That is simply a matter of honoring "donor intent," something that churches and other charities do all the time. In this case the government is the donor of some of the organization's funds.

If religious groups clearly keep the funds for these social services separate from other funds, then, if the government in the future started to try to exercise control over the entire content of the programs used by these religious groups, the groups could relinquish the funds without any wrongful government intrusion into their specifically religious activities.

Since the use of any of these social services is entirely voluntary on the part of the recipient, it does not seem to me that such a program comes anywhere near to having the government "compel religion" with respect to all its citizens or even any single citizen.

Of course, such government aid should be open to *any* religious *or nonreligious* group that is carrying out these services. Roman Catholic, Protestant, Mormon, Muslim, and Jewish groups and so forth should all be eligible based simply on an ability to provide the social services for which the funds are being requested. Such a program is certainly not a violation of the First Amendment as the authors originally intended it.

Should the government, in giving faith-based funds, be able to require that ministries *refrain* from any specifically religious activities or conversations in carrying out these social services? Should they insist, for example, that Catholics not have a crucifix on the wall or that evangelicals not hold a Bible-teaching time in a prison or homeless shelter? Should government require that evangelical Christians *refrain* from encouraging drug-addicted people to trust in Jesus as their personal Savior for forgiveness of sins and a change of heart?

No, I do not think that government should ever make such restrictions regarding faith-based organizations. That would be a wrongful prohibition of the "free exercise" of religion. For these groups, the religious component is an essential part of the ministry that they carry out. People who give food and clothing to the poor do it "in the name of

Jesus" and out of obedience to him and as a means of witness to him. I do not think governments should ever object to this. The government funding is given to carry out the social welfare function (feeding and sheltering the homeless, or helping people to escape from drug addiction, for example). If that is accomplished by the faith-based organization, then the government should not object to these ministry-related components of what the organization does in fulfilling its functions. The groups must not be prohibited from their "free exercise" of religion, but those activities should be funded by private donations.

The principle is still preserved that the *choice to participate* in the program is voluntary on the part of the recipient, and the choice to accept or reject what he hears is also voluntary. There is no government compulsion forcing people to give support to any particular religion, so there is no genuine violation of the original meaning of the First Amendment.

D. POLITICAL ADVOCACY BY CHURCHES AND THEIR TAX-EXEMPT STATUS

In 1954 the US Congress amended (without debate or analysis) Internal Revenue Code §501(c)(3) to restrict the speech of nonprofit tax-exempt entities, including churches, requiring that they refrain from any advocacy of or opposition to any specific political candidates by name. The amendment, offered by then-Senator Lyndon Johnson, stated that nonprofit tax-exempt entities could not "participate in, or intervene in (including the publishing or distributing of statements), any political campaign on behalf of or in opposition to any candidate for public office."[21] Apparently Johnson had proposed this amendment, which passed on a voice vote, to "get back" at two nonprofit organizations that had vocally opposed his candidacy for the Senate.[22]

The penalty for violating this policy is a revocation of the tax-exempt status of the church. Churches in the United States have generally followed this restriction since the enactment of the so-called "Johnson amendment" in 1954 that authorized the IRS to make this restriction.

But before the amendment was passed, *there were no restrictions* on what churches could or couldn't do with regard to speech about government and voting, except for a 1934 law preventing nonprofits from using

21. "The Pulpit Initiative Executive Summary for Sermons Addressing Candidates for Office and Their Issues." www.alliancedefensefund.org/userdocs/Pulpit_Initiative_executive_summary_candidates_2009.pdf.

22. Karla Dial, "Aiming at Goliath," *Focus on the Family Citizen* (Aug. 2009), 25–29.

a substantial part of their resources to lobby for legislation. However, since the passage of the 1954 amendment, the IRS has steadfastly maintained that *any* speech by churches about candidates for government office, including sermons from the pulpit, can result in loss of tax exemption. But that has turned out to be a hollow threat, because the IRS has never actually revoked the tax-exempt status of any church for violating this policy.[23]

Of course, many pastors and other church leaders understand that it is often *unwise* for a church to support or oppose a particular candidate. Specific political positions are not required for people to join a church. Every church probably has members who would support different candidates in any given election. Therefore, when churches refrain from endorsing individual candidates, they also avoid offending their members who have different political convictions. I suspect that nearly all Christians and all churches would recognize the wisdom of exercising considerable caution and restraint with regard to advocating specific political positions from the pulpit of the church.

But that still does not answer the question, Is it right for the Internal Revenue Service to prohibit *all* recommendations for or against specific candidates in *all* elections in *all* circumstances? Should such a decision be made by the government, or should such decisions be left to individual churches and pastors to decide according to what they think is wise in each situation?

The Alliance Defense Fund has recently begun to question the validity of this IRS policy because they have concluded that the policy is actually an unconstitutional violation of freedom of speech and freedom of religion. ADF attorneys believe the Johnson amendment is unconstitutional because (in their words):

- The amendment violates the Establishment Clause by requiring the government to excessively and pervasively monitor the speech of churches to ensure they are not transgressing the restriction in the amendment. The amendment allows the government to determine when truly religious speech becomes impermissibly "political." The government has no business making such decisions.

---

23. "The Pulpit Initiative: White Paper," Alliance Defense Fund (May 11, 2009). www. alliancedefensefund.org/userdocs/Pulpit_initiative_white_%20Paper_candidates_2009. pdf. The IRS recently investigated the tax-exempt status of All Saints Episcopal Church in Pasadena, California, over a sermon delivered by a guest speaker who maintained that Jesus would not vote for President Bush because of the Iraq War. After the church refused to cooperate with the IRS investigation, the IRS closed the examination without penalizing the church, even though the IRS claimed in the closure letter that the sermon constituted direct campaign intervention.

- The amendment violates the Free Speech Clause because it requires the government to discriminate against speech based solely on the content of the speech. In other words, some speech is allowed, but other speech is not. The Supreme Court has invalidated this type of speech discrimination for decades.
- The amendment also violates the Free Speech Clause by conditioning the receipt of a tax exemption on refraining from certain speech. Put simply, if a church wants the tax exemption, it cannot speak on any and all relevant issues addressed by Scripture. This is an unconstitutional condition on free speech.
- The amendment violates the Free Exercise Clause because it substantially burdens a church's exercise of religion. The government does not have a compelling reason to burden religion in this way.[24]

The ADF is *not* arguing that pastors *should* routinely endorse or oppose various candidates in political elections. Rather, it contends that there are times when the moral and religious issues on which candidates differ are so blatant and so clearly supported or opposed by biblical principles that *pastors should have the freedom to speak out on various candidates when they think it wise to do so.* The ADF recognizes that pastors will want to be careful in exercising this freedom and would be wise to consult their elder boards or other leaders well in advance, but the ADF holds that such decisions should be made by individual churches or denominations, not by the government.

Therefore, on the last Sunday in September prior to the 2008 presidential election and also prior to the November 2009 elections, the Alliance Defense Fund found a number of pastors around the United States who were willing to preach sermons *publicly endorsing or opposing specific candidates* and were stating from the pulpit why there were biblical moral grounds on which they based these recommendations. The sermons were actually carefully constructed with legal advice from the ADF so that they would constitute a clear challenge to the IRS regulations.[25] The sermons were sent to the IRS well in advance with a notification that this was the intention of the pastors! It was the hope of the ADF that the IRS would actually revoke the tax-exempt status of at least one of these churches, to provide a test case by which the principle of

---

24. "The Pulpit Initiative," op. cit.
25. Laurie Goodstein, "Challenging the IRS," *New York Times* (June 23, 2008); Dale Buss, "Provoking the IRS, Preachers Address the Bully Pulpit," *Wall Street Journal* (Oct. 3, 2008). Pulpit Freedom Sunday was held on September 28, 2008.

the policy could be tested in court. The ADF actually believes that if this policy ever does come to trial, it has a very strong likelihood of winning on appeal to the Constitution's protection of freedom of speech.[26] ADF Senior Legal Counsel Erik Stanley says, "Our hope is that the IRS will respond by opening church tax inquiries against them, and then we'll file multiple lawsuits in federal jurisdictions and seek to have what the IRS is doing declared unconstitutional. That's why we started this initiative—to end 50 years of intimidation."[27]

Until the passage of the law in 1954, pastors and churches had often made statements for and against individual candidates. The ADF writes:

> Historically, churches had frequently and fervently spoken for and against candidates for government office. Such sermons date from the founding of America, including sermons against Thomas Jefferson for being a deist; sermons opposing William Howard Taft as a Unitarian; and sermons opposing Al Smith in the 1928 presidential election. Churches have also been at the forefront of most of the significant societal and governmental changes in our history including ending segregation and child labor and advancing civil rights.[28]

For example, in 1800 the Rev. William Linn of Pennsylvania said, "It is well understood that the Honorable Thomas Jefferson is a candidate for the Chief Magistracy of the United States, and that a number of citizens will give him all their support. I would not presume to dictate to you who ought to be president, but entreat you to hear with patience my reason why he ought not."[29]

In 1864 Pastor O. T. Lanphear told his parishioners why he supported the reelection of Abraham Lincoln, stating, "The man who casts his vote in the election now pending in favor of a peace not won by the conquests of our enemies does the rebel cause more service, if possible, than he could by joining the rebel army."[30]

---

26. See Allan J. Samansky, *Tax Consequences When Churches Participate in Political Campaigns*, Political Law and Legal Theory Working Paper No. 76, Center for Interdisciplinary Law and Policy Studies Working Paper No. 49, Ohio State Univ. College of Law (Aug. 2006), http://ssrn.com/abstract=924770; Shawn A. Voyles, *Choosing Between Tax-Exempt Status and Freedom of Religion: The Dilemma Facing Politically Active Churches*, 9 REG. U. L. REV. 219 (1997).

27. Dial, "Aiming at Goliath."

28. Ibid.

29. The Rev. William Linn: cited in Dial, "Aiming at Goliath."

30. Pastor O. T. Lanphear: cited in Dial, "Aiming at Goliath."

It seems to me that the Alliance Defense Fund is right in this argument. Decisions about what is preached from the pulpit of a church should not belong to the government, but to the individual pastor and the church itself. Any government control of what is said from a pulpit constitutes a wrongful violation of religious freedom and a wrongful violation of freedom of speech. It is the government—the realm of "what is Caesar's"—attempting to intrude into a realm where it does not belong—the realm of "what is God's." So I hope that the ADF will prevail against the IRS and that the courts will rule that this policy is unconstitutional.

Chapter 8

APPLICATION TO DEMOCRATIC AND REPUBLICAN POLICIES TODAY

It is now time to look back on our study and draw some conclusions about the way in which biblical teachings compare to the current policies favored by the Democratic and Republican parties in the United States. (Readers in countries other than the United States can take this list of policy questions and consider how the various political parties in their own nation measure up to these conclusions as well.)

When I was writing this book, some people told me that they hoped it would be "nonpartisan." They hoped I would simply look at the issues and not at the individual parties. They hoped that the book would evenhandedly support Democrats where their policies were more consistent with biblical teaching and support Republicans where their policies were more consistent with biblical teaching.

But the policies favored by Democrats and Republicans today are so different that it is unlikely that anyone with a consistent worldview and a consistent view of the purpose of government will support Democratic policies about 50% of the time and Republican policies about 50% of the time. This is because the parties' basic views of the role of government are so different, and their fundamental principles are so different.

That is why, for example, Jim Wallis's book *God's Politics: Why the Right Gets It Wrong and the Left Doesn't Get It*[1] is not at all nonpartisan. The title makes people think that Wallis is going to criticize both Republicans and Democrats equally, but the book actually turns out to be an extended argument for supporting Democratic candidates and positions and opposing Republican ones.

Wallis ends up supporting Democratic policies regarding war, the economy, and capital punishment and (for the most part) even giving mild support to a more liberal view of same-sex marriage, as I documented earlier. With regard to abortion, Wallis refuses to support the Republican position that we should have *laws* prohibiting abortion (except to save the life of a mother). Rather, he tells Democrats that they should be more tolerant of pro-life Democrats within the party[2] and also tells them they should do more to reduce teen pregnancy and to support low-income women who are at greater risk for unwanted pregnancies.[3] Then he tells readers that the differences between Democrats and Republicans on abortion are not enough reason to support Republicans, because Republicans do not support "a consistent ethic of life" regarding other issues, since they support capital punishment and nuclear weapons and do not do enough to eradicate poverty and racism, all of which are "critical components of a consistent ethic of life."[4]

In other words, Wallis gives readers no reason that they should support Republican policies and makes the entire book an argument to support Democrats and policies favored by the Democratic Party. The entirety of *God's Politics* ends up saying, in essence, that God supports the Democratic Party.

Why does Wallis reach these conclusions? They are strongly informed by (1) his pacifist convictions regarding war and military power and international relations, (2) his view that the primary solution to poverty is more government redistribution of income from the rich to the poor, and (3) his decision that biblical standards regarding abortion and homosexual conduct should not be the determining factor regarding the kinds of laws that governments should make.

Although Wallis says that "God is not a Republican or a Democrat," and although he and his organization Sojourners supported a campaign

---

1. Jim Wallis, *God's Politics: Why the Right Gets It Wrong and the Left Doesn't Get It* (San Francisco: HarperSanFrancisco, 2005).

2. Ibid., 298–99.

3. Ibid., 300.

4. Ibid., 301.

with that slogan,[5] his book in actuality ends up arguing "God's politics" are the politics of the Democratic Party. I encourage readers to read Wallis's book if they want to hear an argument that God supports the Democrats and their positions.

I have come to quite different conclusions in this book, for the reasons discussed in the preceding chapters. Although I disagree with Republican policies at some points, I have concluded that the policies endorsed by the leadership of the Republican Party have been much more consistent with biblical teachings.

Where does that leave us? Wallis and others say that God supports the positions of the Democrats. I think that the teachings of the Bible, as I understand them, mostly support the current policies of the Republicans. How can people decide between these two views? They can decide in the way people have always decided: by reading the arguments, reading their Bibles (where biblical arguments are used), and then deciding which arguments are the most persuasive. They can discuss their thinking about these matters with others, and when they disagree, they can do so while maintaining a respectful attitude toward the other person. This is a healthy process, and it is essential to a well-functioning democracy.

Sometimes people say they "vote for the candidate, not the party." I think this view is naïve. It simply fails to recognize how decisions are actually made in our current political system. Because only parties— not individuals—can get bills passed in Congress and confirm or reject judicial appointments, *every vote for every candidate is a vote for the candidate's party as much as it is for the candidate.* It is impossible today to vote for a candidate and not also vote for and give support to that candidate's party. And the party in power will determine the course of the nation.

In this chapter I summarize the earlier discussions in the book and compare my policy conclusions with the policies favored by the majority of Republicans and the majority of Democrats, or by those who have determined the policy decisions in their respective parties.

A. PROTECTION OF LIFE

In chapter 2 I argued that abortion is the intentional taking of an innocent human life and that this should be prohibited by law in all cases except to save the life of the mother. On this question Democrats in general (not every single Democrat, but uniformly in their national leadership positions) favor "a woman's right to choose," which means

---

5. Ibid., 9.

they do not favor any enactment of laws that would restrict a woman's right to take the life of her own preborn child. By contrast, Republicans in general (not every single Republican, but uniformly in their top national leadership) have favored laws that protect the life of preborn children. However, no significant change to laws regarding abortion can ever happen in the United States until the Supreme Court overrules its 1973 decision *Roe v. Wade*. This will only happen when there is a sufficient number of "original intent" justices to overturn that decision. And they will only be appointed by Republican presidents and confirmed by a sufficient number of Republican senators in the US Senate.

Chapter 3 concluded that euthanasia, in the sense of actively taking steps to put an old or very ill patient to death, is prohibited by the biblical commands against murder. More liberal Democrats have tended to favor the liberalization of laws regarding euthanasia, but some Democrats have opposed this. Nearly all Republicans, at least on the level of national leadership, have opposed giving people the legal right to take the life of a terminally ill or very old patient.

Regarding capital punishment, I argued that the Bible supports the government's right to carry out capital punishment, at least in the case of premeditated murder. The viewpoints of Democrats and Republicans are not entirely predictable on this question, but a significantly larger number of Republicans would favor the use of capital punishment, at least for premeditated murder, and a significant proportion of Democrats would oppose the use of capital punishment in all cases. In 2008 the Gallup Poll found that only 52% of Democrats support the use of capital punishment, compared with 78% of Republicans and 66% of Independents.[6]

Finally, I argued in chapter 3 that governments should allow people to have some effective means of self-defense, and in nations where there are already many gun owners, this would mean permitting private citizens to own guns for the purpose of self-defense (with reasonable restrictions preventing convicted felons and mentally ill people, for example, from owning guns).

Republican candidates in general, by a large proportion, have favored the right of citizens to own guns. On the other hand, as of April 2009, 60% of Democrats would support stricter gun-control laws, compared with 13% of Republicans and 17% of Independents.[7] Opposition to all

---

6. Lydia Saad, "Americans Hold Firm to Support for Death Penalty," *Gallup.com* (Nov. 17, 2008). www.gallup.com/poll/111931/Americans-Hold-Firm-Support-Death-Penalty.aspx.

7. Bill Schneider, "Poll: Fewer Americans Support Stricter Gun Control Laws," *CNN.com* (April 8, 2009). www.cnn.com/2009/POLITICS/04/08/gun.control.poll/.

gun ownership has been a consistent pattern of more liberal political groups in other nations as well.

B. MARRIAGE

In chapter 4 I argued that biblical teachings restrict marriage to the union of one man and one woman. On this issue, Republicans have almost uniformly supported such a definition of marriage in the laws of individual states and the laws of the United States. Some Democrats have supported this position, but the party as a whole—through the judges that it has supported and through the votes of senators and congressmen on the Defense of Marriage Act, for example—has shown that it is far more supportive of same-sex "marriage" in the United States. In October 2009 the Pew Research Center for the People and the Press found that more than seven-in-ten liberal Democrats (72%) favor same-sex marriage, while eight-in-ten conservative Republicans (81%) oppose it.[8]

I also argued that biblical teachings on marriage express that the ideal for marriage is the union of one man and one woman for life. This would lead to the support of laws that aim at protecting marriage by making it much more difficult to divorce than is currently true in most states. Generally speaking, it has primarily been Democrats who have favored the liberalization of divorce laws, thus making it easy for people to get divorced and end their marriage. Republicans, on the other hand, have sometimes supported easy divorce laws, but many times have opposed the liberalization of divorce laws in their states.

Finally, I argued that the production and distribution of pornography brings significant harm to marriages and to society as a whole, and that both national and local governments in the United States should much more aggressively use current antipornography laws and court-defined standards to prosecute those who produce and distribute material that is clearly pornographic and outside the protection of the law. I also showed how Republican-appointed Justice Department officials and local prosecutors have been far more likely than Democratic-appointed officials to pursue antipornography prosecutions.

C. THE FAMILY

In chapter 5 I argued that the Bible views the bearing of children as a positive blessing from God and something that is to be encouraged and

---

8. "Majority Continues to Support Civil Unions," *Pew Research Center for the People and the Press* (Oct. 9, 2009). http://people-press.org/report/553/same-sex-marriage.

approved. I also argued that the right to determine the kind of education a child receives should ultimately belong to the parents (within certain broad guarantees of educational competence that the state might require).

This led me to conclude that there should be much more involvement of parents (as opposed to teachers and administrators) in deciding what knowledge children are taught and what moral and behavioral standards children are taught in schools.

I also reasoned that the state should not remove the right of parents to discipline their children, even to use physical discipline (such as spanking) so long as there is no actual physical harm that comes to the children (and this of course means that actual abuse of children should be punished by law).

I also argued that a widespread system of school vouchers given to parents, by which they could pay for their children's schooling at any private or public school of their choice, would lead to much higher quality in the educational system, much greater choice and competition among schools, and a much better educational outcome for the children.

With regard to the positions that I advocated in this chapter, by far the most common approach of Democrats is to place the views of the government and the teachers regarding what is right for children above the views of parents. Republicans, by contrast, largely believe that the views of parents must take priority over the viewpoints of government officials.

The opposition to the ability of parents to use physical discipline with their children comes almost entirely from Democrats, who would often support laws outlawing spanking of children completely. Opposition to the use of vouchers for parents to choose their children's schools comes almost entirely from Democrats, especially because of the political clout the National Education Association and other teachers' unions have in the Democratic Party. Republicans, by contrast, tend to favor the protection of parents' rights regarding raising their children, tend to favor protecting the right to exercise physical discipline, and tend to favor programs that would give vouchers to parents for school choices.

D. FREEDOM OF SPEECH

In chapter 6 I argued that freedom of speech is an essential policy for any free nation.

With regard to campaign finance restrictions, I argued that they are mostly wrongful restrictions on freedom of speech. They have not kept money out of politics, but have given unfair advantage to incumbents and to independent candidates who are extremely wealthy. It seems to me appropriate that all campaign finance restrictions should be abolished, with only the requirement that contributions above a certain amount be made public.

Democrats have tended to favor these campaign finance restrictions, because it seems that they give to Democrats (who are largely favored by the media and Hollywood) an advantage in the political system. Such restrictions also provide an endless maze of regulations by which candidates can be inadvertently tripped up and then held liable for breaking the law. Unfortunately, some Republicans have also supported these campaign finance restrictions (the most prominent being John McCain), but a number of Republicans have also opposed them.

I argued that the "hate speech" codes on university campuses are a wrongful and also unconstitutional restriction on freedom of speech and are often used to give privileged status to liberal policies and ideas and to criticize the speech of Christians defending biblical values or promoting the Gospel.

Democrats and political liberals in the academic community have tended much more strongly to support such hate speech codes. This has not been much of an issue among Republicans in politics.

Finally, with regard to the Fairness Doctrine that would require equal time for broadcasting alternative viewpoints on controversial issues, I argued that it would be a wrongful restriction on freedom of speech and would basically be used to try to destroy conservative talk radio, which is the primary media outlet available to conservatives in the United States today. Some Democrats have supported the idea that the FCC should reimpose the Fairness Doctrine; Republicans uniformly oppose this.

E. FREEDOM OF RELIGION

In chapter 7, regarding freedom of religion, I argued that neither the Bible nor the US Constitution (in its original intent) excludes individual people or even government agencies from giving expression to particular religious views or beliefs in the public square. It has been a morally and legally mistaken promotion of the myth that the Constitution requires a complete "separation of church and state," promoted particularly by some mistaken Supreme Court decisions, that has led to an increasing exclusion of religious speech in the public square in the United States.

These inappropriate restrictions on religious expression in the public square have largely been imposed on the nation and on the individual states by the decisions of more liberal judges who have been appointed (largely but not exclusively) by Democratic governors to the various state courts and by Democratic presidents to the federal judicial system. Republicans, by contrast, have generally (but not always) appointed judges who rule more consistently according to the original intent of the US Constitution or the various state constitutions.

I also argued that faith-based programs, by which religious organizations receive government funding to carry out social welfare programs, seem to me to be legitimate in terms of both biblical teaching and the US Constitution. It also seems to me that they do not pose any significant danger to a loss of religious freedom on the part of these organizations.

Republicans (but not uniformly) have tended to favor allowing government funding to be given to such faith-based programs (such as shelters for the homeless, job training, drug rehabilitation, and prison ministries), while Democrats have largely (but not entirely) been much more reluctant to support them.

Finally, I argued that the Internal Revenue Service's prohibition against political advocacy by churches and religious organizations seems to me to be an unconstitutional restriction on freedom of speech by churches. The decision of whether to express a viewpoint for or against an individual candidate should be left to the individual church and the individual pastor or priest or rabbi, not made by the government. I do not think that many Republicans or Democrats have expressed an opinion about this question (although the restrictions were first put into place under the leadership of then-Congressman Lyndon Johnson, a Democrat who later became President).

F. BUT AREN'T DEMOCRATS BETTER AT CARING FOR THE POOR, PROTECTING THE ENVIRONMENT, AND PROMOTING WORLD PEACE?

Some readers at this point might feel persuaded that conservative or Republican policies are closer to the Bible's values on issues related to protecting life, marriage, and the family. But they might think that liberal policies, or policies of the Democratic Party, are more Christian on issues such as caring for the poor, protecting the environment, and promoting world peace. If that is the case, how should a Christian vote?

I encourage such readers to consider the companion volume to this book: *Voting as a Christian: The Economic and Foreign Policy Issues*. In that volume I argue that biblical teachings also lead to conservative positions on these other issues, because conservative positions truly care for the poor, more wisely steward the environment, and better protect the world from violence and evil.

G. WHY DO THE TWO PARTIES ADOPT THESE DIFFERENT POLICIES?

Is there a reason why Republicans have far more often ended up supporting policies that are consistent with biblical teachings, whereas Democrats have far more frequently ended up opposing these policies? I suggest that there are several factors that account for this difference. I have listed them here in an order that moves from the obvious political differences that anyone can see to the deeper factors that involve a person's entire worldview and deeper spiritual commitments.

(1) *Abortion:* Beginning in the 1970s, the Democratic Party became increasingly dominated by people who favor the protection of abortion rights for women. Behind this commitment is a conviction that we cannot know any absolute moral standards for human conduct, particularly sexual conduct, and if unwanted pregnancies result from sexual intercourse outside of marriage or within marriage when a child is not "wanted," then the more liberal commitment to moral relativism means that there is an unwillingness to have the government say that taking the life of this preborn child is wrong. Protecting people's sexual freedom has become, for the Democratic Party, a much higher value.

Thus the Democratic Party's increasingly uniform support for abortion rights (at least on the national leadership level, among national candidates, and in national judicial appointments) means that the Democrats have committed themselves to a position that is fundamentally opposed to the biblical teachings on the value of the preborn child.

Republicans, by contrast, have more and more become a party in which, on the national level and increasingly on the level of each state, no significant leadership positions can be held by people who favor the continuation of a legal right to abortion (except to save the life of the mother). This means that, on the question of laws to regulate abortion, Republicans and Democrats have strayed farther and farther apart, and the biblical values are clearly on the side of the Republican position on this issue.

This difference regarding sexual moral standards has then naturally led to differences about the question of homosexual "marriage." Since the abortion controversies started and pro-abortion people gravitated to the Democratic party, that resulted in a large number of Democrats who were convinced that no one could know any universal moral standards with regard to sexual conduct between consenting adults. Therefore, once the issue of homosexual "marriage" came up, Democrats tended almost uniformly to favor "equal rights for homosexuals" and therefore homosexual "marriage."

Most Republicans, whether because of the Bible's teachings or because of an instinctive sense of moral right and wrong, have held that marriage should be limited to a union between one man and one woman. Therefore Republicans have also largely ended up on the side of the Bible's teachings on homosexuality and marriage.

(2) *Individual human responsibility for good and evil:* With regard to the existence of good and evil in the heart of every individual, and therefore the rightness of holding people accountable for the choices they make, it seems to me that Republicans have, in general, come down on the biblical side of this fundamental question as well. Therefore they have tended to favor stronger military forces (to defend against evil from other nations), stronger police forces, and stronger enforcement of criminal laws (to defend against evil deeds done by people within the nation). Democrats, on the other hand, have been more likely to blame the evil things that people do on forces outside the individual, such as family or society or guns or corporations or national governments. This tends to minimize an emphasis on individual accountability for one's own actions, and this, in turn, makes people think that those who do wrong can simply be persuaded to change their minds with more conversation and more negotiation, whether it be with a criminal within the nation or with leaders who attempt evil things from outside the nation.

(3) *Beliefs about whether we can know right and wrong:* If a person does not believe that absolute truth and absolute right and wrong can be known, then it follows that one person's views are just as good as another's. There is no way to know whether someone is right or wrong. Once a person reaches that conviction, he or she no longer feels accountable to any moral standard, or any standard of truth that is higher than any other, and certainly not to any God (who probably can't be known anyway, even if he does exist).

It follows that if there is no right and wrong that can be known, the people who are *most dangerous* are those who have strongly held religious convictions (such as fundamentalist Muslims and fundamentalist Christians!). These people must not be allowed to have their viewpoints influence the society.

Taking this reasoning one step further, if there is no absolute right and wrong, then the people who can have the most beneficial influence on society (according to what they personally think is "good" for society) are simply those who have the most power. It follows, then, that if you think there is no absolute right and wrong, it is right to seek more and more power, and that power comes, in most nations, through the attaining of political office and the power of the government. Therefore the Democratic Party tends to attract to itself people for whom gaining power through the government, and then increasing that power, is the best way they know to do something "good" with their lives (as they understand what is "good"). That is why Democrats seek to continually increase government power over individual lives.

Republicans, by contrast, have many more people who believe that there are absolute moral standards (as found in the Bible, or for some conservatives in traditional Jewish teaching, or the Bible plus Roman Catholic Church tradition, or the Book of Mormon, and so forth). These people also tend to think that they will be held accountable for their actions to a personal God who will one day judge them. This means that they believe there are absolute moral standards, and the *attainment of power* is not the ultimate goal, but rather *being obedient to the moral code that God has given to us.* They will tend to resist increases in government power, thinking that God has given to government a limited role.

In addition, these people tend to think that the religious system on which they base their beliefs places a high value on individual responsibility and individual freedom of choice. This is another reason why they tend to want smaller government — government that allows more individual freedom. But this individual freedom should be limited to prevent evil people from harming others through murder or rape or theft or breaking contracts and so forth. Therefore Republicans tend to emphasize individual freedom (within certain boundaries of the law).

(4) *Religious beliefs:* There is a significant difference in the religious beliefs of Republicans and Democrats taken as a whole. Conservative evangelicals, who tend to believe that the Bible is God's Word in its entirety, have tended to align with Republican principles. So have others whose religious views lead them to believe in absolute moral right and wrong, such as Roman Catholics, Mormons, and more traditional Jews.

But people who have no religious belief at all, or who do not believe that we can know what God has told us with regard to moral standards, tend to be moral relativists, and this aligns them much more closely with the Democratic Party and its emphasis on allowing people to choose abortion or choose homosexual marriage and so forth.

(5) *Conclusion*: The differences between Democrats and Republicans today have great significance. These differences are not accidental, but stem from differing convictions about several moral and theological issues.